P9-CAT-920

IDIOT'S GUIDES.
AS EASY AS IT GETS!

Starting and Running a Marijuana Business

FEB – – 2019

Starting and Running a Marijuana Business

by Debby Goldsberry

ALPHA

A member of Penguin Random House LLC

Publisher: Mike Sanders
Associate Publisher: Billy Fields
Acquisitions Editor: Jan Lynn
Development Editor: Phil Kitchel
Book/Cover Designer: William Thomas
Photographer: Mark Rutherford, dopeimages.work
Compositor: Ayanna Lacey
Proofreader: Lisa Starnes
Indexer: Brad Herriman

First American Edition, 2017
Published in the United States by DK Publishing
6081 E. 82nd Street, Indianapolis, Indiana 46250

Copyright © 2017 Dorling Kindersley Limited
A Penguin Random House Company
17 18 19 10 9 8 7 6 5 4 3 2 1
001-304721-June2017

All rights reserved.
Without limiting the rights under the copyright reserved above, no part of this publication may be reproduced, stored in or introduced into a retrieval system, or transmitted, in any form, or by any means (electronic, mechanical, photocopying, recording, or otherwise), without the prior written permission of the copyright owner.

Published in the United States by Dorling Kindersley Limited.

IDIOT'S GUIDES and Design are trademarks of Penguin Random House LLC

ISBN: 9781465462060
Library of Congress Catalog Card Number: 2016960065

Note: This publication contains the opinions and ideas of its author(s). It is intended to provide helpful and informative material on the subject matter covered. It is sold with the understanding that the author(s) and publisher are not engaged in rendering professional services in the book. If the reader requires personal assistance or advice, a competent professional should be consulted. The author(s) and publisher specifically disclaim any responsibility for any liability, loss, or risk, personal or otherwise, which is incurred as a consequence, directly or indirectly, of the use and application of any of the contents of this book.

Trademarks: All terms mentioned in this book that are known to be or are suspected of being trademarks or service marks have been appropriately capitalized. Alpha Books, DK, and Penguin Random House LLC cannot attest to the accuracy of this information. Use of a term in this book should not be regarded as affecting the validity of any trademark or service mark.

DK books are available at special discounts when purchased in bulk for sales promotions, premiums, fund-raising, or educational use. For details, contact: DK Publishing Special Markets, 345 Hudson Street, New York, New York 10014 or SpecialSales@dk.com.

Printed and bound in USA

Contents

Introduction

Have you heard about the marijuana industry and wondered what it takes to get involved? Are you curious to know more about marijuana's transition from prohibition to America's new billion-dollar industry? Do you have a good business idea, but need help moving it to the next stage? If so, this book is for you.

Both new business owners and experienced entrepreneurs will find information here to help. The book starts with the history of marijuana and explains how it became illegal in the first place. It walks readers through the long and difficult efforts undertaken by advocates to create medical marijuana and adult use laws, and explains the work that still needs to be done to change the federal regulations.

It's a business manual, designed to give small businesses a chance to compete. It will help you decide what type of business to start and advise you on how to get it funded and permitted. And, once you do that, it will show you how to get your marijuana business open and operational. Your company has to stand out, and this book will help you be bold.

Now is the time to start planning your marijuana business. The laws are changing fast, and only the most organized and prepared companies will succeed. Get ready, or you might be left behind!

How This Book Is Organized

Part 1, Introduction to the Green Rush, provides a brief overview of the history of marijuana prohibition and the efforts to end it. It discusses why now is the perfect time to open a marijuana business, and what types of marijuana businesses and products exist in the marketplace. It ends with a look at the future of the marijuana industry for adults and medical users.

Part 2, Distilling Your Concept, walks you through the different permits and licenses you will need to secure for your marijuana business and how to get them. It shows you how to form your starting team and explains the need for strong mission, vision, and values statements. It also helps you develop income streams and locate clients.

Part 3, Building the Foundation of Your Marijuana Business, guides you through the toughest parts of starting the company. Review the main corporate structures used by marijuana businesses, and learn how to incorporate. Learn to create your business plan, and how to use it to secure your start-up funds. And, review the difficulties faced by marijuana businesses on the real estate hunt, and learn to secure the best location for your needs.

Part 4, Setting Up Your Cultivation Facility, teaches readers how to choose the best plant genetics and grow methods for their needs. Learn how to design your indoor, outdoor, or greenhouse grow space, and take a close look at a wide range of hydroponic operations. Find out what elements your plants need to live, like lights and nutrients, and learn how to protect them from contamination.

Part 5, Dispensary Operations and Management, shows you the ins and outs of designing your facility, with a focus on safety and security. It will teach you what medicines need to be on your menu and in what ratios, and will show you how to purchase the supply. It guides you through the process of selling the marijuana to patients or legal adult users, providing time-saving tips that will make you money.

Part 6, Heavy Lifting: Accounting, Human Resources, and Marketing, guides you through three key operational processes. It offers advice on hiring and training employees, and shows you how to supervise and retain the team. It also guides you through the hard process of terminating employees. This chapter shows you how to create and supervise your accounting plan, and teaches you the importance of creating a marketing plan to measure the success of your campaigns.

At the back of the book, we've included a glossary of terms, a list of resources, operation and management checklists, and sample standard operating procedures (SOPs) to further your understanding of starting and running a marijuana business.

Extras

Throughout the book, we include four kinds of sidebars to enhance the text. Here's what to look for:

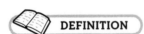

DEFINITION

I will reference several terms that may be unfamiliar to people new to cannabusinesses. These sidebars explain what these words mean.

HASHING IT OUT

These discuss specific information in detail, in order to help your marijuana business save time and money.

HIGH POINTS

These contain an important fact or highlight interesting facts related to the section.

(**HIGH ALERT**)

Take heed of these sidebars that will provide warnings about certain pitfalls of the cannabis trade.

Acknowledgments

This book was written in consultation with the finest group of experts in the industry. It would have been impossible without Dave McCullick, general manager at Magnolia Wellness and professor at Oaksterdam University. He poured his words, knowledge, and experience into the book, and spent an enormous amount of time researching and providing encouragement. Thanks to Stacy Pershall for her assistance with edits, and to Mark Rutherford (dopeimages.work) for the beautiful photos.

The book covers a broad spectrum of information, and I consulted with several experts to provide readers with the most accurate content. Many thanks to Green Rush Consulting for the help with tips on business plan writing, to Investing in Cannabis for their knowledge on raising cannabusiness funding, and to Doug McVay for assistance understanding the state and federal laws. Thank you to Liana Held for taking all of my calls about human resources, accounting, and organizational formation, and for always pushing our companies to the cutting edge. Michael and Michelle Aldrich, your review of and additions to the history chapter are greatly appreciated. And, thank you to Amber Senter, Tom Donohue, and Mary Patton for your input, assistance, and kindness.

I am incredibly grateful to Cheri Sicard of Marijuana Lifers for contacting me about the opportunity to write this book, and to the people who made it all possible, Sheree Bykofsky and Janet Rosen of Sheree Bykofsky Associates, and to Jan Lynn of DK Books for her hard work keeping the book on schedule and creating the final product.

Thank you to my loving family, Barbara, Steve, David, Teri, Jenny, Kyle, Joe, Kirby, Aaron, Mike, Bailey, Noah, Josh, Liana, Jeremy, and the kid.

Shout out to the hardcore marijuana advocates, who worked all those years so you didn't have to: Rick Pfrommer, Diane Fornbacher, Steve Bloom, Aundre Speciale, Steve Hager, Elvy Musikka, Bill Panzer, Kristin Nevedal, Steve DeAngelo, Angel Galvan Raich, John Sajo, Loey Glover, Vivian McPeak, Ngaio Bealum, Jeff Jones, Dale Sky Jones, Dennis Peron, Michelle Aldrich, Anthony Johnson, Ellen Komp, Mikki Norris, Madeline Martinez, Chris Conrad, Yami Bolanos, Dale Gieringer, Omar Figueroa, Amanda Reiman, all the various *High Times* staffers, past and present, all of the great people who volunteered for Cannabis Action Network over the years, and many others. Thanks to Jack Herer, Ben Masel, Dr. Tod Mikuriya, Franco Loja, Michael Rich, and Cypress. You are greatly missed.

I want to give a giant special thanks to everyone at Magnolia Wellness dispensary in Oakland, CA, and to Dave Prinz, Marc Weinstein, and everyone at Berkeley Compassionate Care Center. I am looking forward to everything ahead!

Introduction to the Green Rush

This section (briefly) examines 10,000 years of marijuana's global history and reviews the 1937 tax act that created prohibition. It tells the story of how marijuana users started fighting back in the 1960s, and finally succeeded in 1996, with the passage of California's medical marijuana initiative. Today, 28 states and the District of Columbia have workable medical marijuana laws, and 8 states have legalized adult use and sales.

Right now is the perfect time to get involved in the marijuana industry, as it's bursting with opportunities. Read about the various types of businesses that are starting and the products that are manufactured and sold in this unique space. Learn more about the difference between the medical and adult-use sides of the marijuana industry, and start to think about where you might fit in.

History of Marijuana Commerce

People have used marijuana for thousands of years. Our ancestors carried its seeds around the globe on ancient migration and trade routes. These were planted for medicine, fiber, food, and spiritual purposes. The plant itself evolved to fit the ecosystem, depending on where the seeds flowered. Over the millenniums, indica and sativa plants formed, each with a different appearance and effect.

Marijuana prohibition originated in the early 1900s in the United States. Back then, most people referred to the plant as cannabis. However, the prohibitionists preferred the Mexican word *marijuana*, attaching its users to the racial and anti-immigration sentiments of the times.

Through widespread and determined efforts, marijuana prohibition is finally slowly ending. At the local, state, and federal levels, the worst of these prohibition laws are now fading away, and a new era is being ushered in. In this chapter, we explore marijuana's fascinating journey and the transition of the anti-prohibition movement into the modern cannabis industry.

In This Chapter

- Explore the documented history of marijuana use
- Discover how reefer madness led to prohibition
- Learn how advocates created an industry
- Consider the changing views on marijuana

History of Marihuana Use and Its Prohibition

After roughly 100 years of prohibition, marijuana is finally making a long awaited comeback. Before 1937, it was found in a variety of over-the-counter and pharmaceutical medicines, and used to treat everything from corns to coughs. It was even sold as an aphrodisiac, in pill and liquid form, to a society that had not yet caught *reefer madness*.

 **DEFINITION**

Reefer Madness is a 1936 propaganda film in which marijuana use turns a group of teens and their pushers into murdering lunatics. It helped bolster public opinion in advance of the 1937 congressional vote to prohibit marijuana. Nowadays, the term is used to describe the mindset that swept the nation back then and led to cannabis prohibition.

By the 1930s, Harry J. Anslinger, head of the Bureau of Narcotics, had started the federal attack on marijuana. Using scare tactics and building on racial tensions, he painted marijuana as an addictive drug with criminally insane users. In response, Congress created the Marihuana Tax Act of 1937. The intent was to stop its use by creating a tax so high that compliance would be impossible.

 HASHING IT OUT

Marijuana is part of the nettle family, cannabaceae, genus name cannabis. It has three species: cannabis sativa, cannabis indica, and cannabis ruderalis, each with different attributes. Marijuana, sometimes spelled marihuana, is the name most commonly used for the ingestible strains. Hemp designates the industrial versions, meaning more fiber and less medicine. Other popular names include weed, pot, medicine, boo, ganja, chronic, and kush. Prohibition creates the need to be secretive, so people use code words like "safety break" to mean it's time to smoke marijuana.

This tactic virtually eliminated marijuana use in the states, other than by counterculture groups such as the jazz musicians, beats, and hippies, until one of their heroes, Timothy Leary, struck back. In 1969, he won a U.S. Supreme Court case to have the tax act thrown out. The success was short-lived, though, as President Nixon launched the "War on Drugs" soon after, creating even harsher penalties for marijuana use, cultivation, sales, and manufacturing. Despite many advances at the local, state, and federal levels, it's these laws that are still being fought by marijuana advocates today.

10,000 Years of Documented Use

Not long ago, researchers discovered a 2,700-year-old Shaman's tomb in China. Inside, they found bridles, archery equipment, a harp, a medicine bag—and, surprisingly, a bowl and leather pouch containing about two pounds of marijuana. All the stems, leaves, and male flowers had been removed from it, meaning this marijuana was high grade and meant to be consumed for spiritual or medical purposes. Researcher Ethan Russo, MD, an advisor at GW Pharmaceuticals, makers of Sativex cannabis extract, was sent to review the discovery. He reported being most astonished to find the marijuana had not visibly aged, but actually looked good enough to smoke. After lab testing the sample, he proved it was very potent marijuana.

Cannabis originated long before then, however, evolving on the steppes of Asia, where modern agriculture is more than 10,000 years old. From there, it slowly went global, with seeds located everywhere from a 3,000-year-old Siberian tomb to a Viking ship. However, it didn't arrive in the United States until the early 1900s when Mexicans brought it northward. They had a 100-year head start on us, having attained marijuana seeds via South America in the 1800s. South American marijuana originated from Africa about 200 years before that. Written documentation of marijuana's use as medicine starts in the oldest Chinese pharmacopeia, the *Materia Medica Sutra* by Emperor Shen Nung, who lived around 2000 B.C.E.

By the 1900s, marijuana had gone global, and in the United States, it was available in a variety of prescription and over-the-counter forms. A long time cannabis advocate, Don E. Wirtshafter, created and now curates a Cannabis Museum to showcase these marijuana medicines. The collection of more than 100 historic bottles, some still full and unopened, date back to the late 1800s to the 1930s. The biggest pharmaceutical companies of the day were making marijuana medicines, including Upjohn, who merged with Monsanto, and Parke Davis, who are now a part of Pfizer.

Cannabis Apothecary Jars, circa 1894. (Photo courtesy of the Don E. Wirtshafter collection.)

The Marihuana Tax Act vs. Timothy Leary

The prohibition of marijuana rests firmly on a few people, none more so than Harry J. Anslinger, the nation's first Commissioner of the Federal Bureau of Narcotics. He ran the office from 1930 to 1962, and his influence on cannabis policies has been felt ever since. He was serious about his job, believing marijuana use caused violence and that its users were degenerates. Anslinger's accusations that its use led to pacifism and communism and his Jim Crow-era attacks kept his crusade in the headlines for decades.

During his tenure, Congress passed the Marihuana Tax Act of 1937, effectively creating a national prohibition on cannabis use. Anslinger had pushed to let each state dictate its own law, much like today's policies, but Congress wanted a united federal law. This act instituted a system mandating that every person who handled the marijuana be taxed. By design, it was so cumbersome and expensive that no individual could ever receive the proper tax stamp, yet failure to carry it resulted in huge fines and jail time. Despite initial misgivings, Anslinger heartily coordinated its implementation until he was booted from office during President Kennedy's tenure.

HIGH POINTS

Birdseed companies lobbied against the Marihuana Tax Act, saying marijuana seeds gave feathers a glossy sheen. They were successful in carving out an exemption to the law for marijuana seeds, when used in birdseed. This still exists today, but only for sterilized seeds. The American Medical Association lobbied against the law, too, saying that marijuana was extensively used and nonaddictive, and should not be taxed in a burdensome manner. They were unsuccessful in their efforts, and both pharmaceutical and over-the-counter cannabis medicines disappeared in 1937.

Timothy Leary, former professor of psychology at Harvard University, was arrested just before Christmas 1965. It was no surprise to Leary that this was a possibility, as both New York, where he had picked up about a half ounce of marijuana, and Texas, where he was taking it, had laws making it illegal. In fact, every state did by that time. And, although the federal Marihuana Tax Act required that he get a tax stamp, Leary was too worried to get one. To top it off, he had taken the marijuana on a trip to Mexico with his daughter and a few others. They were busted in Texas on their way back by the Laredo border guards.

Leary and his daughter lost the first trial in district court, and he was convicted of violating the Marihuana Tax Act. He appealed, lost, and took the case to the United States Supreme Court. Leary's argument was that by registering for the tax, he would have been targeted by state law enforcement in Texas and New York. It was basically a Fifth Amendment case against self-incrimination, and the Supreme Court agreed. Leary won the case in 1969, and the Marihuana Tax Act was struck down.

The War on Drugs Begins

The victory in Timothy Leary's case was short-lived. By 1969, President Nixon was in office, and he was a well-known opponent of marijuana legalization. He labeled drugs "America's public enemy number one," making speeches that sounded much like Anslinger's. By the end of 1970, Nixon had pushed Congress to create the Comprehensive Drug Abuse Prevention and Control Act. Within it was the Controlled Substances Act, which categorized drugs, Schedule I-V, according to their potential for addiction and medicinal value.

Schedule I is reserved for the most dangerous substances—those with no medical value and a high potential for abuse. Marijuana was placed here, along with heroin and psychedelics. For perspective, cocaine and morphine are Schedule II drugs and can be prescribed by doctors. Schedule I drugs are considered so dangerous that even most researchers are denied access to them.

By 1971, Nixon had declared a "War on Drugs." Marijuana's association with hippies and anti-war protestors irked him, and the Controlled Substances Act was a tool to use against these ideological opponents. After he was forced to resign, public sentiment softened a bit on marijuana. Legalization started to look possible during President Carter's administration, and states started decriminalizing marijuana. Groups like the National Organization for the Reform of Marijuana Laws (NORML) got started, *High Times* magazine was in its heyday, and head shops were opening up across the nation.

Just Say No

President Reagan, and his formidable First Lady, Mrs. Nancy Reagan, had zero tolerance for drugs. They picked up the anti-drug rhetoric like the 1970s decriminalization movement had never existed. Mrs. Reagan launched her "Just Say No" campaign in the mid-1980s, in Oakland, CA. The DARE program started around that same time, placing police officers in classrooms across America to promote abstinence, and the Partnership for a Drug-Free America began their national advertising campaign. These anti-drug laws promoted marijuana as a gateway drug that leads to crack and heroin abuse, drawing no distinction between the substances in terms of harmfulness or potential for addiction. Congress also authorized a wave of harsh new drug laws in the mid-1980s, increasing federal penalties for marijuana sales, cultivation, and manufacturing. The Comprehensive Prevention and Drug Control Act was amended in 1984, expanding *forfeiture laws*. The Anti-Drug Abuse Act passed in 1986, creating mandatory minimum sentences for marijuana and other drug crimes. During these years, jails and prisons began to fill with drug-related offenders. Incarcerations ramped up during President Bill Clinton's administration, with the creation of the "three strikes" laws.

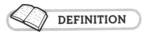 **DEFINITION**

> *Forfeiture laws* allow prosecutors to file claims against property owned by the person or people accused of a crime. These charges are filed in civil, as opposed to criminal court, requiring defendants to fight two cases, one for their personal freedom and one for their property.

Marijuana Advocates Fight Back

I joined the reform movement back in 1986 while in college, and started attending Hash Bash, the Great Midwest Marijuana Harvest Festival, and Hash Wednesday. These annual smoke-ins were spread around the Midwest in Ann Arbor, Madison, and Champaign-Urbana. They were founded in the 1970s by the hippies and Yippies, and in the mid-1980s, annual smoke-ins could still be found in Washington, D.C., and New York City.

Everything changed in 1988, when the police started busting up smoke-ins. On my campus, University of Illinois, we heard that President Reagan had sent word to the campus to crack down, and the school pledged to make sure we never returned. Our local NORML chapter disagreed, and we returned the next year with legalization rallies on all of the University campuses in the state. Major efforts such as these have continued the movement to end marijuana prohibition.

Artists, Authors, and Hippies Get Inspired

It's no secret that drug laws don't prevent people from consuming marijuana. Louis Armstrong started smoking cannabis in the 1920s, using it daily to inspire his jazz performances. Poet Allen Ginsberg started speaking out about reforming the marijuana laws in the late 1950s. Author Shel Silverstein wrote the *The Great Smoke-Off* about marijuana. Jack London smoked hash, as did countless other writers, poets, artists, musicians, and romantics. This is not surprising, as when consumed, the effect of marijuana challenges users to think differently, inspiring new mental connections and creativity.

Despite the conservative laws, the 1960s hippies turned marijuana use into a lifestyle. Many of my associates in the marijuana movement started smoking it in 1967, during the Summer of Love. The nation's youth were following Timothy Leary's advice to "tune in, turn on, drop out." Its use was rumored to cause synesthesia, where users could see music or hear colors, leading to its prominence at music and other counterculture events.

Marijuana in the 1960s and 1970s

Attorney James R. White founded America's first marijuana law reform group, Legalize Marijuana (LEMAR), in 1964. He was defending Lowell Eggemeir, who had walked into a police station one day and lit up a joint. They lost the case, but spawned a movement. Allen Ginsberg co-founded a chapter of LEMAR in New York and John Sinclair in Michigan. Michael Aldrich, a scholar and collector, formed a student chapter in Buffalo, and soon moved to California to take the movement west.

Once there, Aldrich, with his wife Michelle and others, ran AMORPHIA, the Cannabis Cooperative. They sold branded rolling papers to fund the distribution of information to counter the Nixon-era drug propaganda. These funds nearly single handedly paid for the 1972 legalization initiative, which lost two to one. Despite the loss, the yes vote was strong enough for then Senate Majority Leader George R. Mascone to call for hearings that ultimately decriminalized marijuana in the state.

LEMAR inspired the formation of NORML in 1970, whose founder, Keith Stroup, soon gained a national voice for marijuana users. A lawyer by trade, Stroup believed that marijuana users needed information and good lawyers in order to stay out of jail.

By mid-decade, the hippie lifestyle was going out of fashion, but the Yippies were still hard at work. These politically active hippies used street theater, rallies, parades, and smoke-ins to motivate people to get involved in marijuana law reform. Ben Masel, a Yippie organizer from Madison, Wisconsin, founded the annual Great Midwest Marijuana Harvest Festival, which drew marijuana enthusiasts from all over the Midwest. Annual events like this were an essential part of exchanging information and community building in pre-Internet days.

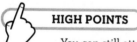 **HIGH POINTS**

You can still attend the Great Midwest Marijuana Harvest Festival each fall in Madison, Wisconsin. Its 46th annual event was held in 2016.

The Hemp Revolution of the 1980s

The revolution continued into the 1980s with Jack Herer, a former military man and Goldwater Republican, becoming a hero of the marijuana reform movement with his groundbreaking book, *The Emperor Wears No Clothes*. Herer and his assistant, Maria Farrow, scoured the Library of Congress and other sources, finding proof that marijuana had once been used for food, fuel, paper, fiber, and medicine. Herer and Farrow set out to tell the nation about marijuana's potential.

Jack Herer, author of The Emperor Wears No Clothes.

Herer and Farrow toured with me back in the late 1980s and early 1990s on the Cannabis Action Network's Hemp Tours, which crossed the states teaching marijuana advocates to fight back against the harsh drug laws. These tours carried a Hemp Museum, with paper, cloth, oil, and other products made from marijuana. Willie Nelson was also interested in advocacy and manufactured the country's first modern hemp product, a denim long-sleeved shirt with pot-leaf stamped buttons.

In 1976, Robert C. Randall won a landmark case, becoming the first legal medical marijuana patient since the start of prohibition. The D.C. Superior court gave him the right to use marijuana to treat his glaucoma. Elvy Musikka, another glaucoma patient registered in the *Investigational New Drug Program* (also known as the Compassionate IND program), traveled nationwide with these Hemp Tours, talking to editorial boards, speaking at town meetings, and giving lectures on college campuses. Everywhere she went, Musikka showed off 300 joints, supplied by the government marijuana each month. She hit the front pages and airwaves nationwide, educating Americans, often for the first time, about the medical uses of marijuana.

 **DEFINITION**

The **Investigational New Drug Program** is part of the drug approval system, supervised by the U.S. Food and Drug Administration (FDA). It allows the FDA to license experimental substances for researchers to use during drug trials. It's also used to distribute drugs on an emergency basis, when lengthy approval processes would harm lives.

Ending marijuana prohibition has been no easy feat. In the 1980s, the government took a lot of aggression out on marijuana users. Together, advocates coordinated one of the most effective grassroots campaigns to hit America. By the 1990s, America was ready for performers like Cypress Hill, the Black Crowes, Willie Nelson, and Woody Harrelson to drive marijuana back into popular culture. After years in hiding, consumers were finally emerging from the closet.

Legalization of Medical and Adult Use of Marijuana

Elvy Musikka was not the only patient on the Compassionate IND program. Among others, there were several glaucoma patients, a cancer patient, and a married couple with HIV/AIDS, Kenneth and Barbara Jenks, who spent their final years spreading the word about medical marijuana. In fact, the Compassionate IND Program was flooded with applications for medical marijuana. However, rather than embrace the potential, the FDA closed the program to new applicants. Today, only Musikka and two others are licensed to receive federal medical marijuana.

When the public rediscovered marijuana's medical applications, demands for the end of prohibition grew. Currently, 28 states now allow its use. Colorado and Washington were the first states to change their adult-use laws, with Oregon; Alaska; and Washington, D.C., soon following. In 2016, nine states—Arizona, Arkansas, California, Florida, Maine, Massachusetts, Montana, Nevada and North Dakota—had ballot measures to legalize either medical or recreational use; only Arizona failed to pass. Federal laws have also begun to evolve, first by de-prioritizing federal spending on enforcement in states with legalization laws, and hopefully soon, with a full rescheduling of marijuana.

The Medical Marijuana Tipping Point

Kenneth and Barbara Jenks' message was heard loud and clear. With the AIDS crisis underway in the 1980s, people were willing to try anything to help ease the suffering brought on by the condition and its various treatments. Longtime marijuana enthusiast, Dennis Peron, was the first to give the idea credence. His partner, Jonathan, needed help, and if marijuana offered the solution, they were up for trying. Dennis had been a pot dealer since the 1970s, when he opened the Big Top Pot Supermarket, and he still had easy access to medical grade strains. They found that marijuana use combated some of the worst side effects of his partner's condition, increasing appetite and stopping nausea, resulting in Peron becoming an evangelist for the medical marijuana cause.

HASHING IT OUT

Fighting cannabis prohibition has not been easy. Dennis Peron was variously raided by local, state, and federal police at his medical marijuana dispensary. He was even shot once in a 1978 bust at his Big Top Pot Supermarket. Although Peron is an extreme example, cannabis entrepreneurs continue to be arrested for running dispensaries or for cultivating marijuana, even in regulated states.

Advisors like the Aldrichs and Herer had all worked together on the failed 1972 California legalization initiative, and, after much input, Peron was ready to take medical marijuana to the San Francisco voters. Proposition P passed by a large margin in 1991, inspiring nearby cities like Berkeley and Oakland to pass similar laws. Peron wrote a statewide medical marijuana initiative next, Proposition 215, passed in 1996, which won the entire nation's attention.

Dr. Tod Mikuriya was a Bay Area physician who wanted to see the Compassionate Use Act of 1996 go into effect. A former National Institute of Mental Health marijuana researcher, Mikuriya had published a collection of studies called *Marijuana: Medical Papers, 1839 to 1972*. Under this new law, a patient needed a doctor's recommendation in order to legally use medical marijuana, and Mikuriya was determined to take away the stigma of providing them with it. Along with other knowledgeable physicians, he trained doctors across the state and met with patients whose primary care physicians refused to issue recommendations.

Peron became the first person to open a medical marijuana dispensary to serve patients with recommendations. This type of retail distribution was not legal, but it was what the patients wanted. Peron's dispensary on Market Street in San Francisco was five stories high, with different services and types of cannabis available on each floor. Peron relocated and was eventually closed by the feds, but other dispensaries sprang up to fill the void. Nowadays, there are thousands of storefront and delivery outlets in California alone, all thanks to the pioneering bravery of Dennis Peron.

HIGH POINTS

The Compassionate Use Act of 1996 requires patients to have the "recommendation" of their doctor, not a prescription. This can be issued by the physician in oral or written form, but patients prefer written, as this is required for entry into dispensaries. Prescription drugs are governed under the *Federal Controlled Substances Act*, whereas a recommendation is merely advisory. California law says that doctors can recommend marijuana for any condition they believe will be benefitted by its use.

Changes to the Medical Marijuana Laws

After California's law changed, other states like Arizona, New Mexico, Colorado, and Washington created statewide regulations to allow medical marijuana production, sales, and use. These new laws were passed by voter initiatives, meaning advocates collected signatures on petitions to qualify for statewide ballots, and citizens voted to change the laws. Depending on each initiative's sponsor, the laws varied between liberal, where access is widespread, to conservative, in which patients still find it difficult to access medical marijuana.

In some states, the legislatures passed the laws, rather than the voters. These laws are often strict and burdensome to implement. They also include limits on qualifying conditions, multilayered tax schemes, and high barriers to entry for supply-side businesses. The good news is that 25 states and Washington, D.C., have passed laws ending such prohibition on medical marijuana, and the plant is available in some form to qualified patients in those locations.

Cannabidiol (CBD) -only laws have passed in 16 states. CBD is one of the main active ingredients in marijuana. Its physical properties are used to treat epilepsy and seizure disorders, especially when combined with low doses of tetrahydrocannabinol (THC). These CBD-only laws are flawed, in that the *entourage effect* of both molecules has the best results.

 **DEFINITION**

Marijuana has two main active ingredients, molecules called THC and CBD. Each has an individual effect, and together they have what's called an **entourage effect**. Anecdotally, THC creates the mental feeling people get from marijuana, making it good for treating depression and inspiring creativity. It also has variety of physical effects, such as increasing appetite and lowering ocular pressure. CBD is known for reducing seizures, without the psychoactive effect of THC. However, CBD should be combined with a small amount of THC for use. In high doses, CBD without THC causes anxiety, and vice versa. They work best together, which is why patients often choose to use whole-plant medicines, as opposed to molecular extracts.

Although the results have been mostly positive, there have been unintended consequences of legalizing medical marijuana. For example, arrests for street consumption have gone up in some areas, as the laws rarely create consumption centers for patients or adults. People who can't smoke at home due to issues such as living in federal public housing are at risk of violating the law by consuming outdoors. Not surprisingly, considering prohibition's history, people of color have been disproportionally targeted by law enforcement under these consumption laws as well. Equity is a problem across the board, as the competitive processes established to issue marijuana permits favor well-established businessmen. This issue is currently being discussed, as the existing underground industry and the new regulators search for solutions.

Adult Personal Use Laws

In 1972, California voters had a chance to legalize marijuana, as did Oregon the following year, but neither passed. It seems that 1970s America was not yet ready to make the leap into legalization, but the advocate's efforts did not go unnoticed. As a result, the laws changed legislatively state-by-state, reducing criminal penalties for possession in places such as Ohio, California, and Oregon. This decriminalization of marijuana meant that in many places possession was no longer a jailable offense, but simply a misdemeanor.

In Berkeley, the voters passed a radical marijuana legalization law in 1973, making all use legal. The California Attorney General threw that law out, but advocates returned in 1979 with a law that stuck. This new law mandated that the local police were to treat marijuana as their lowest priority, and said the city could not spend any money enforcing marijuana laws, effectively putting teeth into decriminalization. This law inspired the legalization efforts that followed, including successful local decriminalization drives in Seattle and Oakland, and the failed 2010 California initiative, Proposition 19.

HIGH POINTS

Richard Lee, a Texas native living in Oakland, California, wrote the Proposition 19 initiative and directed the marijuana legalization campaign. He had already succeeded in passing Measure Z, a local initiative decriminalizing marijuana possession and sales. He founded Oaksterdam University, ran local medical marijuana dispensary Cafe Blue Sky, and operated the Bulldog Coffeeshop. His bold work moved the anti-prohibition movement forward, but came at a great personal cost. His dispensary and Oaksterdam University were raided by the DEA in 2012, and he is currently facing charges.

Despite not winning, Proposition 19 convinced advocates in Colorado and Washington to create their own legalization initiatives. The two campaigns were quite different, with Colorado's organizers using a "Safer than Alcohol" message, and Washington taking a more conservative tax-and-regulate approach. Both passed with implementation mirroring the campaigns. Colorado now has a thriving marijuana industry, yet Washington's law has had implementation challenges. Oregon and Alaska followed in 2014, creating laws to allow commerce and consumption. Washington, D.C., also passed a legalization law, but only for consumption and no monetary distribution. More states are expected to pass legalization laws soon, including California, Arizona, Nevada, and Maine.

Changing State and Federal Laws

There are plenty of good reasons to change the marijuana laws. Ending marijuana prohibition takes a billion-dollar underground economy, and turns it into a taxed and well-regulated industry. It's a historic change, creating a chance for entrepreneurs and potential employees to enter the industry at its roots. In addition, it will also save our communities money, by lessening the burdens caused by arresting and incarcerating people for marijuana.

Note that there are downsides to ending marijuana prohibition. Regulatory schemes are cumbersome, and implementation and enforcement is indeed patchy. It will also take years to correct the mistakes in the current laws. In addition, not everyone agrees on the terms. A majority of support is lacking for the legalization of marijuana for adult personal use, and medical marijuana struggles to gain margins in the 25 states without laws. Opponents are well funded, and anti-prohibition stakeholders are not always organized or cohesive in their approaches. For a comprehensive marijuana law reform strategy to be effective, all of this must change. One day, maybe Americans will have an inalienable right to use cannabis, which can never again be taken away.

Congress Must Act

Congress must fix the old and outdated drug laws and reschedule marijuana. Nixon may have believed it should be classified as Schedule I back in the 1970s, but both research and anecdotal evidence have since shown its safety and efficacy. Programs like forfeiture, three strikes, and mandatory minimums laws have also failed, and need to be scrapped. It falls on today's Congress to initiate change, but for that to happen, the citizens must convince them and elect representatives who agree. Make sure if you're thinking about starting and running a marijuana business that you are working with others on a strategy to change federal law.

Congress must implement forward-thinking ideas as well. These include funding more research into marijuana's medical potential, including the prevention of Alzheimer's, the treatment of seizure disorders, and the care of cancer patients. They need to reprioritize federal law-enforcement budgets, and provide oversight to assure that funds aren't spent enforcing marijuana prohibition. Internal Revenue Code Section 280e must also be changed so that marijuana businesses are not taxed in a manner reminiscent of the Marihuana Tax Act. Finally, they need to tell the Department of Justice (DOJ) and the IRS to allow marijuana businesses to open bank accounts and have access to credit card processing.

States Cannot Wait to Take Action

Congress has a lot of work to do if advocates continue to make headway ending prohibition, and so do the states. When marijuana prohibition started, it began state by state, then federally, and as it ends, the same is also true. Twenty-five states have replaced marijuana prohibitions with regulations, which have evolved as each explores implementation. Most of the current medical marijuana laws are flawed, some so much so that no one can qualify. In other states, regulators are dragging their feet and won't issue the permits. All of this must be corrected for headway to be made.

Advocates, lawmakers, allies, and the marijuana industry must join together in each state to promote and pass sensible marijuana regulations wherever possible. Certainly this should begin with medical marijuana laws, as patients need access to help immediately. Then, states should move toward evaluating changes to their adult use laws. There likely will be some states resistant to these changes, where medical or adult use is rejected in the future. Hopefully, through votes of the legislature or voter initiatives, marijuana prohibitions will slowly end.

Big Businesses Cashing In

As I've discussed, both the laws and the marijuana marketplace are rapidly changing. Five years ago, most patients had never heard of vape pens, and now they are one of the best-selling items at dispensaries. Ten years ago, edible marijuana products were baked and plastic-wrapped in home kitchens, and now they are made in food-safe kitchens by master chefs. Consumer expectations for flavor, packaging, and dosage have also changed with the times. Big businesses have noticed the potential for serious monetary gain in the marijuana industry and are not likely to let those monies pass them by.

All of this means serious competition for people in the existing marijuana industry. Cannabis cultivators and sellers have been outsiders for a century, hiding in the hills or quiet backrooms to ply their trades. These new entrepreneurs, however, come from the business establishment, with well-funded teams and ready business plans. The former knows the marijuana market inside and out, but have little real-world business experience. The latter are ready to step in without core knowledge of the plant or its uses, but see an opportunity and want to take it.

Starting and running a legal marijuana business sounds like an ideal life change to people on both sides. The time to create well-rounded teams is now. Advocates can share the industry's long-standing dedication to ending prohibition with these new entrepreneurs, and in return, can learn key skills and business management knowledge.

The Least You Need to Know

- Marijuana has been used around the globe.
- The first written reference to marijuana's medical use was in 2000 B.C.E., with archeological evidence of use going back even further.
- Cannabis was made illegal in 1937, when the United States Congress passed the Marihuana Tax Act.
- Advocates have fought a long battle to end marijuana prohibition, which is currently still underway.

Why Open a Marijuana Business?

Cannabis commerce is being touted as America's next billion-dollar industry, and suppliers are stockpiling supplies readying themselves for legalization just like Seagram did with whiskey during the days of Prohibition. During that time, the Seagram Company began selling alcohol for medical and industrial purposes. They anticipated a change, though, so they began stockpiling their whiskey. This enabled them to step into the new alcohol market with a ready supply when federal prohibition ended. Their company grew quickly, posting more than $50 million dollars in annual profits within 10 years. In fact, they currently are still a thriving, billion-dollar company.

Marijuana businesses could follow this same path as marijuana's prohibition is repealed. Getting into the industry before the end of prohibition can provide businesses with a head start on their competition. However, the decision to start a business now should only be made after you evaluate and understand all your personal and legal risks, which could potentially be devastating.

In This Chapter

- Learn the qualifications of business ownership
- Consider the risks of being in the marijuana business
- Preserving your rights through advocacy
- Discover how changing the federal laws is essential

Even with such risks, the cannabis industry continues to be vibrant, and widespread entrepreneurship is creating contagious excitement. The laws of prohibition are changing and opportunities to get into a potentially profitable business can be very appealing.

Is This Business for You?

Entrepreneurship is difficult, and less than 20 percent of Americans own their own business. Most people are simply content to be employees. In the marijuana business, each step of starting a business is like an exam: if you can't pass one hard exam after another, you simply won't succeed. Marijuana entrepreneurs must have the right knowledge, skills, and abilities to compete. There's a lot of competition for permits and funding in this increasingly crowded space, and businesses need to be savvy in order to survive.

The first step in deciding if the marijuana business is for you is to research the legality of marijuana businesses where you want to operate. Never open a *cannabusiness* without doing your research and obtaining the proper permits, as this will lead straight to jail.

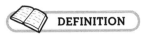 **DEFINITION**

> The word **cannabusiness** is used in the industry to denote marijuana businesses that touch the plant, including dispensaries, extraction labs, and edibles manufacturers. It sometimes refers to companies that serve these businesses, too, such as packaging manufacturers or point-of-sale (POS) software companies.

If your research shows such businesses are not allowed in a specific location, check the legality and ease of obtaining a permit in nearby cities and counties within a commutable distance. You need to live near your business for fast access in emergencies and to prevent commuter burnout. Keep in mind that many cities and states have residency requirements ensuring long-time residents get priority preference.

Profit Potential

There will never be a better time to enter the marijuana industry. This ancient trade is resurfacing from antiquity, and quickly becoming America's next billion-dollar industry. Entrepreneurs from the fields of finance, manufacturing, retail, and marketing are all looking for a way in. Cannabis users are partnering with business experts to create their dream companies. There is an immense amount of excitement about marijuana, and plenty of money available for people with smart business plans.

Creating profitable companies is the goal, and getting involved now will give you a lot of advantages. Your company can get the scoop on prime real estate, as forward-thinking property owners are looking for marijuana tenants immediately. Secure your location and your permit, while others are cautiously waiting in the wings. Future dynasties are being made right now, and you do not want to miss out.

Develop your brand and build its client base now. Satisfied clients will stick with you into the future, and will help bring others in. This is the base of your income, and the more people served, the better for the bottom line. Start amplifying your brand in the media, online, and at events, before the marijuana field gets too crowded. The longer you wait to build a brand, the costlier it will be to find future clients.

The potential earnings are high. Even at small dispensaries, annual sales peak into the millions. Gross margin is close to 50 percent, and pre-tax profits are universally strong. Executive pay and benefits are well above the median, and entry-level pay is often $15 or more. Lenders can expect elevated interest rates in this risky industry, but defaults are rare. And investors are right to be intrigued by the potential future returns. Valuations are on the rise, as prohibition fades away.

This is a fascinating time in American history, where for the second time a failed prohibition is in its waning days. New laws are being passed across the county, and marijuana users and providers are creating them. Get involved now, and you can help write the rules that will govern this burgeoning industry.

Team Qualifications

Marijuana business founders must be experienced in leadership, marketing, and financial management. In addition to you, your business team also needs at least one person experienced in the marijuana industry on board to give sound advice. It's essential that each of your employees is ready to face potential arrest, asset forfeiture, and other drastic side effects of prohibition. Thankfully, the 9th Circuit Court recently upheld a federal budget clause defunding enforcement actions against cannabusinesses in legal states. These laws are confusing, though, and police will still occasionally arrest business operators. Owners will need the fortitude to fight an enforcement action, until federal prohibition ends.

Owner Qualifications

State and local laws will set various qualifications for marijuana business ownership. All company founders and investors must meet these qualifications in order to operate a business. Most laws establish the residency requirements for the length of time applicants must live in that state or city in order to qualify for ownership. Colorado's law initially disqualified any applicant or funder who could not prove two years' residency. However, this changed in mid-2016 with new guidelines for accepting out-of-state investments. California's state law has no limits on residency for owners or funders, but allows individual cities and counties to establish their own requirements.

In California, Oakland's their new law gives permitting priority to applicants who can prove two years' residency in neighborhoods with high marijuana-arrest rates. Their goal is to get marijuana permits to those most affected by the old laws, preventing out of town entrepreneurs from moving in, driving up rents, and diverting profits out of town.

HIGH POINTS

In 2016, the California legislature passed the comprehensive Medical Marijuana Regulation and Safety Act (MMRSA). Bill AB 266 created the Bureau of Medical Cannabis Regulations to govern the system, and established rules for 17 types of marijuana licenses. Bill SB 243 regulates cultivation and establishes environmental protections. Bill SB 643 created rules for applicants, including limitations for felons, and gives more physician oversight to the California State Medical Board.

Expect to be fingerprinted when you go into the marijuana business. State licensing laws include provisions to screen out violent criminals and people convicted of fraud. Many states, such as Massachusetts, also do not allow people with felony drug records to hold licenses. In fact, several approved candidates there were recently denied final permits due to past marijuana convictions. New laws in Oregon and California, however, reverse this trend, exempting marijuana crimes or allowing reformed felons to be considered for ownership on a case-by-case basis.

Other Hurdles to Ownership

There are also other hurdles to consider. Medical marijuana and adult use laws often contain age requirements for users, workers, and founders. Most limit applicants to people over 21 with zero exceptions. Active law-enforcement officers are precluded from owning marijuana businesses, as are seated government officials. Physicians are also often forbidden to own cannabusinesses, especially dispensaries. Regulators must assure that marijuana recommendations are given for medical reasons only, rather than to drive profits at specific retail outlets. Lawyers must carefully consider the risks of ownership, too, as violating federal laws can result in criminal charges and loss of their licenses to practice.

High Safety and Legal Risks

Prohibition is not over yet, and the risks are potentially serious. Federal, state, county, and city laws are all different, with varied consequences for violations. Always carefully review all of these regulations, both for your business's proposed location and for your home. If marijuana transportation is necessary, be sure to check the laws for each jurisdiction along the road. Cities and counties in legal states can and do ban marijuana businesses, especially in areas with low voter support for the issue. Police departments in these areas cling to prohibition-era beliefs, and will arrest operators for perceived offenses. It's expensive and difficult to fight such cases and penalties range from minor fines to felony prison sentences. Before entering the marijuana business, you should retain an attorney to learn your rights during police encounters. Consider all of these factors carefully before making the decision to open a marijuana business.

> **HIGH ALERT**
>
> There are two magic phrases a marijuana business owner should learn. The first is "I choose to remain silent and want to see my lawyer." Once said, the police must stop all direct questioning until your lawyer is present. However, they may still continue to make scary comments or even lie to get you talking. Once you state that phrase, remain silent until legal help arrives.
>
> The second is "I do not consent to this search." Stating it won't stop a search in progress, but it preserves your right to fight back in court.

Running a marijuana business can put you at risk of burglary and robbery. People think cannabusiness owners are flush with cash and products, so it's important to be aware of the crime potential. Never buy, sell, or warehouse cannabis at your home. It's an unsafe practice, and also violates most state and local laws.

Serious Time Commitment

Starting a marijuana business requires an enormous time commitment. Until it's *scaled*, expect to spend your waking hours thinking about how to perfect it. It will take a few months to register the company and write its operational documents, and raising start-up funds can take more than a year. During this period, plan to attend marijuana business conferences and events, and make time to work your connections made there. Founders will spend numerous hours phoning, sending emails, and meeting with potential investors before ever getting funded and launched. Some founders will need to also work a second job for income while their business is in start-up mode.

> **DEFINITION**
>
> A **scaled** business is a fine-tuned operation and ready to expand. It has sustainable procedures and the ability to ramp up or slow down its operations as needed. This business is stable to the point that it could be franchised, sold, or replicated with ease.

Securing a marijuana business permit is the top priority, as investors will have high expectations for a timely launch. However, there could be a long wait between the company's founding and the issuance of a marijuana business license. Along the way, expect your business funders to watch its income and use of funds closely. Be ready to explain any variances and to correct any initial assumptions that fail.

Challenges to Entering the Business

There are other big challenges to also consider. Competition for permits is tough. For example, the dispensary permit process in Berkley, California, started with more than 150 potential candidates and narrowed to a field of only 15 applicants. There were 6 finalists considered by the city council, and 3 eventually received permits. In Maryland, 150 groups applied for the 15 medical-marijuana cultivation licenses granted in 2016, and in Marin County, California, 15 candidates are currently competing for 4 permits. Marijuana businesses need stellar teams, a qualified location, and ready funds to survive these cutthroat competitions.

Raising funds for such businesses is also difficult. Investors and lenders are wary of the quasi-legality of the industry. Federal forfeiture is a concern to investors, who envision their money vanishing in an instant. The nonprofit business requirements found in many state laws limit access to start-up money, leaving loans as the only funding source. Banking is a big problem, too, as most banks will not create accounts for marijuana businesses, making it impossible to secure traditional loans. Many marijuana businesses cannot even take on funding, as they have no bank to receive it.

Large taxes and fees are another concern. Federal IRS rule 280e says that marijuana businesses cannot deduct their normal and regular operating expenses from their taxes, only the cost of goods sold. This means they generally pay 25 percent or more than other companies in federal taxes. Additionally, licensing fees for marijuana businesses are always high. In Oakland, California, cannabusinesses pay 5 percent of all gross income to the city. This means $50 out of every $1,000 goes to the city, compared to the 60 cents charged to grocers or the $1.20 for car dealerships. Excise taxes are even worse, as in Washington state, where cultivators, manufacturers, and retail companies are all charged 25 percent on sales. When combined, these taxes and fees can take away most or all of the profit generated by marijuana businesses.

The final big challenge is finding real estate. Most building owners refuse to rent to marijuana businesses, and if they do, the rent is higher than normal. Most mortgage contracts allow the bank to forfeit properties for violations of federal law, and this includes allowing marijuana businesses onsite. Buying property is also hard, as banks will not issue mortgages to cannabusinesses.

HASHING IT OUT

The squeamish truth is that arrest, forfeiture, robbery, and financial scrutiny are all deal-breaking possibilities. Do not go into the marijuana business without making an informed decision after careful evaluation. It might be the perfect moment to join this burgeoning industry, but only do so with a full understanding of the existing risks.

Being a Marijuana Advocate

Changes in federal and state laws must occur to end marijuana prohibition, and marijuana businesses must contribute to making this happen. Pledging funds to one of the prominent advocacy groups working for reasonable regulations is one way to help. They include reform groups such as Americans for Safe Access and the Drug Policy Alliance. Local marijuana reform groups can be found coast to coast, from California's NORML to Florida's Cannabis Action Network. You won't have a hard time finding an organization that supports your corporate values and goals.

Marijuana businesses can also take direct action to change the laws by reaching out to city, county, state, and federal officials. They are often curious to learn more about marijuana and how the industry works. You should attend city council meetings to speak up about proposed laws, and visit elected officials at their offices to voice your opinions and learn theirs. Don't expect to receive universal support, but it's important to educate those that need it and to build connections with supporters. Marijuana business owners need well-connected lobbyists and should consider joining groups like the National Cannabis Industry Association to pool resources for congressional campaigns.

The Laws Need to Change

State and federal laws are in conflict about marijuana. Twenty-five states and Washington, D.C., have legalized the medical cannabis industry, but it's still considered a felony to the feds, who continue to arrest more than 750,000 people annually for simple possession—that's more than one arrest every minute.

Marijuana is in the *laboratory of democracy* right now. Legalization is being tested at the state level, where trial and error can flourish without mistakes that could affect the entire nation. Liberal states like California, Oregon, and Colorado have laws that allow widespread accessibility. Yet in states where voters are more conservative, such as in Illinois or Maryland, the laws are restrictive. This dynamic plays out inside each state, too, where cities and counties can opt in or out of licensing marijuana businesses.

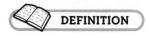 **DEFINITION**

Laboratory of democracy is a phrase coined by Justice Brandeis in the 1932 Supreme Court case, *New State Ice Company v. Liebmann*. This ruling determined that the 10th Amendment gives states the right to exercise autonomy and to act as laboratories for social change. This way, new laws can be tested on a smaller scale, without affecting the whole country. Congress can then evaluate these ideas and adopt successful ones at the federal level.

Legalization could take several paths, depending on how advocacy efforts shape future laws. Congress or the Department of Justice (DOJ) could move marijuana to Schedule III, like aspirin, or to another schedule that allows limited distribution through pharmacies. Or, it could be removed from the Controlled Substances Act altogether and regulated like alcohol, tobacco, or herbal medicines. Decriminalization is also a possibility, with penalties reduced from prison sentences to fines.

Besides ending criminal penalties for marijuana, other federal laws also need to be changed. Cannabusinesses need access to banking and merchant services. The Marijuana Business Access to Banking Act has failed to pass Congress since 2013, but it could soon, thanks to the ongoing efforts of advocates and state regulators. IRS ruling 280e must also be eliminated, so marijuana businesses can take regular tax deductions, and mandatory minimum sentences and forfeiture laws must be changed.

The Public Needs To Be Educated

Although the marijuana issue may be important to you, not everyone shares this view. To be motivated to take or support action, the public must be educated about the high costs of prohibition, the importance of medical marijuana, and the relative harmlessness of adult use. They need to learn facts like how Colorado's crime rates lowered after they legalized adult use, as did instances of drug overdose and highway accidents. People need to hear stories about how medical marijuana is preventing seizures and easing intractable pain.

As a cannabusiness owner, you must dedicate time to ending the stigma attached to marijuana by sharing information about medical marijuana with your friends, family, and community. Most people don't understand how its active ingredients have specific medical benefits. Take time to research the *cannabinoids* THC and CBD, and learn how their effects vary based on potency and method of ingestion. Study the difference between the two types of marijuana, indica and sativa, and how they act together in hybrid plants. Learn how to explain and demystify this plant medicine with this knowledge.

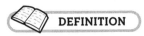 **DEFINITION**

> **Cannabinoids** are the main active ingredients found in marijuana. They are neuro-regulators, facilitating communication between cells. The most important are tetrahydrocannabinol (THC) and cannabidiol (CBD). THC creates the marijuana "high," with benefits such as easing of muscle spasms and reducing nausea. CBD is a nonpsychoactive pain modulator, often used for treatment of seizures.

Patients Need More Information

More people could benefit from the use of medical marijuana, but they are reluctant to try it. As an analgesic, it's safer than aspirin, and Professor Gary Wenk's research at Ohio State University shows that just a puff a day reverses memory impairment and restarts brain cell growth in seniors. This means that marijuana might prevent Alzheimer's disease. But, using a plant medicine is not as simple as taking a pharmaceutical drug. Patients need to be educated about marijuana strains, its potency, and the potential methods of ingestion, and they need help choosing the right products to treat their symptoms.

Patients also need to know the risks. They can still be arrested in legal states, unless in possession of a doctor's recommendation for marijuana. Purchasing outside of dispensaries is generally forbidden, and home cultivation is strictly limited. Violations can lead to arrest and incarceration, so it's important for patients to understand and follow the laws. Marijuana businesses should educate their customers on what to say if confronted by law enforcement. Overzealous law enforcement is still a problem in areas where support of medical marijuana is low.

Getting Involved in the Campaign to End Prohibition

As a marijuana advocate, you have countless ways to get involved. Lobby your elected representatives, sharing facts and personal stories to influence their votes. Provide court support to people on trial for marijuana offenses, showing the prosecutor and judge that voters care about the outcome. Coordinate *jury nullification* campaigns, educating jurors on their right to find cannabis defendants not guilty, despite laws saying otherwise. Join election campaigns to help candidates with cannabis law reform platforms. Coordinate marijuana voter initiatives to change laws and create workable regulations. Teach others to do the same, and you'll help supercharge the efforts to end cannabis prohibition.

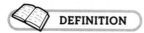 **DEFINITION**

Jury nullification is when a defendant is found not guilty, even though the jury believes a crime was committed. They essentially refuse to apply the law because it's wrong or being misused against the defendant.

Talking About Marijuana

The marijuana plant has faced down a 100-year eradication effort, and bounced back stronger than ever. Early adapters and new recruits alike are fanatical, spreading the word about its uses and the harms of prohibition. Marijuana consumers and entrepreneurs form instant friendships, crossing social and economic boundaries to share experiences. The cannabis community is diverse, thriving, and strong, and joining it is highly enjoyable.

These supporters want the indisputable and inalienable right to use marijuana, and for it never to be taken away again. However, voters are not ready to accept full legalization without more information, and the cannabis users and entrepreneurs themselves need to provide it. Physicians need proven data about the medical applications, going past anecdotal reports and into peer-reviewed and published studies. Your family will also likely question the sanity of risking personal safety to start a marijuana business, so get ready to explain your passion and the importance of this cause.

Discussing Medical Marijuana with Your Doctor

Physicians hold the power to approve use of medical marijuana in states where it's legal. Patients must seek a doctor's recommendation before qualifying for these protections. There are two ways to do this. Patients can find a clinic specializing in medical marijuana, with doctors who are knowledgeable about its uses and can answer questions about the type of marijuana to choose and how to ingest it. However, such clinics are often high-volume clinics, and doctors lack the time to establish a true doctor-patient relationship.

Patients can also seek medical marijuana recommendations from their primary-care physicians, but those physicians may be wary of providing it. Those doctors are in need of information about the effects of marijuana to support its use, so it's important that patients bring supporting data to the appointment, like research studies and credible medical marijuana fact sheets. A doctor won't recommend its use if he cannot understand the benefits. Physicians may also be concerned that their medical licenses might be compromised. In California, the medical board polices doctors for marijuana policy compliance. Several prominent physicians have faced reviews and won, but the fight is costly and time-consuming.

Talking to Your Family About a Marijuana Business

Telling family that you want to start a marijuana business is complicated due to marijuana's perceived bad reputation. The government says it's dangerous; cultivating, manufacturing, and selling marijuana is a federal felony; and people are locked up for life sentences right now. At the same time, it's legal in 24 states for medical purposes and in 4 for adult use. This disconnect in the laws is bewildering and your family may wonder if the risks are worth it.

Prepare your case before broaching the subject. Gather easy-to-understand literature about medical marijuana. Cue a couple of patient testimonial videos showing first-hand accounts. Locate reputable articles about the high costs of prohibition and the successes of state legalization programs. If you are a patient, find specific data about how medical marijuana helps your condition. The discussion will be easier if you are armed with the facts.

Help your family understand that now is the time to open a marijuana business. *First mover advantage* gives ground-level entrepreneurs a jump on future competition. The potential earnings could be extremely high! Today's marijuana businesses will develop consumer loyalty and secure vendor contacts long before less entrepreneurial people get involved. And it's rare that the federal government raids a state-legal business, so the risk of arrest or forfeiture low. Take time to educate and excite your family, so they become your biggest cheerleaders and a support system in hard times.

 **DEFINITION**

> **First mover advantage** is the competitive advantage gained by companies founded early in brand-new industries. This can take forms of securing exclusive vendor contracts and developing market share and consumer loyalty.

The Least You Need to Know

- Marijuana might be the next billion-dollar industry, but there are risks to getting involved now.
- Starting a marijuana business requires a lot of effort over a long time period.
- Cannabusinesses must get involved in campaigns to educate voters and help reform the laws.
- Educating your family, physician, and community about marijuana will help you succeed.

Types of Marijuana Businesses

In today's budding marijuana industry, there are many types of cannabis businesses. It's not just the cultivation and sales of marijuana that bring in revenue or create jobs. Entrepreneurs have entered the space creating entirely new lines of business. These break into two categories, including companies that touch the plant and those that do not.

On one end of the spectrum are manufacturing facilities, distribution companies, and testing labs. All of these handle marijuana, so they are required to operate under a high level of regulatory scrutiny. The same seed-to-sale tracking process and safety protocols found in cultivation and sales facilities are required for these cannabusinesses. On the other side, which is much safer for business owners and investors, are companies that do not touch the plant, but serve those that do. This includes marijuana magazines, point-of-sale (POS) software companies, marketing agencies, and packaging and counter display producers.

You have a lot of choices on where and how to deploy your talents. It's important to research the risks and benefits of each option before getting started. Take your time to find the industry sector that fits your skills and drives your passion.

In This Chapter

- Learn about the various types of marijuana businesses
- Discover the difference between medical marijuana dispensaries and adult-use facilities
- Review both for profit and nonprofit business models
- Explore the history and future of lab testing

Remember, this a rapidly expanding field, so innovation and creative exploration is key. Be inventive and start something new!

Choosing the Right Business for You

There are a multitude of cannabusiness opportunities with just about any function you can imagine. Some of these jobs were previously segregated to the illicit market and available only to those few who dared to operate outside the law. Or, they were isolated to the medical industry where participation was limited to people with existing medical conditions and doctor recommendations for marijuana, or to the few researchers working in licensed research facilities. Nowadays, both groups are becoming mainstream, fashionable, and available to more people.

Start by learning about the different types of marijuana businesses. Research how much they cost to launch and what kind of profits you can expect. Learn the potential roadblocks and explore the likelihood of getting permitted. If these factors add up, this might be the right business for you. All cannabusinesses have the potential to be lucrative, but some more so than others, so do your homework. The industry is in its infancy, and as it grows so will the types of businesses and opportunities.

As more states move to legalize some form of marijuana cultivation, manufacturing, and sales, the blossoming industries' revenues will continue to soar. For example, in California, where medical marijuana has been legal for two decades, there is an estimated $1 billion in annual sales of medical marijuana alone. A report from ArcView Market Research predicts that legal marijuana sales could approach $22 billion by 2020.

HIGH POINTS

Legal cannabis has been recording high dollar sales in all regulated medical or adult-use markets. Revenues are poised to skyrocket, as more states deregulate marijuana. Ending the arrest and prosecution of people for cannabis cultivation and sales will also save millions of additional dollars. This revenue will revert back to local communities and states, providing extra needed funds for public services and education.

Retail Dispensaries

Retail dispensaries have become common in states with medical-marijuana laws. These brick-and-mortar stores sell medicines to approved patients only, under strict regulations and governmental oversight. If you are not privy to what happens inside a dispensary, you might believe what you see in the media, which stereotypically reports that dispensaries are multi-million dollar fronts for recreational users, that they serve mostly those under 25, and that they create a risk for neighborhood children. The opposite is actually true: dispensaries are generally caring nonprofit organizations, serving mostly people over 40 with serious and chronic health conditions.

Another misconception is that people go into a dispensary and smoke marijuana. This is also not true, as most state and local regulations do not allow on-site consumption of any kind. When they do, smoking is generally forbidden in favor of vaporization only. Smoking marijuana and use of open flames are banned. In total, only Oakland, San Francisco, and Berkeley have laws allowing consumption at dispensaries, and less than 10 facilities have the required special use permit necessary to do so. This is because the rules and conditions are strict, and most operators don't want the hassle of providing extra oversight and security.

Dispensaries do not just sell marijuana flowers, which are called buds. They also sell concentrated cannabis products, including hashes, oils, and waxes. They provide topical creams and salves, bath balms, and hair care products. Ingestible marijuana goodies are abundant, with items like cookies, brownies, candy bars, cotton candy, and popcorn available. Capsules and *tinctures* are offered in a variety of potencies and for different specific uses. In all ways, patients and producers alike are getting more sophisticated in their respective needs and abilities.

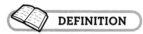 **DEFINITION**

> Marijuana **tinctures** are cannabinoids extracted from the plant using ethyl alcohol, glycerol, vinegar, coconut, or olive oil. THC and CBD bond to these carriers, leaving an infused liquid behind after the plant matter is strained. They are packaged in dropper bottles, so patients can take measured doses straight or infused into beverages.

Types of Retail Dispensaries

Many retail models have popped up since the first dispensary opened in California in 1996. Most are like pharmacies or old-time apothecaries. Patients go into a dispensary with a doctor's note or recommendation. They are assigned to a peer counselor, often called a budtender or patient service clerk, who guides them to products that match their medical needs. Many people find this service useful, especially if they are new to using medical cannabis.

Many dispensaries operate like community centers. They offer adjunct services like massage therapy, chiropractic treatments, acupuncture, and yoga. Members are able to access cannabis-growing classes and patient support groups. Most community-based dispensaries offer compassion programs to provide free and discounted medicine for disabled or low-income patients, and some have other free programs like food closets and clothing drives.

In legal states, visiting a dispensary has become as common as going to a grocery or clothing store. They even have express lines for patients in a hurry and pharmacy-style pick-up lanes for pre-ordered marijuana. Some dispensaries are a lot like Chinese herb stores, where the marijuana is weighed in front of you, and other types of herbal medicines are provided. Lavender, sage, and other herbs with healing properties can also be found at dispensaries.

People who have traveled to Amsterdam are familiar with the "coffee shop" style of marijuana store. Dispensaries that operate on this model offer coffee, tea, and a place to hang out, besides just providing marijuana. This style of facility is not often seen in the United States, although it's certainly coming soon. Magnolia Wellness in Oakland and SPARC and Green Door in San Francisco all operate with this lounge-style model.

Many people who previously purchased marijuana in the illicit marketplace now have medical-marijuana recommendations. They arrive at dispensaries experienced with the medicines and knowledgeable about what works for them. However, the most surprising and fastest growing segment of this business is older patients. Those 60+ are coming into dispensaries like deer caught in the headlights. They have not used marijuana before and need guidance to choose the right medicines. These patients grew up in a different generation believing in reefer madness. Now older and increasingly more health-conscious, they are looking for alternative ways to treat their illnesses. These patients often have the most questions and fears about using marijuana, so it's important for dispensary staff to give them all the information and attention they need. It also ensures a happy and hopefully returning customer.

> **HASHING IT OUT**
>
> I often hear complaints from patients aged 45 and up saying they wish more people their age worked as budtenders. These positions are generally entry level, lower-waged jobs, which attract a younger and less skilled workforce. To stay in tune with the needs of all patients, dispensaries should establish wages and benefits to attract mature and well-trained workers.

Adult-use dispensaries are more akin to regular retail stores rather than like cafés, pharmacies, or community centers. The market in legal states is competitive, so the cannabusinesses focus on quick, safe access, in pleasant and friendly environments. The key to return customers is availability of top-shelf, fairly priced cannabis products. Adult-use customers want the same selections found in dispensaries. Buds, hashes, tinctures, and topicals are all found in these facilities. None of the legal states allow onsite marijuana consumption, so all products are sold to go. It's expected that clients will consume their cannabis products when safely at home.

Size Limitations Matter

Marijuana dispensaries face limitations on where they can locate in each city or county. This includes zoning restrictions that dictate where they are permitted, and exclusionary rules mandating distances from schools, parks, and residential neighborhoods. Finding willing landlords within these limited areas is tough, and dispensaries have very few choices. The size of the rental space determines what goods and services the dispensary is to able offer.

Small spaces are serviceable, with a minimum requirement of about 800 square feet. This is enough room for a reception desk, a small dispensary bar, and a backroom for purchasing and packaging. More space is ideal, with an industry average of about 3,000 square feet. Ideally, each dispensary needs room for an entryway and reception area, a dispensary room with space for four to six retail stations, administrative offices, a purchasing room, and packaging space. Larger dispensaries have community centers and therapy offices, providing needed complementary services to their members.

For-Profit vs. Nonprofit Businesses

State laws dictate whether marijuana businesses can be organized as for-profit or nonprofit businesses. States like Oregon and Colorado allow for-profit companies to own marijuana businesses, while Massachusetts and Illinois require nonprofit operations. In California, the Secretary of State has limited registration to nonprofit businesses for the last decade. This will change in 2018, when the new state medical marijuana laws take effect.

Both for-profit and nonprofit business models have advantages, so familiarize yourself with the benefits and limitations of each. The main difference is that for-profit businesses can pay out profit-sharing bonuses and dividends, whereas nonprofit businesses cannot. Nonprofits can give both regular and performance-based bonuses to staff members. But as there are no shareholders, there are no dividends to be paid. All of the profit stays within the organization to be invested in accomplishing the mission or is saved for the future.

Nonprofit businesses can get special tax breaks and incentives from the city, state, and federal government. That has not yet been the case with the IRS and marijuana businesses, though, as they target cannabusinesses with higher rates instead. These groups operate for a mission, so the organization can act for the good of the community rather than for the profit of the owners. Nonprofit organizations are also eligible for public and private grants that aren't available to for-profit businesses. However, they do face a higher level of public scrutiny to maintain their nonprofit status, and must regularly prove compliance to regulatory agencies.

HASHING IT OUT

Being a nonprofit organization does not mean that your company cannot be successful and make a profit. It simply means that you will pay a corporate tax on those profits like any other business. Being nonprofit also doesn't automatically mean that you are tax exempt. Many nonprofit companies pay corporate taxes. The IRS has yet to grant a tax-exempt status to a canabusiness.

Another concept is blending both for- and nonprofit visions by using a Beneficial Corporation (B-Corp) business model. A B-Corp is a type of for-profit entity that operates for a mission, rather than strictly for a profit. This includes acting for a positive impact on workers, society, and the environment, as well as for-profit goals as defined by the shareholders. They differ from traditional corporations in purpose, accountability, and transparency, but not in taxation. Thirty states allow formation of these corporations, but medical marijuana businesses may be limited in their ability to register this way, due to their for-profit status.

Cultivation Facilities

Marijuana cultivation is difficult, and there are real risks. These facilities can only be opened in legal states and in cities and counties that permit marijuana use. Starting an unlicensed grow can be a devastating mistake. The legal and financial consequences are simply not worth it. Enforcement agencies are able to destroy the crop and force growers to forfeit their equipment at will. Owners and workers are subject to costly legal battles, and prison is a real possibility. Before cultivating marijuana, always review your local legalities and prepare to follow the rules.

It's a novice mistake to think that commercial cultivation is the same as home growing. Entrepreneurs who succeed with small crops in garages and closets find the move to large-scale production difficult. It's not just a matter of multiplying formulas for a bigger space. Industrial cultivation requires a familiarity with farming techniques that prevent and eliminate pests, molds, and mildews on a larger scale. Marijuana also has specific lighting needs, and the plants depend on proper airflow and nutrients to thrive. Top cultivators spend years developing strategies to create maximized environments for cannabis growth. Marijuana entrepreneurs should always hire a *master grower* to manage their crop.

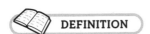 **DEFINITION**

> **Master growers** are cultivators who are experienced in management of industrial-sized cannabis facilities. They have proven experience producing consistent high-test plants. These growers are often marijuana breeders, who have created award-winning strains.

Indoor, Outdoor, and Greenhouse Cultivation

There are three basic types of cultivation facilities: indoor, outdoor, and greenhouse. Indoor cultivation is a product of prohibition and the need to grow marijuana without being detected. The job of the indoor cultivator is to create an outdoor environment inside. They trick the plant into thinking it's outside. Indoor cultivation is good for the creation of high-grade marijuana, as the environment can be manipulated to maximize light, water, and airflow. The cannabis can be kept pure in these carefully controlled environments, limiting the likelihood of pests, molds, mildews, and other contaminants. The downside is the real impact these facilities have on the environment, from the high electrical and water need to the importance of having safe waste-disposal systems for chemicals and plant waste.

Outdoor and greenhouse cultivation are harder to control. Bugs, molds, and mildews have veritably unfettered access to the plants. But the lowered costs and relative benign nature of marijuana contaminants makes these methods attractive to cultivators. And since the plant evolved to grow in natural sunlight, it excels in outdoor environments. The debate between the two schools of thought, indoor versus outdoor, is intense. This is amplified by the fact that indoor cultivation allows for up to four grow cycles a year, whereas outdoor growers are limited to a maximum of two in most regions.

Indoor cultivation is more expensive than outdoor cultivation, requiring the grower to purchase special lighting and apparatuses such as air conditioning, humidifiers, fans, charcoal filters, and timers. Indoor cultivation has its own challenges in controlling things like pests and molds as well as other factors that affect the end product. Walls are porous, air-intake systems bring in molds and mildews, and vents leave room for bugs to creep into the facility.

Your local climate can also be the deciding factor. In regions with extreme heat or cold where the growing season is short, you have no choice but to grow indoors or to try greenhouse cultivation. Greenhouse cultivation offers growers the best of both worlds, using natural sunlight while maintaining the ability to control the environment. Growers can add artificial lighting when needed, and they can control airflow to cool the space during heat waves. Greenhouse growers can cultivate three crops a year, compared to their outdoor counterparts stuck with a maximum of two. Plus, using mainly natural sunlight versus powered light provides a big cost savings, resulting in a competitive pricing edge above indoor crops.

Space Regulations

Like dispensaries, state and local municipalities impose limits on the size of cultivation facilities. The fear is that large indoor and outdoor marijuana grows will attract crime, flooding the illicit marketplace with purloined marijuana that makes its way to children. The reality is that it's illegal cultivation that attracts crime. Licensed cultivation is monitored with the highest security. These facilities are inspected by regulators for leakage and loss, and violators face penalties up to jail time for violations.

State and local size regulations can vary widely, with some setting square-footage limits and others establishing plant-count maximums. For example, California's new state laws will permit licensed indoor cultivation facilities from 2,500 to 22,000 square feet in size. Outdoor facilities can be up to 42,560 square feet (one acre) or 50 plants total if not housed together. Permit fees will be charged by parcel size, with large facilities paying more. Local municipalities can establish additional size limits. Urban areas generally do not permit large outdoor marijuana grows, due to the risk of theft and diversion. They limit space for indoor cultivation, too, as large grow facilities require less staff than nonmarijuana manufacturing uses.

Manufacturing Spaces

Before the legalization of cannabis in Colorado, Denver's industrial marketplace was already in the early stages of economic recovery. The legalization of marijuana contributed to rent growth and drove a decline in vacancy in the local real estate marketplace. Only 67 of the 321 local jurisdictions in Colorado allow medical and retail marijuana licenses, and with marijuana entrepreneurs rushing to deliver their product into the marketplace, they snapped up all the possible spaces. This demand has led to the industry's willingness to pay upwards of three times the normal market rates.

The average size of manufacturing facilities ranges from 2,500 to 20,000 square feet. Licensed marijuana production spaces are tightly regulated in every way, from the size and location of the facility to the type and quantity of the goods made. They are subject to fire, building, environmental, and health department inspections, and failure to comply with regulations can result in immediate loss of any license. Marijuana product manufacturers are held to high safety standards, as the processes often use volatile substances and volatile substances that will be ingested by patients.

HIGH POINTS

State medical and adult-use marijuana laws give control to local municipalities. Each gets to decide whether to permit or ban cannabis cultivation, manufacturing, and sales. Like dry counties after alcohol prohibition, citizens in many areas aren't yet ready to embrace cannabusinesses. If allowed, local zoning regulations designate the areas where marijuana businesses are allowed.

There are a large variety of marijuana manufacturing companies. The most widespread are those that make ingestible food-based medicines like cookies and brownies. Cannabis extraction companies are the next most popular. These break into two categories, based on whether or not they use volatile solvents to extract the cannabinoids from the plant matter. Nonsolvent-based processes use ice or shaking to create high potency cannabis extracts. These processes are used to make hash and keif by breaking the resin off the leaves.

CO_2 and butane are also used to extract cannabinoids from the plant matter. The first process is nonflammable, but the latter creates problems. Butane explosions are rocking America as unpermitted outlaws have set up facilities to supply the demand for this popular marijuana product. These sites need fire and planning department oversight in order to be considered safe. Like the exploding moonshine stills during prohibition, licensing and regulating marijuana is key to ending this problem.

BAS Research is one of California's only licensed extraction labs, permitted and inspected by the city of Berkeley.
©Clifford Lee Nichols

Finding the Right Zone

Finding the right zone for your use is the first step to complete regulatory compliance. Marijuana manufacturing businesses are required to operate in specific areas as determined by local municipalities. Some states have cottage industry laws, allowing small-scale production at home. California's cottage industry law allows up to $50,000 in wholesale baked goods to be manufactured at home. However, marijuana edibles can only be made in homes if local rules also permit it.

Potential locations vary based on the type of marijuana products produced. Making marijuana edibles and sifted hash is generally considered light manufacturing. These businesses are allowed in areas typically reserved for commercial food manufacturing or small-scale production of consumer-ready goods. Heavy solvent manufacturing like butane or CO_2 extraction may be required in industrial manufacturing zones for safety reasons, often on a city's outskirts, away from large population concentrations.

Following All the Rules

Just like any other business, marijuana manufacturers are required to follow all rules regarding fire safety, building codes, and health department regulations. These rules are generally spelled out in local municipal laws or the application regulations. Receiving and maintaining a marijuana license is dependent on following all of these requirements. Cannabusinesses face heightened regulatory oversight and frequent inspection, and it's essential to always be up to code.

Of primary concern is the safety of products being created for human consumption. Manufacturers must follow all codes and protocols to make pure medicines. Marijuana edibles producers are no different than those in the noninfused commercial food service industry. Kitchen managers must be well-trained in handling procedures, and regular health department inspections should occur to assure the facility safety.

Distribution and Transportation

Cannabis has historically made its way to the marketplace in one of three ways. The first is through individual brokers, who act as middlemen between the cultivators and manufacturers and the sellers. They source cannabis from a few farms and supply it to dealers, who sell to their friends. Second is through informal distribution networks. In this scenario, products are gathered from various sources in larger amounts and sold to *brokers* or individuals who sell it to others. Finally, individuals can source their cannabis directly from their contacts with farms or underground manufacturing facilities. These models, which evolved out of necessity, have grown to become the industry standard for distribution in the regulated industry.

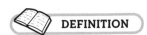 **DEFINITION**

A cannabis **broker** is the person who arranges sales between the supplier and buyer, working directly with cultivators and manufacturers to source a supply. They arrange transportation and manage pricing, terms, and payments from the buyer to the seller. Brokers get paid either a percentage of each sale or a flat rate per unit, with $100 a pound being the current average pay.

Brokers still supply the medical marijuana industry in California, where seed-to-sale production is not yet regulated. They gather marijuana from either regulated or clandestine grows and deliver it to dispensaries. Brokers are responsible for collecting payments—cash on delivery or on consignment—and they pay suppliers, taking a fee for the service. In other legal states, marijuana is produced at vertically integrated farms owned by the dispensaries or is purchased from licensed producers. Specialists deliver the medicine from farms to dispensaries, assuring the purity of the medicine and the legality of the transportation plan.

Distributors are moving into today's legal cannabis industry. They operate much like those in the alcohol industry, buying a variety of bulk products from manufacturers and reselling them to retail shops at wholesale prices. Such entities wield great power in the alcohol industry, and those entering the marijuana industry are getting pushback against their monopolistic tendencies.

Brokers Become Distributors

Today's legal marijuana markets often require officially licensed distributors and transportation specialists. Casual marijuana brokers no longer exist, replaced with drivers tightly controlling the movement of marijuana from producers to sellers. Transporters are required to carry bills of lading and to obtain approval for travel plans. They're often electronically tracked between locations, which prevents unwanted law enforcement encounters and protects drivers from theft. This careful monitoring of transportation and distribution helps assure that marijuana products do not fall into the illicit marketplace.

Distributors gather marijuana products from multiple sources, storing them for sale to a variety of clients. They lab test these products in bulk, verifying purity and potency and eliminating testing fees for dispensaries. Successful distributors offer whole plant flowers, edibles, topicals, and extracts, all available for immediate safe delivery. This means less work for dispensary buyers, who can fill most of their needs with one phone call, and a single delivery and payment.

Alcohol distributors are starting to compete in the marijuana industry, as they have the experience and infrastructure to make headway. They have had decades of practice transporting heavily regulated products to the marketplace, and are well known to state compliance officials. They targeted California's booming industry in a big way, lobbying the state to create a mandatory distribution law. This hotly debated policy, if allowed to take effect in 2018, will mandate that all marijuana products be sold through licensed distributors, eliminating all sales through broker dealers and direct farm to retail sales.

Safe Product Transportation

Law enforcement agencies are not keen on marijuana legalization, and they have a hard time letting go of its prohibition. Police still target distributors and transporters on the road. After the 1996 law passed, the California Highway Patrol (CHP) refused to stop arresting people for medical marijuana. Americans for Safe Access, a nonprofit organization, sued them on behalf of patients. They won the case, so CHP is now mandated to follow the laws.

Most states have strict rules governing the transportation of legal cannabis. Vehicles carrying marijuana need to be registered and insured, and all drivers must have valid licenses on board. Any documentation required by law has to be complete and easily accessible in the vehicle. Cannabis products should be stored in a smell-free and secure manner such as being locked in the trunk or a travel safe. Drivers must follow all rules of the road, using signals when turning or changing lanes, never following too closely to other vehicles, and stopping at all mandated signs and crossings.

 **HIGH ALERT**

The majority of the people stopped while transporting cannabis are pulled over for minor vehicle infractions. Erratic lane changes, cracked windshields, and speeding or driving too slow can each lead to police encounters. It's essential drivers follow all the rules of the road when transporting marijuana.

Door-to-Door Delivery Services

Marijuana sellers have delivered cannabis door to door for decades. They buy a pound from a grower or broker, break it into smaller units, and provide these to clients for a sale at a modest mark up. This mode of sales isn't allowed in most legal states, which limit transactions to licensed and secure dispensaries. Only California allows delivery-based sales, although others, such as Oregon and Washington, allow patients to share cannabis between each other at home. It doesn't mean sales don't happen this way, just not legally. A quick online search will guide anyone to countless unlicensed and illegal marijuana delivery services in legal states.

Legalizing Pot Dealers

Medical marijuana delivery is just like getting a pizza, except your medical recommendation must be verified first. Cannabis orders are phoned in or managed online. After a short wait, the driver arrives at the door with your order. Payment is transacted in cash or by credit. The driver spends only a few minutes at your home, verifying the contents of the order and transacting the payment. Unfortunately, not every patient has convenient access to delivery as few states and cities are willing to license them.

Underground delivery services are prolific in California and several other legal states. In the California Bay Area, the region's finest cannabis is only available by delivery. CRAFT Cannabis is a farm-direct service, with master growers producing indoor flowers and a front office that coordinates direct delivery to members. This vertically integrated method keeps costs down for both the organization and its patients, but is in a legal gray area according to city law. Berkeley, where it's headquartered, only allows sales at dispensaries and in private homes, where there's a limit of 10 clients per day with no available delivery service.

Licenses and Taxation

Delivery services are not currently licensed to operate anywhere, other than a few dispensaries in California whose city regulations allow this adjunct use. Oakland, California, is planning to license independent marijuana delivery companies soon, as a part of an equity-based effort to diversify the industry. Delivery services have a lower barrier to entry than other cannabusinesses, without the costly need to meet the high manufacturing standards required for producers or the security protocols of retail dispensaries. Creating this license will make it easier for small business people to get involved in the cannabis industry, creating more company owners, jobs, and additional avenues of safe access for users.

Licensed delivery companies will need a commercial headquarters where they can conduct business. These headquarters will have to meet minimum security protocols, including proof of safe storage of all cannabis and cash. Once permitted, these delivery services will be required to pay all federal, state, and local taxes and licensing fees, along with funding payroll taxes and workers compensation. Currently, millions of dollars in illicit cannabis is being sold door to door, so licensing this part of the marketplace will create safer communities and add much needed funding to public coffers.

Product Testing Labs

The early days of marijuana testing were filled with questions about what *standards* to use, which equipment to test on, and what type of tests were needed to assure potency and quality. During these initial stages of experimentation, there was little industry confidence in the results being provided by the marijuana testing companies. Each lab took years to create and verify their methods, and early dispensaries were test subjects helping to create these systems.

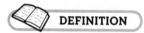 **DEFINITION**

> Lab **standards** are small samples of the test subject material, which are used to calibrate lab equipment. These are generally secured from agencies that produce them for lab use, but marijuana standards are only available to federally licensed facilities. State permitted cannabis labs often make their own standards, calling into question the veracity of their findings.

Data Utilization

Nowadays, sophisticated analytical testing laboratories are part of the marijuana market. Such laboratories measure the medicine's potency, screen for molds and mildews, and detect contaminants from pesticides and fertilizers. Patients and adult users who purchase at licensed facilities know exactly what they're getting for their money due to such testing. Patients no longer have to gamble with the potency of edibles, where eating too much has adverse effects. Molds not visible to the naked eye are now detectible, and immune-compromised patients are more protected from harm.

Cultivators use lab data to standardize production, creating safer, consistently available medicines. In addition, dispensary buyers can now purchase products based on potency and purity, thus providing patients access to reliable medicines. This testing created safety and standardization in a business that long relied on the casual assurances of illicit growers and sellers.

Currently, California hosts more than a dozen cannabis-testing labs, and other medical cannabis states have followed suit. Producers, retailers, regulators and marijuana users all agree that lab testing marijuana products makes sense.

Berkeley's Steep Hill Lab was the first medical marijuana testing facility in America.

Driving Innovation Through Lab Testing

As the first analytical laboratory dedicated to medical cannabis, Steep Hill was able to make market-changing discoveries. They were the first to identify and test for the high-CBD marker in marijuana. These tests identified plants that cultivators and patient advocates then used to develop new medicines for the treatment of seizure disorders. They led the drive for self-regulation of the lab testing industry, in lieu of access to regular lab accreditation processes.

Steep Hill was also a driving force behind the profiling of cannabis-specific terpenes. Terpenes are the fragrance molecules emanating from all plants, including marijuana. These account for the unique scent variations found between strains. Terpenes are also found in essential oils, where lavender is used for calming and tea tree oil is used as a skin care product. Cannabis is unique in that each strain has a specific profile of terpenes, which are believed to exhibit medicinal properties independent from the cannabinoids. Overall, they contribute to a strain's entourage effect.

HASHING IT OUT

Some of the first labs that were available to cannabis businesses did not hire experienced lab technicians to perform their cannabinoid profiling. They instead hired people from the cannabis industry, and taught them how to perform the tests. The best labs quickly abandoned this practice, opting for professionally trained technicians to ensure integrity of the results.

Today, the push continues to assure that testing labs are using sound practices and producing verifiable results. Driven by regulations in legal states, it creates testing regulations and minimum requirements for this new industry. Government oversight and access to third-party standards will continue to help assure accountability for consistent, timely, and trustworthy results.

The Least You Need to Know

- Each municipality sets zoning requirements, which limit the areas where marijuana businesses can be located.
- Regulatory compliance is essential for cannabusinesses, and all building, fire, and safety codes must be followed.
- Most existing marijuana delivery services are unlicensed, and the industry must to keep pushing for regulations and access to these permits.
- Lab testing assures the potency and purity of the medical marijuana supply, and has lead to important discoveries that benefit patients.

Medical Marijuana vs. Adult Personal Use

The line between medical and adult personal use is blurry. Marijuana is an analgesic, and it's safer than aspirin. Many adults who smoke it for recreational purposes are using it to lower pain and reduce stress. In addition, marijuana prevents glaucoma and Alzheimer's disease, with prophylactic effects that are becoming important to our aging population.

Conversely, people without medical conditions sometimes secure marijuana recommendations. These people are afraid of the dangers found in the illicit marketplace, and want access to the variety of cannabis products available at dispensaries. More states are regulating adult use and sales of marijuana, and this abuse of the system will fade as prohibition does. In the meantime, it's important to focus on medical marijuana patients whose health depends on the availability of clean medicines.

In This Chapter

- Explore the difference between medical and adult-use marijuana
- Study the active ingredients in the plant
- Find out why there are so many cannabis strains
- Learn what conditions are helped by medical marijuana

Understanding Marijuana Use

Medical marijuana is legal in 28 States, the District of Columbia, and Guam. Adult use of marijuana is legal in Colorado, Washington, Oregon, Alaska, California, Maine, and Massachusetts. The exact same products are consumed by both user groups. They're produced with the same cultivation methods and manufactured employing identical production standards. Medical marijuana dispensaries and adult-use facilities both operate in similar manners, with membership requirements and point-of-sale (POS) tracking systems.

The differences between these facilities are small, with only their corporate missions, visions, and values distinguishing them. Medical dispensaries serve the chronically ill, and generally offer adjunct services that benefit their members. These dispensaries are likely nonprofit organizations, governed by boards of directors rather than shareholders. Adult-use facilities are profit-driven companies, with most in the industry operating in a socially responsible manner, focusing on the environment, sustainability, and community partnerships.

Patients at dispensaries have a true medical need. They have proven this to a physician, who recommended marijuana as a useful treatment. Cannabis provides these people with specific symptomatic relief, which they understand and can articulate. Adult users like marijuana because it's relaxing and makes them feel good. They use it for the experience, rather than for any specific medical benefit. Some use marijuana to have fun and lower their normal inhibitions, consuming it at concerts, before art openings, and as an accompaniment to a gourmet meal. This type of marijuana use is often labeled recreational.

A lot of people believe that all marijuana use is medical. Dennis Peron, author of the California initiative that legalized medical marijuana, promotes this philosophy. Supporters tout the idea that there's no such thing as recreational use, saying that all users gain some medical benefit regardless of their intent. Studies have proven that this may be true, with results ranging from showing lower rates of alcohol and drug abuse to proving that cannabis helps remove plaque from the brain in recreational users.

What Is Medical Marijuana?

Although it's the same as all marijuana, medical marijuana is an elevated form of the product. It's grown using standardized methods, tested for potency, and screened for contaminants. It's packaged and transported using safe-handling processes to licensed dispensaries with trained staff members who help patients decide what products work for their specific symptoms.

Medical marijuana acts on the human endocannabinoid system (ECS), which is a group of receptor sites found throughout the brain and body. When cannabis is ingested, THC and CBD travel to these sites. It's a *neuromodulator*, meaning marijuana helps smooth communication between neurons in the body, mostly in the central nervous system. Humans make their own internal cannabinoids, called endocannabinoids, which are supplemented by the ingestion of external cannabis. The ECS modulates a variety of body functions, like pain, appetite, and mood.

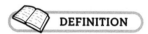

DEFINITION

> **Neuromodulators** facilitate communication between neurons, assuring that each fulfills its proper function. THC acts as a tool, helping to organize these complex actions in the human body.

Two endocannabinoid receptors, CB1 and CB2, have been identified so far. CB1 receptors are found in the brain, nervous system, and stomach. CB2 receptors are found mostly in the skin, immune system, and mucous membranes. Medical cannabis acts on these sites, providing relief for problems related to the functions managed by each. It's no surprise that patients use marijuana for stomach disorders, pain relief, and to ease stress conditions.

Making the Choice to Use Medical Marijuana

People should fully understand the laws before choosing to use medical marijuana. Each state and municipality has varied rules on patient rights, and with those come responsibilities. Patients have to keep their medicine out of reach of children and pets, cannot drive while intoxicated, and must not divert it to the illicit marketplace. Cannabis use, even medical, is not without risks, from social stigma to arrest.

Not everyone will be understanding and empathetic about your choice to become a medical marijuana patient. Be prepared to deal with the uncomfortable situation of encountering a prohibitionist. Decide how you will respond, and be ready with facts about medical marijuana. Many people hide their marijuana use from family and friends, even when recommended for medical reasons. Some become advocates, working to educate others.

Medical marijuana is federally illegal, and participants in state programs are still subject to arrest and prosecution. Many people are uncomfortable violating any law, so they currently refrain from using medical marijuana. Patients also face prosecution for breaking state marijuana laws, which have strict possession and cultivation limits. People in states without a regulated industry should not use medical marijuana, as getting caught can result in arrest and jail time.

Michigan is currently the only state that protects patients from being fired from their job for using medical marijuana. Workers in every other legal state can be terminated, simply for being a medical marijuana patient. California's Supreme Court ruling grants this right to employers, which is unlikely to change soon. People who work in jobs that require drug testing should not use medical marijuana, even if they have a doctor's approval.

HASHING IT OUT

Although Michigan does provide job protections to medical marijuana patients, the legislation doesn't apply to people who work for the federal government. People who live in Michigan, but work for the Department of Transportation (DOT), the Federal Aviation Agency (FAA), and other such agencies are not granted these same rights.

Adult Recreational Marijuana Use

Recreational users consume cannabis to create positive feelings, referred to as being "high." The majority are responsible people, quietly ingesting various forms of marijuana at home. Its use does not negatively affect their daily lives. Despite prohibition, most Americans don't think it's an incredibly deviant pursuit, so the risk of being stigmatized is low.

Cannabis use is still hotly contested, though, and clashes between spouses can divide families. Users have been denied child custody in countless cases. Even in supportive households, the smell can be considered offensive. Consumers are often relegated to the garage in order to keep it out of the house and away from neighbors.

In legal states, consumers have access to a variety of cannabis products. These must be taken home for use, as neither public consumption nor social clubs are allowed. Of course, these laws do not stop recreational users from gathering together to smoke marijuana. California's proposed legalization initiative, Proposition 64, allows cannabis social clubs, which will hopefully set a new precedent for other states to follow.

Medical Cannabis Explained

The medical effects associated with marijuana are created by the interactions of various compounds found in the plant. Cannabinoids like THC and CBD are the main active ingredients, in combination with the smell molecules called terpenes. These work together in various combinations to create specific benefits for patients. It's only in the last decade that the measurement of these compounds has been available on products sold at dispensaries. This essential information aids patients in choosing the right medicines for their medical needs.

Patients choose their medicine based on the effects they seek. Dosage, strain, and method of ingestion all determine what symptomatic relief can be expected. Low potency cannabis in small doses is good for nausea and anxiety. Conversely, high doses of cannabis can cause nausea and anxiety. Patients treating serious illnesses like cancer require a high potency dose, up to 1,000 milligrams a day, as tolerance builds through regular use.

Active Ingredients

The major psychoactive ingredient in marijuana is tetrahydrocannabinol (THC), though its other cannabinoids have medical properties, too. Cannabidiol (CBD) is used for pain relief; cannabinol (CBN) is for sleep; and cannabigerol (CBG) is a muscle relaxer. With more than 100 cannabinoids identified in the plant so far, the potential number of benefits is huge. However, more research is needed to learn about the specific functions and interactions of each.

The potency of cannabis is measured using THC and CBD as the common markers, as most lab tests do not yet include the other cannabinoids. The THC in cannabis grown outdoors generally ranges from 10 to 15 percent, with greenhouse flowers coming in at 12 to 18 percent THC. Indoor-grown marijuana is more potent, with test results showing 12 to 25 percent THC. CBD is limited to certain marijuana strains, which were only recently identified and are just now being widely distributed to cultivators.

Ingestible food-based product doses are measured by the milligram. The average patient consumes between 5 and 25 milligrams for medical purposes. People with serious conditions, or high tolerances, take approximately 100 milligrams per use. There can be serious negative effects from consuming too much marijuana. Users must know the potency and dose of any cannabis they plan to ingest, or they should just say no.

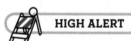

HIGH ALERT

> People who eat too much marijuana can have adverse reactions including racing heart, paranoia, and dizziness. It can result in an emergency room visit, where the patient will be monitored until the effects pass. The feelings peak after about two hours, waning slowly from there.

THC occurs naturally in the plant in its inactive form, which is called THC acid (THCA), which seems to modulate the immune system. When heated, smoked, or baked, it converts to THC in a process called *decarboxylation*. Raw THCA also has medical benefits, although it doesn't act on the endocannabinoid system. Patients juice the raw plant, and drink it much like they do wheat grass, using it as an anti-inflammatory.

DEFINITION

> **Decarboxylation** is a chemical reaction that occurs in cannabis when heated, which removes a carbon molecule from the plants THCA, changing it to its psychoactive form, THC.

Terpenes bind to cannabinoid receptors in the brain. They have specific effects, including making the THC "high" effect more intense. Terpenes are molecules that produce smell. Patients can gather some information about a strain's expected effects by sniffing the dried flower. Using smell, feel, appearance, and potency as guides, it's possible to gauge the general effects of marijuana products.

Major Terpenes Found in Marijuana

Terpene Type	Use
Pinene	An anti-inflammatory bronchodilator
Linalool	A sedative for anxiety and stress
Myrcene	Low dose: an energizer High dose: sedative
Limonene	To treat anxiety and depression
Beta Caryophyllene	An anti-inflammatory with analgesics effects

Excerpted from SC Labs (sclabs.com/learn/terpenes.html)

Terpenes should be consumed at low heat, as their medical value is diminished or eliminated at boiling. Patients seeking the benefits of terpene therapy should use heat-adjustable devices such as vapor pens to consume them. This way the full flavor and the potential for medical benefits are kept intact.

Differences Between Sativa and Indica

All strains are derived from two basic types of marijuana: cannabis sativa and cannabis indica. These started as the same variety, but evolved over eons to separate strains with different appearances and effects. Sativa strains come from warm climates with lots of sun and long days. It originated near the equator in places like Thailand, Jamaica, and South America. Sativa strains take longer to grow and mature than indica plants, in part because they are taller with long branches and arm-sized buds. They grow best outdoors under natural light, but can be raised indoors with proper care.

Indica strains come from cooler climates in places such as Afghanistan, India, and Morocco, which have shorter days and get less sun. Indica grows smaller and faster than sativa, with plants maturing indoors after only 8 weeks, as compared to the 10 to 12 weeks required by sativa strains. The same applies outdoors, where sativa plants grow as big as trees and indicas remain smaller like a wide-leafed bush.

Cultivators choose to grow sativa, indica, or hybrid plants based on their location, grow method, and their potential resale values. Indica has a grow cycle that allows four indoor and two outdoor crops annually. Sativa growers can get a maximum of three indoor crops annually, sometimes less, and two outdoors if *forced flowering* techniques are used.

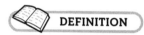 **DEFINITION**

> Outdoor marijuana is planted in the spring, growing tall and wide for several months. It flowers, creating consumable buds, when daylight hours wane in the fall. **Forced flowering** is when outdoor growers cover plants with dark material beginning in the summer. By leaving them in darkness for 12 hours a day, the plants are tricked into believing it's fall and time to flower.

Cultivators breed sativa and indica strains together to create hybrid strains. These are popular at dispensaries, as they bring together the best aspects of each plant type. Sativa strains are known for being uplifting, like coffee, and are used for conditions such as depression and chronic fatigue. Indicas are relaxing and help with pain, sleep, and anxiety. Hybrids combine the two types of effect in one experience. Patients often prefer this to a pure strain, as sativas can be too racy and indicas too sleepy. Hybrids are like the Goldilocks of marijuana—just right.

Sativa sells for more per pound to dispensaries due to its rarity. Cultivators don't like the longer grow cycle and the additional space needs, so fewer produce it. Indica strains are less pricey, as they are quicker and easier to cultivate. Hybrids are priced the same as indicas, unless the strain is well-known and popular. Celebrity breeders and their strains demand higher prices, but they do sell at a higher price point and move faster than other strains.

 HASHING IT OUT

> It's impossible to name the average cost of a pound of marijuana, as the market varies from state to state. Wholesale pounds list for up to $6,000 in Illinois where supply is scarce, and for less than $3,000 in the flooded California marketplace. For perspective, here are the average prices of marijuana in California for high-grade indoor pounds:
>
> - Celebrity hybrid: $2,900
> - Sativa: $2,700
> - Indica: $2,600
> - Hybrid: $2,500
> - CBD strains: $1,800

Why So Many Strains?

Indicas and sativas evolved naturally, developing specific characteristics based on their origin. These heirloom marijuana varieties are called *landrace* strains, and they were locally domesticated and adapted through agriculture to thrive in each region. Once humans started using marijuana, seeds from these plants traveled around the globe. Landrace varietals bred with each other, both purposefully and by spontaneous processes, creating hybrids. These hybrids bred with other marijuana plants, creating even more strains.

Thousands of strains are available in today's marketplace. Each is either a landrace strain or originated with landrace parents. Marijuana breeders carefully select strains to hybridize for specialized effects, creating a constant flow of new types. Naming rights are assigned to the breeder, other than for landrace plants, whose names are historic. Strains created by well-known breeders, with a satisfying bouquet and a stable cannabinoid profile, become world-famous. Modern strains like Jack Herer, Super Lemon Haze, Granddaddy Purple, and OG Kush are sought after in dispensaries, as they are dependable, beneficial medicines.

How Does Marijuana Work in My Body?

The endocannabinoid system plays an important role in the human body, regulating the immune system, pain response, thought processes, and other essential functions. Its CB1 and CB2 receptor sites absorb the THC and CBD cannabinoids when marijuana products are consumed. This starts a process of communication between neurons, providing specific benefits or negative effects, depending on the product's molecular components, its potency, and the dose.

The CB1 receptor seems to attract THC, and CBD goes to the CB2 sites. The CB2 receptor is found in the immune system and mucus membranes, which makes sense as CBD acts as an anti-inflammatory. It's also known to counteract the THC "high" that's felt, and can be used to calm patients experiencing an adverse reaction. CBD research is less pronounced, as it's a new field of inquiry. Steep Hill Lab first spotted CBD in plants coming from a Northern California grower only about five years ago. The plants did not look pretty, but, patients were drawn to them none-theless, and the cultivator was curious to understand why. Testing showed CBD was the reason, and several marijuana varieties that were formerly considered unsalable were discovered to contain this beneficial cannabinoid.

Patients need to understand which product they should use for their specific treatments. For example, people hoping to sleep must avoid sativas, and those with depression should stay away from indicas. Recreational users want to understand how to match cannabis to the activity they have planned. Using sativa before a sporting activity is motivating, and indicas help relax sore muscles. However, a heavy dose of indica makes users sleepy, and a high CBD strain even more so. Athletes should stick to hybrids, or start with sativas and move to indicas after their activity.

Understanding the difference between sativa, indica, hybrids, and CBD is easy, especially at licensed dispensaries where trained staff members can guide clients to the right choices.

Conditions Treatable with Marijuana

Marijuana has been used as medicine for 10,000 years, and was legal until 1937. Its uses are well documented, both through studies done at esteemed institutions and with anecdotal evidence collected by researchers. Even at the height of the 1980s War on Drugs, the U.S. government continued to supply a limited number of patients with marijuana cigarettes to treat cancer, AIDS, and glaucoma. By the 1990s, word was out that marijuana was medicine, mostly thanks to motivated grassroots advocates and evidence showing that prohibition was a failure.

The FDA has approved synthetic THC to treat nausea and improve appetite. It's available by prescription only in Marinol (dronabinol) and Cesamet (nabilone). GW Pharmaceuticals conducted successful trials of Sativex, a whole plant THC and CBD cannabis extract, mainly for people suffering from neuropathic pain. Sativex is not yet available in the United States, but can be found in pharmacies throughout Europe and Canada.

Some patients prefer the stability of prescription medications, but most choose to frequent dispensaries instead of pharmacies. This is in part because people prefer natural over synthetic THC. It's also because dispensaries offer adjunct services and a social scene. The services these facilities provide sometimes can be lifelines for low-income and isolated patients.

Medical Conditions and Recommended Marijuana Strains

Condition	Sativa	Indica	Hybrid	CBD
Cancer	X	X	X	X
AIDS/HIV	X	X	X	X
Chronic Pain		X	X	X
Seizure disorders		X		X
Neuropathy		X		X
Gastrointestinal disorders	X	X	X	X
Insomnia		X		X
Migraines	X	X	X	X
Stress		X	X	X
Depression	X		X	

continues

Medical Conditions and Recommended Marijuana Strains   (continued)

Condition	Sativa	Indica	Hybrid	CBD
Anxiety		X	X	X
Lupus		X	X	X
Fibromyalgia		X	X	X
Anorexia	X	X	X	

Patients have numerous resources to turn to for information about medical cannabis. Social media sites have medical marijuana special pages, as do countless online forums such as Reddit. Dispensary locator apps like Weedmaps, Leafly, and Sticky Guide also provide strain information and patient product reviews. Ed Rosenthal's *Big Book of Buds* series documents strains from around the world, detailing everything from their history to the estimated effects of hundreds of marijuana types. Most dispensaries have online menus, some with strain reviews, so members can see what's offered at each. Once you understand the basic strain types, deciding what marijuana product to use becomes much easier.

The Least You Need to Know

- Marijuana acts on the human endocannabinoid systems and its CB1 and CB2 receptor sites.
- Cannabis medicines provide predictable effects, depending on their strain, its potency, and the method used to ingest it.
- The cannabinoids THC and CBD, along with terpene molecules, are the main active ingredients in marijuana.
- Marijuana can be used to treat a variety of symptoms, but patients need to understand what product to use before using it. Licensed dispensaries provide trained staff to help guide them in making these choices.

Marijuana Products

Marijuana products come in many forms, from dried buds to infused coffee to body lotion. Dispensaries offer an array of products, but some patients in legal states choose to go the old-fashioned route and grow their own marijuana. Whether you grow outdoors in the dirt or purchase infused cotton candy from a dispensary, you'll need to know the best way to consume your cannabis.

Different marijuana products require different delivery systems. When you're faced with bongs, brownies, and dab rigs, rolling papers may seem quaint, but joints remain one of the cheapest and easiest ways to consume cannabis. Edibles, tinctures, and concentrates require greater awareness of the dosage; these products are often much more potent than dried plant material. Learning to dose your medicine right helps to ensure a pleasant experience and maximize symptom relief.

In This Chapter

- Discover how marijuana plants produce THC
- Learn to grade the appearance of cannabis
- Review the vast variety of marijuana medicines
- Study the use of high potency concentrates

Introduction to Growing Marijuana

As cannabis is a plant and plants are not designed to grow indoors, a successful indoor grow requires tricking the plants into believing they're outside. To mimic an outdoor environment, you must recreate the sun, wind, and rain and regulate the climate to simulate an outdoor garden. The five important elements of successful plant growth are light, water, nutrients, oxygen and carbon dioxide levels, and temperature. Any plant needs all five or else it will not grow. More of one element will not make up for the lack of another.

Marijuana plants are male (pollen producing), female (ovule producing), or hermaphroditic. As the male plant blooms, its buds produce pollen. Outdoors, the wind blows this pollen onto the buds of female plants, resulting in fertilization. After releasing its pollen, the male plant has completed its lifecycle, so it wilts and dies. After a female plant becomes fertilized, it begins to devote its energy to seed production, while it too begins to die. The mature seeds fall to the ground to create new plants with the combined genetic traits of the parent plants.

When both male and female marijuana plants flower, they produce sticky resin glands on the leaves and buds; these glands, known as *trichomes*, contain the plant's THC (tetrahydrocannabinol) and other cannabinoids. Females produce the most trichomes, which help to protect the plant and her seed set from the harsh outdoor environment. Male plants produce very low amounts of THC.

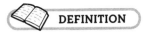 **DEFINITION**

Trichomes are resin glands on the leaves and flowers of the cannabis plant. They consist of a stalk and a head, similar in shape to a mushroom, and contain the plant's cannabinoids and terpenes.

Although the aim of growing plants is to produce cannabinoids like THC, you're looking for growth of the actual trichomes. From a distance, these tiny, glandular, mushroom-looking stalks are difficult to identify, but by using an inexpensive 30X microscope, you'll be able to observe their development before and after harvesting the plant. Trichomes are also largely responsible for the aroma of the plant, as this is where the terpenes reside.

To Grow or Not to Grow

At some point or another, most everyone who enjoys smoking marijuana has at least thought about growing it. Some want to grow so they'll never run out, some want to make a profit, and others want to grow the perfect strain.

With many states passing new, legal-marijuana laws, thousands of smokers now have the opportunity to grow their own cannabis. There are many obvious benefits to growing your own weed, but you just don't want to take on the commitment of cultivation. Growing marijuana isn't easy, and it requires dedication.

Now, if you're living in a state in which you're allowed to grow your own, you must decide if you are able to put in the necessary time to care for plants. If you're thinking of growing indoors, weigh the cost of buying cannabis against the cost of water, electricity, nutrients, lights, and other growing necessities.

One of the benefits of growing your own marijuana is that you control the quality—you'll always know exactly what you're getting. If you planted White Widow seeds, then you know you'll get White Widow plants. If they're taken care of properly, they'll be just as great as anything you'll ever buy in a dispensary. You'll also know the nutrients and fertilizers with which it was grown.

Remember that you'll more than likely make a few mistakes in the beginning. Your first plant or two will be an experiment, and with trial and error you will find what works best. There are a lot of different ways to grow marijuana—indoors, outdoors, in a greenhouse, in soil, with a hydroponic system—which means you'll find the methods that work well and the ones that can destroy your entire harvest.

Another benefit is saving money. When you buy your marijuana from a dispensary, you usually pay a specific price per gram and per ounce. When you grow your own, that changes—you only pay for supplies and utilities. Growing may be the right decision for you if a dispensary is too expensive or too far away. If you're on a budget, growing your own medicine may also be more affordable.

 HIGH POINTS

Follow all electrical safety rules when using electricity to grow. Illegal wiring or stealing electricity brings with it large fines and possible jail time when associated with growing marijuana. Many people who have been arrested for growing marijuana were caught due to illegal wiring jobs.

Always comply with local and state laws when growing cannabis. Even though it's legal, you still have to follow the rules. Be smart and know the local laws and regulations before you start growing your own cannabis. Knowing your plant-count limits is crucial to complying with city, county, and state cultivation programs. Never exceed legal limits on plant count or finished and processed medicine.

Keep in mind that you also are at risk of home invasion and crop theft. Be discreet; telling people you're growing increases the risk of theft.

Home Cultivation Methods

Different cannabis cultivators use different growing methods. The oldest tried-and-true technique is growing outdoors in a combination of soil and a growing medium such as peat moss or vermiculite. Many home gardeners set aside a small space in their home for an indoor garden, such as a closet, basement, or spare bedroom. You can also use a grow cabinet or specially designed tent to produce small amounts of cannabis.

Many use soil as an indoor grow medium, but you can also use a hydroponic or aeroponic system. The method you use matters less to the plant than to the grower. Use the method that works best for you, taking your skills into consideration. If you're a novice, you might want to stick with soil, which is more forgiving should you make a mistake (and you will) while learning to grow. If you jump right into hydroponics or aeroponics, you may very well find it to be beyond your abilities and become frustrated. Ease into the unknown, and start simple.

If growing outdoors, a small plot in the backyard is sufficient if you have the space. You can also set up a small greenhouse, which offers you more environmental control. Some growers use an entire house or grow house, but renting a house for the sole purpose of growing marijuana is a big expense. Cities also frown on this, and most set home-grow plant limits. Cultivators can be arrested for exceeding these numbers.

Whole-Plant Flowers

Whole-plant cannabis flowers (buds) are the most sought-after cannabis product, medical or recreational. However, there have recently been many innovations in cannabis products, such as concentrates like wax, shatter, and jellies, and innovations in delivery methods, such as vaporizing and edibles.

HIGH POINTS

No matter what cannabis product you are making, it all starts with the whole-plant flowers. The better your starting material, the better the final product. It's your job as the grower or person sourcing the cannabis to know what to look for when choosing materials.

Organoleptics

Organoleptics refers to the sensory aspects of a substance, such as taste, appearance, and scent. It's your job as a grower to perform organoleptic inspection procedures to detect disease or pathogen contamination, which can lead to health problems. Organoleptic screening determines which cannabis samples need further analysis.

When judging cannabis, you start with a visual scan (often with magnification) of the bud structure. How much leaf is left on the bud? Was it trimmed well, undertrimmed, or overtrimmed? Are there any signs of mold, powdery mildew, or pests such as spider mites? Next, you smell the cannabis and evaluate the desirability of the aroma while trying to detect the odor of mold (a strong ammonia or cat-urine smell).

The aroma should be one of the first organoleptic elements to greet you. There are about 200 compounds that create the aroma and flavor of the cannabis plant. Marijuana has a wide range of aromatic notes, such as pine, cinnamon, and citrus. Cannabis that hasn't been cured well smells like hay or has no scent at all; good cannabis has a strong, lingering scent.

Organoleptic examination cannot be used to detect potency, but scent and appearance gives some indication of how strong the cannabis is. With a little experience, you'll know what you're looking and smelling for. You must take all organoleptic elements into account when determining the price for which you will sell your cannabis product.

A Buds, B Buds, and Shake

Each wholesale unit (a unit is usually a pound) of cannabis contains three grades of product. The first grade is all of the "A" buds, or nice, big tops of the plant. These are the most developed, largest of all the buds, and are highly sought after. The second grade is the "B" buds, which are about the size of a dime or a piece of popcorn. It's still very good cannabis and in most cases just as strong as the "A" buds. The third product is "shake," which consists of the small pieces of the buds that break off as it dries, gets handled, or moved about.

Most dispensaries break the product into the three categories and turn it into three different products. "A" buds are the top-shelf buds and demand the highest price—around $50 to $60 per eighth of an ounce. "B" buds go for a little less, around $35 to $45 per eighth of an ounce. Shake is generally used for making pre-rolled joints or edibles.

HIGH POINTS

Not all dispensaries grade on the same system. Some use the alphabet (A, B, C buds), while others use a different system with rankings like Private Reserve, Special Reserve, and Connoisseur's Reserve. Dispensaries may also set across-the-board prices, such as $50 per eighth, $45 per eighth, $40 per eighth and so on, depending on the quality of the product.

Sifted Hash

Hash, or hashish, is one of the oldest cannabis products. It's made from trichomes, the most potent part of the plant, and consumed by smoking, just like cannabis flowers. However, you can also consume hash by eating it.

Once separated, the hash can be kept loose, in a form known as kief or kif, or pressed into a cake or ball and saved for later consumption. Because it's so concentrated, hash is much more potent than the herb itself, and is considered a delicacy. Master Hashmakers spend years perfecting the craft, and the wholesale and retail price for their products shows the hard work.

Screen Hash Production

One method of separating the resin from the plant is dry sifting, which uses a fabric screen to produce kief. Screens allow the trichome heads to pass through, but not the raw material. The drier the cannabis, the more likely some of the plant material will sift through as well, producing greener hash. Freezing cannabis before sifting will make the resin more brittle, and therefore, easier to separate.

The size of the trichomes varies with the strain and type of cannabis. Indica plants tend to have bigger, fatter trichomes, while sativa strains tend to have smaller, skinnier trichomes.

Today's modern hash-making techniques can get very sophisticated, with special equipment like washing machines and filter bags that do most of the work.

More traditional hash-making methods vary quite a bit in their technique. Hand-rolling is considered the easiest and least expensive, and still produces high-quality hash. Unfortunately, this method is also the most time-consuming. First, you must dry the plant, then clean your hands and slowly roll the material between your palms. A black film will form on your skin, and continuing to rub will produce small balls of resin. You can then press these balls into whatever form you desire.

Water Hash Production

Sometimes called bubble hash, ice hash, or full melt, hash produced using cold water is among the cleanest and highest-quality varieties. In this method, producers soak the plant material in ice water while filtering. This causes the trichomes to harden and separate more easily.

After being agitated, the water is poured through mesh filter bags, such as Bubbleman Bubble Bags, which aid in extraction. These bags are of different sizes to collect the separated trichomes. Trichomes settle on the mesh filter, while the buds float on the water's surface. Drain the mesh and allow the hash to dry before pressing and storing. It's then ready for consumption.

HIGH POINTS

Makers of ice-water hash often believe they have to completely dry the medicine first. It's not necessary to dry cannabis before getting it wet again. You can make hash right after trimming the buds.

Ingestible Medicines

Edibles are a discreet and convenient way to consume cannabis, particularly for those who cannot tolerate smoking. Edibles are cannabis-infused food, and many people find that they offer a more calming, relaxing experience than smoking. On the other hand, the effects of edibles can be hard to predict and tend to vary among individuals.

Edibles also deliver medication and get the user high more effectively than smoking. Although they take longer to kick in, once they do, they last longer than inhaled cannabis. Most users say they save money by using edibles, which create the same effect with less medicine.

However, you should be aware of the difference between smoking and eating cannabis. The body absorbs the active ingredients differently based on the delivery method. Smoking cannabis has a more immediate effect, but that effect diminishes faster. You may not feel the effects of edibles for up to an hour after ingestion, but you can feel them for 4 to 12 hours, depending on the dose.

The biggest drawback to ingesting cannabis is the ease of overdose. The key is to go low and slow: consume low doses of edibles, and wait at least an hour before eating more. Fatty, heavy, or sweet products such as brownies or chocolate take longer to digest, which means it will take longer for you to feel high. On the other hand, infused drinks and tinctures will begin to work much faster.

Cannabis overdose is not fatal, nor will it do any long-term damage. However, it's a very unpleasant experience. Feelings of paranoia, anxiety, and panic often set in, as well as a lack of coordination. The people who take the time to learn how to ingest cannabis are very grateful that they did. You should eat regular food before consuming edibles to decrease your risk of overdose. If you feel that you've consumed too much cannabis, don't panic. Remain calm, drink lots of water, and eat more food to help mitigate the effects of overconsumption.

Whether you choose indica- or sativa-infused edibles, the high will be more relaxing than if you'd smoked the same strain. You will probably find that edibles give you more of a physical rather than cerebral high.

> **HIGH POINTS**
>
> The effects of edibles are stronger and last longer than those of smoked cannabis due to the different methods of absorption. Controlling the dose of smoked cannabis is much easier than controlling the dose of edibles. The products you choose and the setting in which you consume them also affect the high.

Edibles

There are several ways of making cannabis edibles, and depending on what you're making, some methods work better than others. Whatever method you use, you must be sure to disclose all ingredients on the label, adding as much information about the ingredients as possible.

Some state laws require that the labels include the THC dosage and number of servings per package. In Colorado, one serving contains up to 10 milligrams of THC. There's a high risk of overconsumption among people who have never used edibles or ingestible cannabis, so new users should always be guided to lower dose edibles in order to have a pleasant experience.

In the past, many cannabis edibles were sweet rather than savory, though in today's cannabis market, more and more savory products exist, partly due to patients' desire for healthier foods. Edible choices today range from traditional cookies or brownies to cotton candy, soda, tea, coffee, breads, popcorn, cooking oils, capsules, pills, tinctures, pastes, and spreads.

Tinctures

Tinctures, usually made by alcohol extraction, are one of the oldest forms of medicine and are still popular today. However, many dispensaries will not carry alcohol-based tinctures, as they serve patients under 21. Tinctures may require a liquor license, which dispensaries cannot get. In the case of medical marijuana, many dispensaries feel that alcohol has no business in a medical facility.

Many of today's tinctures sold at dispensaries are glycerin-based, since glycerin is a plant-derived, alcohol-free substance. Other tinctures are oil-based, using sesame or other food-grade oils.

Pills

Cannabis pills, capsules, and gel caps are very common and quite popular, as they offer ingestible cannabis in calorie-free, sugar-free form. These delivery methods may also offer a controlled, time-release option. Suppositories, one of the best methods of delivering medicine to the bloodstream, are also becoming quite popular.

Cannabutter and Edible Oils

Cannabutter, or cannabis-infused butter, is one of the most common ingredients in edibles. Cannabutter is often made with crushed marijuana buds or shake. Butter, which acts as a solvent for THC, is melted on the stovetop or in a slow cooker with the dried flower added and strained after cooking. Using hash to infuse butter or oil saves time, as there's no need to strain after infusion.

For recipes that do not call for butter, you must find another method of infusion. Alternatives to butter include vegetable, coconut, sesame, or peanut oil, or any other food-grade oil. If a recipe doesn't call for butter or oil, you may choose to add hash or kief directly to the food.

Extracted Cannabis Products

There are a wide range of extracted cannabis products available today besides hash, kief, butter, or oil. Other products include topical preparations such as balms and salves, waxes, shatter, *transdermal administration* patches, and personal lubricant. Choosing which product to use depends on what qualities and effects you desire.

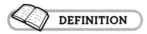

DEFINITION

> **Transdermal administration** means apply patches or creams directly to the skin, or inserting implants in the body to deliver medicine.

Oils

In addition to edible oils, there are also smoking oils. One ingestible form of oil is known as Rick Simpson Oil (RSO) also known as cannabis oil, hemp oil, or Phoenix Tears. RSO is a whole-plant cannabis oil that can be administered orally or applied directly to the skin. It's very popular with cancer patients, many of whom, like its namesake Rick Simpson, swear it cured their cancer.

Whole-plant oils, including RSO, contains cannabinoids such as THC, CBD, and CBN. Many businesses sell their own version of RSO, with some higher in THC and others higher in non-psychoactive cannabinoids. Transmission to the circulatory system via oral mucosal membranes, also known as sublingual delivery, increases the bioavailability of cannabinoids.

Whole-plant cannabis oil differs from hempseed oil, which is made from the cold-pressed seeds of the cannabis plant. Hempseed oil, which is sold in health-food stores, is rich in essential fatty acids and offers multiple nutritional benefits.

Wax

Wax is really just another form of whole-plant cannabis oil. Its wax-like consistency is due to variables in manufacturing, such as temperature. Often extracted using butane, the THC content of wax can be as high as 90 percent when the manufacturer starts with high-quality flowers.

Another method of wax production is carbon dioxide (CO_2) extraction. CO_2, a naturally occurring substance that leaves no residue, turns to liquid under pressure. It's also a common food additive and extraction method for making herbal supplements. CO_2 extraction works by inserting supercritical CO_2 into a high-pressure vessel containing cannabis. When the pressure is released, the CO_2 evaporates leaving pure cannabinoids.

HIGH POINTS

Our bodies produce CO_2 when we breathe. It allows for extraction without the use of petroleum-based solvents, which prevents contamination of the medicine and eliminates the danger of explosion in production facilities.

Shatter

Shatter is made the same way as wax, using butane or CO_2 extraction methods. However, it has a different name due to its glass-like consistency. Shatter got its name because it often snaps or "shatters" when handled. The words budder, honeycomb, crumble, and sap are also used to describe the different textures of wax.

More Marijuana Medicines

There are other steadily growing categories of cannabis products, with more being introduced almost daily. Body- and skincare products are growing in popularity, and several celebrities such as Whoopi Goldberg have even released their own lines of tinctures, bath salts, and balms meant for the relief of menstrual cramps and other localized pain.

Bath Balms

Lotions, salves, and infused oils, also known as topicals, are absorbed through the skin for relief of localized pain and inflammation. Topicals are nonpsychoactive, making them ideal for patients who want the benefits of cannabis medicine without the high.

Strain-specific topicals attempt to harness certain terpenes and cannabinoids for the purpose of targeting specific ailments. Along with THC, CBD, THCA, and CBN, topicals may incorporate other elements for additional relief, including lavender, rose, wintergreen, and mint essential oils. The cannabinoids in topicals usually can't reach the bloodstream—they can penetrate the CB2 receptor system, but not the CB1.

Snoop Dogg, Margaret Cho, and Willie Nelson are among the celebrities getting into the cannabis business. Celebrity endorsements of cannabis products is a trend that is sure to continue, and these products are sure to take a large market share.

Patches

Transdermal patches deliver medicine to the bloodstream through the skin. They help heal injuries by delivering a controlled dose of medicine via a saturated adhesive or porous membrane. Transdermal patches are used to deliver many medications, with cannabis now among them. A Colorado company called Mary's Medicinals is leading the way into the legal cannabis market, driving research and development of transdermal patches and creams. Transdermal delivery is considered very safe, especially for new and first-time users.

Lubes

Marijuana lube or sensual cannabis oil, as it's more accurately called, is beginning to make head-way claiming a small market share of the budding marijuana industry. A number of companies are introducing personal cannabis products, including tampons. Medicated lubricants serve the same function as other personal lubricants, but with the addition of cannabis. Applying the product 40 minutes prior to sexual activity can help enhance the experience without the high. Cannabis tampons and feminine-hygiene products are known to relieve menstrual cramps.

Other Medicines

Cannabis pet-care products are also becoming popular. Outlawed in 1937, cannabis pet-care companies are currently reintroducing products for dog, cats, horses, and other animals, who benefit from it the same way humans do. Using these medicated products on ailing pets can help extend their quality of life.

Introduction to Smoking and Vaporizing Tools

Papers for rolling joints are readily available at most tobacco stores, along with water bongs, which deliver a sudden large dose with every hit. *Vaporizers* are quite popular as well, as they allow users to smoke cannabis without inhaling burning plant material.

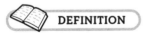 **DEFINITION**

Vaporizing transforms liquid to aerosol at a temperature below combustion, allowing the user to benefit from the cannabinoids found in marijuana without having to inhale the burning plant material.

Papers, Pipes, and Bongs

Pre-rolled joints are a popular product for people who don't know how or don't want to roll their own. Individual joints allow patients to try different strains without purchasing larger quantities. Today's pre-rolled joints come in cigarette or cone style, gummed or not, and can be made from rice, hemp, and bamboo. Some contain only cannabis flower, while others include kief, hash, wax, or oil either inside or painted on the outside of the joint. Some oil-brushed joints are also dusted with kief. Some papers are flavored, with chocolate and fruit flavors being among the most popular.

Pipes also come in all shapes and sizes, and are usually made from wood, glass, or metal. Some change color when heated; some have a carburetor for increased dosage delivery. Bongs are also made of a number of materials, although glass is the most common, and come in many sizes, shapes, and designs. Many people fill them with water for filtering the smoke, while others like to fill them with ice for a cool, refreshing hit. Some headshops sell kits that allow you to make your own bong out of ice or frozen fruit juice.

Refillable Vape Pens and Vaporizers

There are many types of vaporizers available today, including e-cigarette-style vape pens that use pre-filled, disposable oil cartridges. These pens are small electronic devices that vaporize oil or wax, producing an aerosol or vapor, which delivers cannabinoids to the bloodstream when inhaled. Some vape pens use a special attachment that you can refill with wax, oil, shatter, or dry herb. They afford more choices for the consumer and are very discreet compared to joints, pipes, or bongs.

Vape pens are a discrete way to consume cannabis, without the smell caused by smoking marijuana.

Since appearing on the market in 2004, e-cigarettes and vape pens have grown in popularity, especially among younger patients. Reviews of their safety vary. A 2014 review concluded that health authorities may have overstated the risks of vaporizing, but a review of the pens themselves indicated a need for awareness of related electrical waste.

Dabbing—the Phenomenon and Its Tools

Dabbing is a method of cannabis consumption that has been around for at least a decade, but the advent of more advanced extraction methods has led to a wider range of products. Dabbing is especially popular with 20- to 30-year-olds.

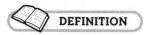 **DEFINITION**

> **Dabbing** delivers cannabis via a dab rig, which looks similar to a bong. Users heat a metal piece called a nail with a handheld torch, and apply a small amount of concentrate to the hot nail with a metal dab tool. The concentrate instantly vaporizes, and the user inhales. It provides a strong hit, and is a faster and more efficient delivery of cannabis than smoking.

Although dabbing itself is not dangerous (though you do need to control your intake and pace yourself), attempting to extract the oil yourself can be very dangerous. The process of dabbing can also be a bit intimidating, largely due to the use of the blowtorch, which has led to comparisons between dabbing and smoking methamphetamine or crack cocaine. Although dabs, unlike cocaine and meth, are nonlethal, using too much concentrate can lead to an unpleasant high.

Dabbing requires some new, strange tools with names like torches, nails, and carb caps, and they can be expensive. Electronic nails run on electricity, but can cost upwards of $300.

Carb-cap and dabber-combo rigs have become the most popular choices among consumers in recent years. Which dabber or dab tool you prefer often depends on the type of concentrate you prefer. Dry, crumbly concentrates work better with different dabbers than sticky concentrates such as sap, shatter, or budder.

The biggest benefit of dabbing is that it supplies a powerful dose of medicine to those who truly need it. Patients who dab to help alleviate severe or chronic pain or extreme nausea report overwhelmingly positive results.

The Least You Need to Know

- Marijuana plants can be male or female, with the males producing pollen and females producing seeds, and can be grown indoors or outdoors.
- Grading cannabis requires examination of the smell, taste, size, and appearance of buds.
- Cannabis can be consumed using a wide range of delivery systems, such as joints, bongs, pipes, dab rigs, edibles, topical concentrates, and transdermal patches.
- Different delivery systems allow users to consume different cannabis products, such as dried flowers, concentrates, and hashish.

Distilling Your Concept

Every aspect of your marijuana business has to be well thought out. This starts with a thorough examination of the federal, state, and local laws. The company has to rigorously adhere to state and local laws, and must work hard to stay on the right side of those at the federal level. Read about how each branch of the federal government has passed laws or regulations about marijuana. Find out how state laws differ from these, and how local laws fit into the scheme. All of them affect your marijuana business.

After dissecting this, you likely know where you fit in. Now you need a founding team. So learn how to create the best group, and how to develop your corporate identity. You need a name and a mission, vision, and values to guide the company. Learn here how that team works together to establish your income streams, locate your client base, and lead the group to profitability.

Federal, State, and Local Policies

Congressional policy on marijuana is defined by the Controlled Substance Act of 1970, which lists marijuana in Schedule I, meaning that it's dangerous and has no medical value and a high potential for abuse. Congress made those determinations politically, not based on science, yet it remains the law of the land. Since then, advocates have been trying to convince Congress to change marijuana's scheduling, either lowering it to Schedule II or III or removing it from the law altogether.

Beginning in 2009, the United States Attorney General implemented a series of policies to reconcile federal laws with state and local medical marijuana and recreational use laws. These deprioritize law-enforcement activities in states with legal marijuana. The one caveat is that states have tightly regulated programs to assure that marijuana isn't diverted from its intended users. Cannabusiness owners face tough scrutiny and mountainous regulations, but if they follow them all, they are unlikely to have problems.

In This Chapter

- Review the Department of Justice (DOJ) policies
- Learn about key federal court rulings
- Get briefed on state-by-state laws
- Explore state residency requirements

Federal Policies

As previously discussed, possession, cultivation, and sale of marijuana are all prohibited, first by the 1937 Marihuana Tax Act and later in 1970 with the Controlled Substances Act (CSA). Despite this, the federal government has allowed states to create and operate medical marijuana and adult recreational use programs. The fact that 28 states have legal medical marijuana has not swayed enough members of Congress to agree on a bill to amend the CSA.

Instead, the federal government has tolerated state marijuana laws, mostly standing aside where strong regulations exist. Federal enforcement priorities have largely shifted away from targeting marijuana users and businesses, except those in violation of state laws. Instead, they are using their time and funding to fight more important crimes.

All three branches of the federal government have weighed in, each creating policies or laws about marijuana. This makes it hard to understand the laws and how they might affect your marijuana business. Take time to research each one, and decide for yourself how to best comply.

HIGH ALERT

The main thing to know concerning federal policies is that marijuana is illegal under federal law.

Constitutional Issues

This current situation came about in part because of a combination of tolerance from the executive branch and support from the legislative branch. The federal government could assert the right to close all the programs, but it has chosen a more compassionate approach. It's possible to contend, though, that the federal government should not be able to do anything about state marijuana programs anyway. This is due to two things: the Tenth Amendment to the Constitution and its Commerce Clause.

The Tenth Amendment states simply that, "The powers not delegated to the United States by the Constitution, nor prohibited by it to the States, are reserved to the States respectively, or to the people."

The United States Constitution's Commerce Clause gives Congress the power "to regulate commerce with foreign nations, and among the several states, and with the Indian tribes." That's how Congress has authority to regulate interstate commerce. But, nowhere in the Constitution is the federal government given the power to regulate *intrastate commerce.*

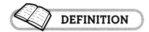

DEFINITION

Intrastate commerce is economic activity that takes place entirely within a state's borders, such as medical marijuana programs, for example.

It seems like marijuana programs should be protected by the Constitution. But, the Supreme Court has already decided that those rules don't apply where cannabis is concerned. In a 2005 ruling in the case of *Gonzalez v. Raich*, the Supreme Court rejected the Commerce Clause/ Tenth Amendment argument in a 6 to 3 decision. The majority decision found that concerns over marijuana use and the possibility of *leakage* into other states was sufficient to override the Constitutional questions, even though the Raich case only involved noncommercial, intrastate cultivation.

Executive Branch

The position of the Obama administration was laid out in a letter signed by then-Deputy Attorney General James M. Cole on August 29, 2013. It was sent to United States Attorney General offices around the country in regard to medical marijuana businesses operating in their jurisdictions. The Cole Memo clarifies that the Justice Department still regards marijuana as illegal and dangerous, and that they still intend to enforce the Controlled Substances Act. However, it seeks to reconcile the conflict between the department's attitude and the reality of state laws.

The Cole Memo expresses that the federal government will use their "limited investigative and prosecutorial resources" to focus on these marijuana enforcement priorities in states with legal programs:

Preventing the distribution of marijuana to minors;

Preventing revenue from the sale of marijuana from going to criminal enterprises, gangs, and cartels;

Preventing the diversion of marijuana from states where it is legal under state law in some form to other states;

Preventing state-authorized marijuana activity from being used as a cover or pretext for the trafficking of other illegal drugs or other illegal activity;

Preventing violence and the use of firearms in the cultivation and distribution of marijuana;

Preventing drugged driving and the exacerbation of other adverse public health consequences associated with marijuana use;

Preventing the growing of marijuana on public lands and the attendant public safety and environmental dangers posed by marijuana production on public lands; and

Preventing marijuana possession or use on federal property.

There were actually two Cole memoranda. The first was issued in 2011 to clarify a 2009 memo to U.S. Attorney Generals issued by Deputy Attorney General David W. Ogden. The Ogden Memo was a much more positive statement about Justice Department policy in regard to medical marijuana. It said, "prosecution of individuals with cancer or other serious illnesses who use marijuana as part of a recommended treatment regimen consistent with applicable state law, or those caregivers in clear and unambiguous compliance with existing state law who provide such individuals with marijuana, is unlikely to be an efficient use of limited federal resources."

At the time of writing, we don't know what policy will be pursued in the coming years. It's possible that Department of Justice policy will remain unchanged, though it's also possible that it could change as soon as January 2017.

HIGH POINTS

The Drug Enforcement Administration (DEA) announced a rule change in summer 2016 that will allow entities other than the National Institute on Drug Abuse and the University of Mississippi Research Center to cultivate marijuana for scientific and medical research. This could provide a path toward re- or de-scheduling. It also allows researchers access to marijuana of a viable quality for Phase III research studies, which must be conducted before medicines can be approved for the market. Although this new process will take time to implement, it's a promising development, as it creates a way for medical marijuana producers to get involved directly with medical research.

Legislative Branch

Congress passed the Rohrabacher-Farr Amendment to prevent the Justice Department from interfering with state-legal medical marijuana programs. It was first successfully attached to the 2015 Commerce, Justice, and Science Appropriations Bill, and was included again in the 2016 Appropriations Bill. Because it's a rider to an annual Appropriations Bill, the amendment has to be reintroduced and approved every year.

The language of the amendment is simple: "None of the funds made available in this Act to the Department of Justice may be used ... to prevent such States from implementing their own State laws that authorize the use, distribution, possession, or cultivation of medical marijuana."

Advocates had been concerned that this language was too vague to provide real protection for growers or dispensary operators. The Justice Department originally thought so, and asserted in federal court that the amendment only prohibited them from interfering with state agencies and their employees. However, in 2016, a three-judge panel of the U.S. Court of Appeals for the Ninth Circuit ruled to affirm the position of Representatives Rohrabacher and Farr that the amendment did indeed stop the Justice Department from being able to go after medical marijuana dispensaries and growers. In fact, the Department of Justice's asset-forfeiture cases against two California dispensaries, Harborside Health Center and Berkeley Patients Group, collapsed due to this ruling on spending.

The amendment has to be passed each year, but the court ruling would still apply year after year so long as the amendment's language is included in the annual Appropriations Bill. The Rohrabacher-Farr amendment was added to the 2017 Appropriations Bill. The 2016 federal fiscal year ended on September 30, and Congress had not yet agreed on the budget. They postponed its consideration, and instead passed a *continuing resolution*, which keeps the government funded as previously approved. At this writing, it's unclear if the amendment will be renewed past its April 2017 expiration date.

 **DEFINITION**

> A **continuing resolution** is a short-term funding bill passed by the U.S. Congress to keep government agencies open and operating in lieu of an annual Appropriation Bill.

Judicial Branch

Federal courts, all the way up to the Supreme Court of the United States, have weighed in on state marijuana reforms. There are three particularly significant historic cases. The first was *United States* v. *Oakland Cannabis Buyers Club* (2001). In this case, the Supreme Court held that medical necessity is not accepted as a defense against charges relating to medical cannabis distribution, overturning a lower court decision. This ruling forced this dispensary and all others operating at that time to close their doors to patients.

The second case was *Conant* v. *Walters* (2002). This was a class-action suit against the federal government for threatening to bring action against physicians for recommending medical marijuana to qualified patients in California. The physicians prevailed, winning the right to discuss and recommend medical marijuana. The Supreme Court held that the government can't threaten or punish doctors for speaking to their patients about medical marijuana and even recommending medical marijuana.

Gonzalez v. *Raich* (2005) is the final case. In this case, the Supreme Court ruled that the Commerce Clause of the Constitution should be interpreted broadly enough to allow the federal government to exercise authority in regard to marijuana. This includes even the intrastate, noncommercial cultivation of medical marijuana for seriously ill patients. The 6-3 decision provoked a scathing dissent from Chief Justice Rehnquist, who called the states laboratories of democracy wherein innovative social policies may be developed.

State Policies

Changes in the marijuana laws have mainly been driven by citizen initiatives. Voters wrote the proposed laws, collected signatures, qualified for the ballots, and won the popular votes. California and Arizona were the first two states to pass medical marijuana laws by initiative, and others like Colorado and New Mexico followed soon after. States including New Hampshire and Illinois legalized medical marijuana through their legislatures. Citizen advocates worked with elected officials in these states to create these laws and to push for their enactment.

All eight states with adult-use laws were passed through voter initiatives, as was the law in the District of Columbia. Lawmakers in the other 42 states will watch and wait to see the outcome of programs in these states before any legislatures take action to change the laws themselves. In the meantime, advocates in medical marijuana states with voter-initiative processes are weighing the chances for a ballot effort for 2020.

State-by-State Marijuana Laws

Forty-two states have medical marijuana laws, but they are not all created equally. There were 25 states with effective medical marijuana programs of some sort before the 2016 election. The Marijuana Policy Project defines "effective" programs as those that remove criminal sanctions for medical marijuana use, define the eligibility of qualified patients, and allow some means to access medical marijuana. This is typically either through retail dispensaries or by allowing limited home cultivation.

> **HIGH POINTS**
>
> States with effective medical marijuana laws include Alaska, Arizona, California, Colorado, Connecticut, Delaware, District of Columbia, Hawaii, Illinois, Maine, Maryland, Massachusetts, Michigan, Minnesota, Montana, Nevada, New Hampshire, New Jersey, New Mexico, New York, Ohio, Oregon, Pennsylvania, Rhode Island, Vermont, Washington, and the District of Columbia.

Seventeen other states have laws that are not considered effective. There are several reasons these laws don't work. Some contain key clauses that create irreconcilable conflicts with federal law. Others set unreasonable barriers to access medical marijuana, such that no patient can secure their medicine. And finally, some states limit the allowable marijuana strains to those with low-THC and high-CBD only. CBD-only medicines are not widely available, and patients in these states are left without access. Regulations have yet to be set for states with new laws, but patients in North Dakota, Arkansas, and Florida remain hopeful that access won't be unreasonably limited.

Colorado, Washington, Oregon, Alaska, and the District of Columbia all legalized adult use and possession before 2016. In the recent election, California, Nevada, and Maine joined the list, with voters in each state passing laws to implement adult-use legalization. The original four states have already created systems to regulate cultivation, processing, packaging, and distribution. The new states will take a year or more to create regulations to license manufacturing and sales chains.

 HASHING IT OUT

All the state programs for both medical and adult-use marijuana vary to a considerable degree. There are, however, several elements that are fairly consistent from state to state. These include:

- Monitoring of recommending physicians
- Patient registries and identification cards
- Owner and investor residency requirements
- Owner and employee criminal background checks
- Facility location restrictions
- Facility security requirements
- Limits on hours of operation
- Seed-to-sale product tracking
- Restrictions on allowable products
- Packaging regulations
- Limits on promotions and advertising
- Bans on public consumption

The Thousand-Foot Rule

The thousand-foot rule is just one example of bad state policies that are a direct result of the federal prohibition. This typically involves limiting marijuana businesses from locating less than a 1,000 feet from schools and other facilities that cater largely to people who are under 21. U.S. Criminal Code includes a sentencing enhancement for controlled-substance violations based on the proximity of the offense to school property, parks, and a number of other facilities. This means federal penalties are increased when such violations occur. This rule became part of nearly every state law, due to federal pressure from the DEA and the Justice Department. Only California bucked the trend a bit, lowering the distance to 600 feet.

Some laws allow state agencies and regulators to cut applicants a little slack on this rule. For example, if some part of the property line around a proposed facility is just 20 feet inside the 1,000-feet line, regulators might be willing to grant a waiver. You may also be able to get a waiver if a school moves in after you were permitted, or if the city decides to build a park nearby. There are no guarantees, though, and you may lose your space due to this carried-over federal law. That's why, to have a thriving marijuana industry, federal marijuana policy has to change.

Investor and Owner Residency Requirements

Taking a look at the experiences of Oregon and Colorado, which have both medical and adult use programs, is informative when trying to understand the future of residency requirements. Oregon's adult-use law originally contained no residency requirement for owners or investors, but the state legislature added them in 2015 before the law could go into effect. In 2016, they removed them again, before the Oregon Liquor Control Commission had even begun issuing licenses. They were originally supposed to stay in place until 2017, but legislators wanted to let out-of-state dollars come into the Oregon industry as quickly as possible.

Oregon's medical marijuana program originally allowed people from out of state to register as patients, as long as an Oregon-licensed physician signed their recommendation form and if they could find a state-based grower. In 2016, the Oregon legislature amended the medical marijuana law to require that patients must be state residents. Proponents of this new law said they were concerned over leakage, pointing to farms in southern Oregon that grew marijuana for out-of-state patients. Now, retail marijuana sales can be made to anyone over the age of 21, no matter where they live. So out-of-state visitors can still come to Oregon to purchase marijuana at the adult social-use shops; they just can't register as medical patients or shop at dispensaries.

 HIGH POINTS

According to the Oregon Department of Revenue, the first 9 months of legal adult-use sales generated more than $40 million in tax revenue for the state.

Colorado set up an implementation task force prior to their adult social-use law kicking in. That group recommended a two-year residency requirement be imposed on the new legal industry, just as it had been imposed on the medical industry. Those rules were changed somewhat in 2015, and then in 2016 the state legislature enacted more changes in the rules that have opened a very broad door for out-of-state and even institutional investors to get involved in the Colorado industry. Out-of-state people are still limited in the portion of a company that they can own, though, under new definitions for "direct" and "indirect" beneficial interest owners.

As of January 1, 2017, any U.S. citizen can qualify to become either a direct or indirect beneficial interest owner in Colorado. The state still maintains limits on how big of a piece out-of-state people can own, and they limit the total number of direct beneficial interest owners to 15 percent in any marijuana business. Colorado also created the category *qualified limited passive investor* for marijuana businesses to make it easier for out-of-state people to invest. This category of investors is for people with no daily operational control and less than 5 percent interest in the company.

Local Policies

A number of municipalities in legal medical marijuana states have enacted bans, moratoriums, and other restrictions to keep marijuana businesses out of their jurisdictions. Others have been more welcoming and supportive.

Local Bans and Moratoriums

Strictly speaking, states cannot force municipalities to accept marijuana-related businesses in their jurisdictions. This is because of the Supremacy Clause of the Constitution, which says federal law "shall be the supreme law of the land." Marijuana is illegal federally, per the Controlled Substances Act, and efforts to turn control to the states have failed at the Supreme Court. Congress gave a nudge forward with the Rohrabacher-Farr appropriations amendment, and the Cole memo has been helpful, too. But neither fully protects state marijuana laws, and the Controlled Substances Act still rules.

So if local or county jurisdictions were required to have marijuana businesses, it would create a conflict with the Controlled Substances Act. In Oregon, for example, the head of the Association of Oregon Counties (AOC) testified before the state legislature's legalization implementation committee, warning lawsuits were imminent if they were not given an opt-out provision. Their concern was that state-regulated cultivation and distribution of marijuana violates the federal Controlled Substances Act.

The Oregon law-enforcement community was particularly sensitive to this problem and not because they strongly oppose marijuana use. Instead, it's due to the fact that they swear to uphold the Constitution and to enforce the laws of the land. Forcing law enforcement and other elected officials into the position of breaking federal law creates a *positive conflict* with the Controlled Substances Act, and they can use this as grounds to sue and stall implementation.

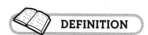 **DEFINITION**

> A **positive conflict** is when two jurisdictions both claim legal supremacy over a situation.

The Oregon AOC lobbyist argued that with the opt-out clause in, they would have no standing to sue. The legislature had no choice but to add it to entice cities and counties to opt into the program. Under Oregon law, only cities and counties that allow cannabusinesses get a share of the tax revenue from statewide legalization. Unfortunately, there are generally still more municipalities banning marijuana businesses than not in legal states.

Codes and Regulations

Municipal laws contain a lot of details marijuana business owners have to learn and follow. State laws require that you locate in a city or county that allows marijuana businesses, and your local regulations will be found in the municipal codes. There will either be a competitive process, with a limited number of permits given only during limited application periods, or there will laws allowing any number of marijuana businesses to locate there as long as they locate in green zones and meet all distance regulations. Research your local zoning regulations, and review the laws before you rent a space and apply for a license.

You must get a local business license and pay any fees related to your marijuana application. These fees will likely be higher than normal, due to the extra oversight required by city and state laws. All marijuana businesses have to meet building and fire codes, and, depending on the type of business, you will have to follow health and environmental codes. Your facility will have to be successfully inspected by each department in order to open, so never do any unpermitted construction or remodeling. You will get caught, and face fines and delays.

The Least You Need to Know

- Federal law has supremacy over state law when it comes to marijuana.
- Congress passed a budget amendment that prevents the DOJ from spending enforcement funds in legal marijuana states, but this could change.
- The Supreme Court ruled that physicians cannot be targeted by the government for recommending medical marijuana.
- Marijuana businesses have to follow multiple municipal regulations, including zoning, building, fire, and licensing laws.

Creating Your Company

Your cannabusiness needs great founders, a board of directors, and advisers willing to mentor and coach your team. Your job as chief is to put this group together and create the company with their guidance. Work with them to choose the company's name and to establish its mission, vision, and values, which are important decisions that will have a lasting effect.

Make sure you understand your company's income streams and know exactly when and how the business will become self-sustainable. Your start-up funds are surely limited, so you'll need to ramp up quickly in order to survive. Know where your clients are well in advance of opening day and be ready to serve them efficiently. Don't try to do it all alone—work with allies in the marijuana industry and with the people you serve to build a dedicated base.

In This Chapter

- Find out how to build your founding team
- Learn how to create your corporate identity
- Discover why you need a mission statement

Putting Together the Founding Team

Success requires putting together a team with the skills, knowledge, and abilities needed to execute your vision. This group will be required to work together, cooperate, and solve problems. The challenge is finding the people with the right qualifications in a relatively new field. Look for people willing to contribute their time and knowledge to the effort.

It's hard to launch a business alone, and you're likely to need co-founders. Having people dedicated to a shared vision from the start can help supercharge your company's launch. You also need an experienced board of directors who have a variety of specialties and a willingness to say "no" when needed.

The Founders

The founders consist of the person or people who came up with the product or idea, and those they bring in early whose skills make it viable. This group develops the company's business plan and three-year financial projections. They also help establish the culture of the company, and set its original mission, vision, and values.

Many founders feel that they alone can carry out the vision, but the reality is that if the company fails to make money, founders can be forced out of the company or pressured into stepping aside. Surround yourself with talented and motivated co-founders to ensure you can launch and reach profitability on the projected timeline.

Select talented co-founders with knowledge, skills, and abilities that complement yours. The company needs a chief executive officer (CEO), a chief operating officer (COO), a chief financial officer (CFO), and a chief marketing officer (CMO) or the equivalent. If your founders can fill these roles while you are getting started, the company will save money and time. You can find full-time employees later, after you are funded and the company can afford it.

 HASHING IT OUT

Besides industry-specific experience, these are some of the attributes to look for in your founding team members:

- Good interpersonal skills
- Experience in leadership and team building
- Decisive and competent problem solving
- Proven ability to organize and execute projects
- Strong analytical abilities
- Motivated and accomplished self-development
- Flexibility

The Board of Directors and Advisers

If you are a nonprofit organization, the board of directors holds responsibility for your marijuana business. The board elects a chairperson to organize their agenda and to lead meetings, which is a position you may want to hold yourself. In addition, they are responsible for choosing the group's executive director and the officers who supervise its daily operations. Your organization also must designate a president, a secretary, and a treasurer, but they can all be the same person. Most groups try to fill each role with a skilled adviser so they maximize the talent on their decision-making team. Board members generally serve 1- to 2-year terms, and nonprofits boards are self-nominated and elected.

Your for-profit company likely has a board of directors, too, with members who are elected annually by your shareholders. Shareholders don't want the burden of corporate oversight, so installing a board ensures that talented individuals are watching and running the company. The board picks the CEO, who supervises daily operations, and a president, secretary, and treasurer to manage the big picture.

If your marijuana business is a Limited Liability Corporation (LLC), it might have a board of managers or a managing director to supervise operations. Partnerships are governed by partnership agreements, which may assign oversight to a board of directors and officers or not. The partners hire the CEO and work together to make important decisions. It's important to carefully consider each business model before you incorporate, and to determine how decisions will be made into the future.

 HASHING IT OUT

The board of directors oversees company management and ensures that its supervisors perform their day-to-day duties. Most boards of directors have between three and fifteen members, but yours can have as many as you want. Consider appointing an odd number of board members to avoid voting deadlocks.

A board of advisers is not a requirement, but many marijuana businesses use them. The idea is to create a team of experts with a wide range of skills and knowledge willing to add their talents to your team. Good advisers bring clout to the company, and they can make introductions to regulators, vendors, customers, and other key people. Generally, you only need them occasionally when help is needed within their specific field of expertise. They don't have the same obligations as the board of directors, and they do not answer to shareholders. They support your team and help it grow.

Make sure you don't surround yourself with "yes" people. Your marijuana business will be stronger if the directors and advisers are willing to question your ideas and say no when needed. Don't appoint family members to either board, unless they have a required skill set or understand your need to be challenged. Informed diverse boards help keep your company current and relevant. Consider compensating your boards for their time, especially for any travel expenses they incur to attend meetings. You are more likely to attract top people if they don't have to pay their expenses to participate.

Hiring Professional Services

Your corporate lawyer is the most valuable professional you will hire. Find an attorney experienced in cannabis law to incorporate your company, create its operational documents, and to assure that your plans comply with state and local regulations. They will help create your fundraising documents, review your leases and contracts, and manage the company's copyrights and trademarks. This is an enormous amount of important work and will be costly to complete. Don't skimp on it; you need the best attorneys beside you on this journey!

Retain a criminal defense attorney, too. You need someone to advise your team on the laws to protect yourself and your company from police intervention. You must follow both state and municipal laws, and it's complicated to learn and understand the details. Take advantage of your professional assistance. Make sure to learn about the federal marijuana laws, too, and be ready to face the consequences if you are targeted by a federal law enforcement action.

Hire an accountant who understands IRS 280e regulations. Make sure they review your business plan and evaluate the tax consequences of your proposed fundraising methods and how you will use those funds. You need to fully understand the long term financial implications for the company, before you take on startup funds. Finally, consider hiring a well-connected government relations person. It's helpful to have guidance as you go through the regulatory process and apply for your marijuana business license. A good government relations person will act as your mentor and coach, planning appointments with elected officials and regulators. They'll go with you to the meetings and help pitch your proposal. They can also make sure your team is informed about any proposed municipal or state legislation and that your voice is heard.

Establishing Your Corporate Identity

Your cannabusiness needs a memorable name that captures its essence. It needs to be distinct yet simple to remember.

Work with the interested board members, advisers, and founders to create succinct mission, vision, and values statements. The mission statement should be simple and easy to repeat. It should express exactly what it is that your company does in two sentences or less. Use it to focus your strategy and to illustrate to customers and employees the goals that drive your business. Your mission statement should motivate people and make them want to get involved.

Your vision statement looks to the future. Whereas a mission statement tells why you're in business, a vision statement tells where your business is going. It's a transformational statement that discusses your company's mission, and how wonderful life will be when you reach the goals. It's a short statement, too—no more than a sentence or two. Each word matters on the mission and vision statements, so take time to consider each and make them count.

The company's values statement lays out the ethical principles the cannabusiness pledges to follow. This includes ideals like social responsibility, green business operations, and giving back to the community. This statement can be as long as you want, spelling out the company's views in detail and listing specific programs to address each issue.

Choosing Your Company Name

Your business name should represent your mission, values, and vision. Take the time to come up with a name you'll be happy building branding around for many years. Avoid using your own name, as it will be hard to build brand awareness (unless you are well known) and may also limit who wants to buy the business if you decide to sell in the future.

Brainstorm with your co-founders to come up with the company name. Decide on a few keywords and list synonyms to expand the options. Combine them in various ways, and eliminate ideas that don't work. Think about names that match your mission, vision, and values. Try to find unique ideas that are appealing to the marijuana market.

Do your research before deciding on your company's name. Make sure the social media handles are available, and that you can secure the web domain name. Check with your state's filing office to make sure that nobody else has the name in your region and that it's not already trademarked by someone else. At the end of this process, meet with the founders and pick the best option. Finalizing the name is worth celebrating; you should be able to cheer it loudly!

 **HIGH ALERT**

If you want to trademark the name, find a good lawyer and be diligent in the process to avoid future trademark litigation.

You don't necessarily have to trademark the name unless you think you might grow into a large, national company. If so, it can be expensive and tricky, but it's well worth the investment. Trademark protection is available for logos, names, and symbols, with each trademark category offering different levels of infringement protection.

Brainstorming Your Mission Statement

Your job is to create a guided process that leads to the mission statement. Get a focused group of stakeholders involved, and choose a good team of people from all parts of the organization. Invite interested board members, shareholders, and staff members to join the process. And, consider taking input from potential clients and suppliers as well. This will help you get to know your target market and what they expect from the company.

Host a focus group with the people who want to participate. Settling on the right mission statement requires asking the right questions.

> Why are we in business?
>
> Who are the customers?
>
> What level of service do we provide?

Consider how you differ from the competitors, especially in terms of core values. Record all of the ideas, and ask the group to vote on their favorites at the end of the session. Use these to write the mission statement.

The mission statement can only contain a couple of key concepts, and you have to express these with laser clarity. Combine the best ideas from the focus group into three to five sentence combinations. Ask key people to comment on each and be open to modifying them based on this feedback. Your final statement has to flow like the refrain of a song if you want people to remember and repeat it. Take time to make sure each word is meaningful.

 HASHING IT OUT

Here are some cannabusiness mission statements to review:

We are dedicated to developing innovative ways for people to consume cannabis, which nurture, enhance and improve lives.
-Kiva Confections

To provide cannabis medicines and life enhancing services in a welcoming, in-formed and compassionate manner.
-Magnolia Wellness of Oakland

To deliver experiences that inspire expansion of the mind, community, and overall wellbeing of humankind.
-Oaksterdam University

To promote the growth of a responsible and legitimate cannabis industry and work for a favorable social, economic and legal environment for that industry in the United States.
-National Cannabis Industries Association

Creating a Forward-Thinking Vision

Your marijuana company starts with its mission, but the goal is to complete the plans and reach the future. Your vision statement describes the path and what can be found at the end. It must be serious but also creative and forward thinking. And, like the mission statement, the entire concept should be captured in one catchy, memorable line.

It requires planning and thoughtfulness, so plan a specific meeting to brainstorm ideas. Ask attendees where they see the company in the future, what goals they want to accomplish, and what the world will look like when that is done. The answers to this will help you write sample vision statements. Like before, provide a couple of sample statements to a group of core advisers. Elicit feedback on which best captures the company's goals and which will motivate the team into the future. Choose the best idea based on this feedback and write your final statement from them.

Guiding Your Company Based on Clear Values

Create a set of core values to shape your company's development. These are the guiding principles that should be considered when making each of the company's decisions. Use them to prioritize resources and to help you make seemingly impossible decisions. Your values help determine how to handle conflicts and challenges as your business grows.

Core values are a source of inspiration and organizational pride. They help you differentiate the brand and attract customers who are aligned with it. These values should be ingrained in your company culture. Clearly explain and articulate these values to the entire organization, and hire employees who agree to uphold and enforce them.

The Least You Need to Know

- You need a talented co-founder, a board of directors, and officers to guide the company in startup mode.
- A skilled attorney and an accountant help ensure that the company is created right.
- Company decisions should meet the standards set by your mission, vision, and values statements.

Building the Foundation of Your Marijuana Business

Your marijuana business needs a firm foundation to last into the future. This starts with a careful consideration of its corporate structure and meticulous design of its guiding documents. In this part, learn how hiring an attorney and an accountant to help now can save you time and money in the future.

Finding your funding won't be easy. You need a well-researched business plan and a strategy for locating investors. There is a lot of competition right now, and catching people's attention takes planning. Learn how to build your three-year projections and discover what it takes to give a winning pitch.

Once funded, your company needs a brick and mortar location to operate. Learn here how to pitch your business to landlords. Just like funders, they want proof you will run a safe and profitable business. This part of the book will help you face these challenges and prepare you to succeed!

Incorporation Logistics

Marijuana business owners have to make one important decision after another. Your mission, vision, and values statements provide guidance, but the real control is spelled out in your company's operating documents. Its articles of incorporation, by-laws, and any subscription agreements detail the company's decision-making structure.

Your founding team has to pick a corporate structure and then register the company with the state and federal governments. It's a good idea to seek professional advice from lawyers and accountants when choosing your business structure. The form your company takes will determine your personal liability and will influence its ability to raise money.

In This Chapter

- Review the different corporate structures
- Learn how to incorporate your business
- Find out what operational documents you need
- Consider how to make company decisions

Choosing Your Structure

Research all the options before choosing a structure for your company. Learn the positives and negatives of each and understand the liabilities and responsibilities before you make the decision. If you have co-founders, each person should be consulted about this, and the group should determine which works best. There's a lot of shared liability in corporations, and each person should understand and agree before signing on.

Considering hiring an attorney to help your marijuana business with the incorporation process. There are numerous steps to complete and having professional assistance assures you complete them all correctly. Expect to spend a minimum of $3,000 in legal fees, and likely more, before you have completed the process. Of course, you can always do it yourself, but only if your team has the time, skills, and determination.

Do Your Research

State and municipal marijuana laws identify the types of businesses that can hold licenses. Start with a thorough review of the laws in your area before you dive into forming your company. Some state laws limit operations to nonprofit organizations only, and others allow for-profit companies, too. After doing your research, make sure to look closely at each possible type of corporate structure. You need to pick one that protects your board, officers, and staff from liabilities while establishing the best tax benefits for your company.

Following is a brief description of various business structures used by marijuana businesses. Each has detailed and nuanced rules and regulations, so be sure to do further research or consult with an attorney for details.

Nonprofits. A nonprofit company is a charitable corporate entity registered as such at the state and/or federal levels. Many cannabis businesses are state-registered nonprofits, but not federal nonprofits as the feds have restrictive regulations that screen out marijuana businesses. There are nonprofit structures for charitable, social-welfare, agricultural, and labor organizations; social clubs and fraternal societies; employee-benefit associations and funds; and veterans' and political associations. Some marijuana nonprofits can acquire state tax-exempt status, but they still will not qualify for federal exemption.

Nonprofits are run by a board of directors and can have voting members and nonvoting members. Voting members play an important role in running the company, as they elect the board of directors. Nonvoting members are often just financial supporters, with no real rights or responsibilities. Some nonprofits give nonvoting members the right to inspect or audit meeting notices and minutes and may give other records-inspection authority.

The board of directors appoints the organization's officers and hires the executive director. They generally supervise the company through regular financial and operational reviews, and are tasked with making essential decisions for the company. They also have personal liability for any underpaid sales tax and for any labor law violations.

HIGH POINTS

Most of the original state medical marijuana laws required that medical marijuana businesses be either nonprofit or not-for-profit entities. This idea was to stop funds from the sale of marijuana from being used to fund organized crime. If marijuana businesses have no profit, none can be misused. These laws have started to shift in recent years with California and other states now allowing for-profit companies to enter the space.

Cooperatives. Co-ops are groups of like-minded people working together for a common cause and mutual benefit. There are two types of co-ops: worker-owned and member-owned. In worker-owned co-ops, staff members jointly own the company and have voting and decision-making rights based on their years of service and position within the company. Member-owned co-ops are businesses that require anyone using the facility to register as a member. This often comes with a small fee to start, and then each member gets voting rights.

In both, the members vote to elect the board of directors, which governs the organization. They hire the executive director or chief executive officer (CEO) and appoint the group's officers. Members also share in the company's annual profits. Dividends are given based on the membership shares of each person. For example, in retail co-ops, dividends are often distributed to members based on the amount each person spent over the year.

The downside of co-ops is that each member is an owner, and the possibility exists for a large voting block to form amongst its members. This means membership on the board of directors, and hence the officers and executive director, could quickly change based on the whims of a splinter group of members, possibly creating havoc for the company.

Sole Proprietorships. You can also own your own marijuana business with no partners and no board of directors. Sole proprietorships don't even need to incorporate. They are not distinct from you as an individual. The income is all yours, and you personally pay the taxes. You still need a local business license and have to pay sales taxes and fees just like any other marijuana business, though. And, if you want to use a name other than your own, you have to register to operate under a fictitious name.

> **HASHING IT OUT**
>
> Fictitious business names are also known as *DBAs*, which is short for "doing business as." Your sole proprietorship will be required to use your personal name for all official paperwork and filings, unless you have a DBA. Several states don't require these to be registered, but most require that you file the DBA with the state government or county clerk's office.

The upside of a sole proprietorship is that you have complete decision-making control. The downside is that you also take on unlimited personal liability. Any unpaid taxes, liens, or levies against the company and employment law violations all become your problem, without the corporate shield to offer protection for your personal assets. It's also hard to raise money for these types of companies, so it's likely not a good choice unless you have your own funds.

Partnerships. A partnership is when two or more people share ownership in a business. These organizations are tricky, as each person holds an equal decision-making vote. Be sure to carefully vet any potential partners, and take time to write a partnership agreement that outlines how decisions will be made and how problems will be solved. Partnerships are required to register with their state's filing agency, which is generally its secretary of state. They also have to choose a name and file a DBA.

Partnerships are easy to form, saving money and time. Partners pool their resources, both time and money, and good partners motivate each other to accomplish hard tasks. They can go wrong easily, though. Disagreements amongst partners are inevitable, so be ready to compromise in order to stay in business. There are complicated tax implications, too. The company's profits pass through to the partners, meaning each person is responsible for adding the total to their personal income and paying the taxes for it all. Liabilities also pass through to the partners, and each person is responsible for any mistakes made by other team members. Deep-pocket partners can find themselves paying personally for problems created by others.

You might consider forming a limited liability partnership (LLP) instead, where voting rights and responsibilities are given to each person based on their investment percentage. This is likely a more attractive organizational formation to investors who might not be willing to assume the full brunt of the partnership's potential liabilities.

Limited Liability Corporations. Limited liability corporations (LLC) are hybrid companies that provide liability protections like a corporation and tax benefits like a partnership. For tax purposes, the company's income and losses are passed through to the owners, who are called members. Most states require more than one owner, although not all do, and the members themselves decide how much control each person has and how much profit they share in.

LLCs have to file with their state's filing organization, likely the secretary of state. They also need an operating agreement that creates rules and regulations for the company, specifying how decisions are made within the company, how profit distributions are handled, and what rights are given to each member.

Unlike in partnerships, LLCs protect the personal assets of members from corporate liabilities. This is a big upside for both founding members and potential investors. LLCs also have more leeway in determining how profits are distributed, so people that give more capital or put in more sweat equity can receive more. The downside is in tax complications. For example, the company's entire net income is subject to self-employment taxes, and Medicare and Social Security must be paid on it all. Some states require the LLC to dissolve if any single member leaves, so be cautious when moving forward in those locations.

 **HIGH ALERT**

Your marijuana business has to file tax returns with both the state and federal government. This is particularly complicated for LLCs, as it's a state-only tax status. LLCs have to file their federal returns as corporations, partnerships, or as a part of the owner's personal tax returns. This decision is made based on the number of members in the LLC and on the way the company votes to file. Some LLCs are automatically assigned a federal status by the government, which can be appealed if needed.

C Corporations and S Corporations. A C Corporation, or C Corp, is the most common business tax status in the United States. These companies have numerous benefits, including protection from most liabilities for the board of directors' members, officers, shareholders, and staff. There are still a few liabilities that can pass through, though, such as unpaid sales taxes and certain human resources situations. This also includes collecting, but failing to pay, employment taxes or personally committing labor law violations.

Investors like to join C corps, as they can be given equity shares for their contribution. The company can issue multiple classes of stock—each with different voting rights—and can have as many shareholders as desired. This tax status comes with lots of tax benefits and a lowered risk of audit. However, there are problems with taxation in that some money is double taxed. The corporation has to pay taxes on all of its income, and then when the profit is distributed to shareholders, it is taxed again as income to them. C corps require a lot of paperwork and clear oversight of the financial management. Hire a lawyer and an accountant to help your marijuana business stay compliant.

Companies that wish to avoid the double taxation in the C corp structure can hold an election to become an S corp. If successful, the company is not taxed itself. Instead, the profits and losses pass through to the shareholders. S corps require an even greater level of oversight to assure compliance, including copious recordkeeping of meeting minutes and corporate decisions.

Benefit Corporations. Thirty-one states have laws allowing benefit corporations to register. These are companies that form not just for a profit, but also to accomplish social or environmental goals. The requirements for filing vary state by state, so consult your local laws to find out more. Generally, you are required to state your beneficial purpose in the company's articles of incorporation and list them on each stock certificate. The shareholders must understand that the company will sometimes make decisions that move the goals ahead but do not create profits.

Benefit corporations attract clients who like the added value of shopping at places with missions they support. They also attract top staff, too, as people like meaningful work. But, there are downsides. You'll have to constantly prove to shareholders that the social goals are being met, and that the company has a healthy balance between its spending and its work building a profitable business.

HIGH POINTS

If your state does not allow benefit corporations, consider becoming certified as a B Corporation. This is a rigorous privately regulated program, managed by B Labs of Berwyn, Pennsylvania, which gives a stamp of approval to a participating company who meets "rigorous standards of social and environmental performance, accountability, and transparency." Getting B Corp status does not convey any tax benefits to the company, but it's meaningful to your staff, clients, and to the community.

DIY vs. Hiring a Lawyer

Relying on the advice of business professionals versus incorporating yourself can have very different results. Choosing your corporate structure and establishing it properly is important work and mistakes can be costly. DIY incorporation carries the possibility of future problems if you make a mistake. It does you no good to save money now, but to be unprotected against litigation later.

It's fairly easy to choose your business entity without assistance, especially if your team does its research, but you should consider hiring an attorney to help register the company properly and to write your articles of incorporation and operating agreements. There are books and websites that will guide you through the process, too, including the well-used NOLO Press guides. Either way, make sure to choose a corporate structure with decision-making, profit-sharing, and tax-paying processes you can live with long term.

Establishing Your Corporation

Once you decide what kind of organization to form, it's time to start filing paperwork. You have to register with the state, the federal government, and with your local municipality. To do this, you need a corporate address and an agent for service of process who acts as the point person for lawsuits and paperwork for your company.

You can complete these steps yourself or have your corporate attorney manage them. It's not that hard to complete these forms or to manage the filings, but it can be time consuming, especially if you have to walk in your state and local applications. If nothing else, have your corporate attorney on call to answer questions along the way.

Getting an Address and a Registered Agent

Establish a corporate address early in the process of forming your company. You'll need one in order to file your incorporation paperwork and to apply for your city business license. And, you definitely need an address to apply for a state marijuana business license. Without an established address, you cannot become incorporated or licensed.

Your established corporate address cannot be a post office box or mail service. It must be a physical location. Consider renting an administrative office to get started, where you incorporate the company and operate the business before your marijuana permit is granted. You can always update your address with your state's filing agency when you move into the marijuana facility. If you cannot afford or don't need an entire office, rent a co-working space, and register your company there. Neither of these rental scenarios is likely to allow marijuana inside, so expect your lease to specify this.

Your company also needs a registered agent to act as the official contact for the corporation. Their job is to ensure proper receipt of any lawsuits and legal documents for the corporation. Some have their lawyer act as the registered agent. Others use a firm like V-corp, who act as registered agents for various companies, charging a small annual fee for the service. You can also act as your own agent for service of process. But, because registered agents are the official point of contact with regulatory agencies, it's to your advantage to have someone with a knowledge of legal intricacies manage your service.

 **HIGH ALERT**

Law-enforcement officers are often the ones who serve papers, and most companies don't want the police coming to their corporate headquarters. The registered agent usually holds a different physical address for this reason.

Filing with the Secretary of State

You have to register your cannabis business with the state's filing agency, unless it is a sole proprietorship. Generally, you register with the secretary of state, but not always, so research the laws in your area to learn more. The document you file is called your Articles of Incorporation. The state will require certain data to be included, and may even provide a template for your company to use. Otherwise, hire an attorney to write them or create them yourself. Your state agency will provide you with a list of detailed information to include, and if any is missing, your incorporation will be delayed.

Before filing, check with your secretary of state to verify that your proposed name is available. They should have a way to do this on their website. Have a few potential names in mind in case yours is already taken. Or, consider adding to or subtracting from your proposed name. For example, if Green Flower Shop is already taken, try revising your name to Green Flowers. The meaning stays the same, and the name remains salable across multiple markets.

Your Articles of Incorporation should include this information:

- The name of corporation

- A statement of the corporation's purpose

- Information for the agent for service of process

- The corporation's street and mailing addresses

- The number of total authorized shares

- The incorporators' signatures

This may not be all that is required, so be sure to check with your state's filing agency for details. Expect to pay a fee for filing. In California, this is $100, but each state varies. Once your application is accepted, the state will likely send you a stamped copy to mark the official start date of your company.

It's likely that you also have to complete a statement of information. California companies have 90 days after filing their articles to submit this form. Your state's rules may differ, so be sure to research this and comply. The statement of information gives the state more data about your company. They are required to be updated periodically to help keep the government informed about any changes. The statement of information notes the corporation's name and address, the officers' names and addresses, and information for the agent for service of process. It's generally easy to file online, and the fees are negligible.

 HASHING IT OUT

In states including California and Delaware, when filing your articles of incorporation, you are also registering to pay state corporate income tax. California's Franchise Tax Board is the state's tax collection agency. They require that every corporation pay a minimum annual tax of $800 and more depending on your company's annual profits. Be sure to research how to file with your state tax agency, as each has different laws.

Attaining a Federal Employee Identification Number (EIN)

After you get your articles of incorporation, you can file for your federal Employee Identification Number (EIN). The Internal Revenue Service (IRS) issues EINs for the purpose of tax administration. It's how the IRS identifies your business. You must have an EIN if you are a corporation or if you have employees.

It's fairly easy to apply for an EIN at the IRS website. It only takes a few minutes to fill out the form, and if there aren't any problems, your number is issued on the spot. However, it's not always simple. For example, if your new name is someone else's old name, reassigned to you by your state, the IRS may require more details before issuing an EIN. And, you can only apply for one EIN per day, per Social Security number, so plan accordingly. You may want to have your accountant or lawyer procure the number for you, as they will be able to manage any problems.

Companies use an EIN to conduct activities that generally require a Social Security number. Beyond paying taxes, this includes opening bank accounts, getting credit cards, and applying for business permits. If your marijuana business is a sole proprietorship, you are not required to get an EIN, but you might want to regardless. EINs are also used to issue 1099s to independent contractors, and without one you will have to list your personal Social Security number on each.

Paying State Sales and Use Tax

Most states, but not all, require medical marijuana businesses to apply for a permit to sell and then pay sales tax for each transaction. These are licenses called *seller's permits, sales tax certificates,* or by another similar name, and you must file for one with the right agency in your state. For example, in California, you file with the Board of Equalization; in New York, with the New York State License Center; and in Colorado, with the Department of Revenue. Most states have online applications or you can walk in and file.

Technically, it's your clients who owe the taxes on each purchase, not your company, but because individuals are highly unlikely to ever pay the taxes on their own, your business acts as a vessel for the state, collecting them at the time of each sale. You also have to pay use tax on any retail products given away for free. The state still wants their taxes on these items, but only on the wholesale value. Keep careful track of all gifted items so you can pay this properly.

Even in states without sales tax, you may be required to register for a seller's permit, or you may choose to do so voluntarily. Wholesalers from other states will charge you sales tax on purchases unless you can provide them with proof that you are a resale business. In Oregon, the Department of Revenue has an option for retail companies to apply for resale certificates to use when buying goods from out of state.

HIGH POINTS

You may be required by law to post your seller's permit visibly in your retail store, so consumers can see that you are properly licensed, and that when you collect their tax, it is really being paid to the state. Check your state regulations to find out for sure.

Getting a City or County License

State marijuana laws grant local control, meaning each city and county has the right to ban or allow these uses. Those that allow it can establish rules that limit certain rights of users and businesses. For example, California's new marijuana law allows adults to grow six indoor- or greenhouse-grown marijuana plants per parcel of land. Local laws are not allowed to limit this right in any way. However, cities and counties are allowed to ban outdoor cultivation, and many have chosen to do so.

If you want to start a marijuana business, you have to research your city's laws and find these limits. It may or may not be possible to accomplish your goals where you hope, so have several options in mind for your location. Where it's allowed at the city or county level, you have to secure two different approvals: a zoning license and a marijuana business permit.

The first is secured from the zoning department of the city or county in which your facility is located. These permits are not easy to get, even for normal retail and manufacturing companies. Be prepared to prove that your building is located in an area approved for marijuana uses and that your landlord approved the use. You will likely be required to hold a public hearing, so be sure to canvass the neighborhood for support. Oppositional neighbors can kill your project if the zoning officer is compelled by their complaints.

Once you have your zoning license, which gives your business the right to occupy the building, you still have to secure a marijuana business license to open. This might be a competitive process, depending on the local laws, limited to occasional rounds of open applications. If so, expect to face fierce rivalry from multiple candidates and plan for high costs. It might be a non-competitive process, with a small green zone and major exclusionary zones designed to stop cannabusinesses from overpopulating neighborhoods.

Some cities and counties wrap both the zoning license and the marijuana business permit into one special use permit. The processes are still the same—a public hearing with neighbor input weighing in on the project and a complex application process to secure the license. Marijuana businesses often hire multiple consultants to assist, including a government relations expert, a community organizer, and an attorney.

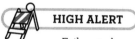 **HIGH ALERT**

Failure to be regulation-compliant can lead to penalties and leave you subject to litigation with no legal protections. Never open a marijuana business without a permit or in an unlicensed facility.

Corporate Governance

By now, you are surely starting to see why most people are content to be employees, rather than entrepreneurs. Starting a business is hard work, and you have to accomplish one challenging task after another to succeed. This is also why most businesses fail; after you start, you have to stay compliant. It means constantly renewing your licenses and paying all of your annual taxes and fees. Don't fool yourself into thinking you can't afford a lawyer to help now; this will, in fact, prevent you from paying them more later when things go wrong.

Nothing is more important than establishing the means of governance you'll use for your corporation. There are several important documents that affect the company's decision-making structure, ability to raise funds, and its systems of management and diligence. Some of these documents you might be able to write yourself, but it's advisable to work with an experienced attorney instead.

Your marijuana business needs operational documents that outline how it runs. Depending on the type of company you form, this starts with your operating agreement. It can be in the form of bylaws or as shareholder, membership, or partnership agreements. These agreements contain the rules and guidelines governing the board of directors, shareholders, or partners in your company. You also need a subscription agreement in order to attract and contract investors, and a buy/sell agreement stating how shares or ownership can be transferred.

Operating Agreements

These are contracts between the board, shareholders, partners, or members of the corporation—starting with the founders—that explain their rights. In for-profit companies, operating agreements also detail how equity can be sold and distributed. Depending on the type of corporation you form, your marijuana business will have bylaws or a shareholder, membership, or partnership agreement.

All four of these establish:

- The size and term limits for the decision-making board
- Rules for the removal of directors
- Officer titles and terms of service

- Rules for creating committees

- Regulations for calling and running meetings

- Requirements for preventing conflicts of interest

- Voting rules of the board, members, partners, or shareholders

- Limitations on liability

- How to dissolve the corporation

Additionally, shareholder, membership, and partnership agreements contain information on:

- Capital contributions to the corporation

- How to transfer or sell shares

- Salaries and equity distributions

- Managing disputes between shareholders

 HIGH POINTS

Many startup companies write their own bylaws or shareholder, membership, or partnership agreements. You can find online templates at the SBA website, through NOLO Press, or through a variety of other reputable sources.

Buy/Sell Agreements

A buy/sell agreement establishes the process if someone decides to sell their equity in a privately held company. These agreements generally give other shareholders the right of first refusal before anyone else can purchase the shares. They are used in the event of a retirement or disability and detail the process of selling a partner's company's shares or interest in the event of a death. In addition, they also specify any situations that trigger mandatory sales of a shareholder's stock. They often contain a clause mandating that the company hold life insurance policies on each shareholder to help the other shareholders purchase the equity of a deceased partner.

Subscription Agreements

A subscription agreement is a contract that binds the seller to sell and the buyer to buy, all at a set price for the amount of shares established within. It also contains warranty and representation information for all involved parties, which includes listing the percentage of ownership the shareholder will own in the company once all of its shares have been distributed. It also establishes the rights attached to the shares, including any voting rights or board positions being offered.

The Least You Need to Know

- You need an agent for service of process to accept any lawsuits and official documents for the company.
- Your marijuana business needs to apply to the federal, state, and local governments for various licenses to operate.
- You need an operational document for your company that clearly outlines how decisions will be made, including how the company could be transferred or closed.

Creating a Business Plan

Every marijuana company needs a business plan to guide its mission and vision. These documents take time and effort to create and must be carefully researched and written. The financial projections are complex, often requiring the assistance of a paid adviser. The package must then be given to a competent designer who will finesse it into a final package for investors to review.

You are the magnet that attracts funders to the plan. Get your tools ready, starting with the business plan narrative and financials. Make them simple to digest by preparing a PowerPoint presentation that summarizes the opportunity in a simple and attractive manner. Create an "elevator pitch," which you can deliver in less than 30 seconds, to offer investors a quick look at the opportunity and a chance to size up your personality. You have to inspire confidence quickly to open doors and be ready to justify your plans in detail when you are invited in to pitch.

In This Chapter

- Learn how to organize and write a marijuana-focused business plan
- Do targeted market research to validate your business model
- Build financial models to show investors that your business has a good chance of success
- Create a convincing pitch deck and elevator pitch to use to woo investors

Preparing to Write Your Business Plan

For anyone starting a new business, the idea of writing a business plan might sound daunting for any number of reasons. Look at the big picture, though, and you'll realize that much of the value in writing a business plan is in the process itself and what it teaches you about the business you're preparing to launch. A good business plan should provide you with a to-do list and a roadmap that will help guide your team as it moves forward.

When you embark on a business plan project, be prepared to research market information, analyze it, and explain how your business model will succeed over both the short and long term. Going through this research and writing process is critically important for your own understanding of the market, your competitors, and where you fit into the picture. As with any writing project, you want to keep the audience squarely in focus and communicate your ideas as clearly as possible.

HASHING IT OUT

There are always problems and solutions in a business market, but that doesn't mean they're easy to identify or solve. You will be forced to question the validity of your ideas and go through all the necessary steps to make your case—if you can convince yourself of it, you should be able to convince others, too.

If you are manufacturing marijuana oils that patients will use to alleviate their pain, there is a clear benefit for your customer base that most people understand. But if you are developing a new machine to perform these oil extractions, you'll have to establish why it's superior to existing machines and why manufacturers will be tempted to purchase it.

Reviewing the Industry

In many ways, the marijuana business is vastly different than a traditional business, and your plan should acknowledge and respond to the unique circumstances of this unpredictable and high-stakes industry. One of the first reality checks that would-be marijuana operators and investors must confront is that marijuana is still illegal on the federal level. If you're planning to open a business bank account, you'll find that most banks will not even entertain that conversation. However, the legal market obviously exists in many states, both for medical and adult use. It's possible to open legal businesses under these laws, and the Department of Justice (DOJ)and Drug Enforcement Administration (DEA) generally stay away.

Think about your business plan from the investor's perspective and envision the questions investors' have about an industry with so many legal issues. Some of the unique sections in a marijuana business plan should include:

- A compliance section providing an overview of local and state licensing regulations and how your company plans to comply with these rules moving forward.

- A financial overview providing transparency on taxes, cost of goods, deductions, and other areas where marijuana is treated differently than other businesses.

- An overview of the products you plan to produce or sell and what makes them appealing and/or unique to patients or recreational buyers.

Know Your Chosen Field, Inside and Out

Depending on the state you live in, marijuana may be classified as a medicinal product, a recreational product, an illegal product, or some combination thereof. Learn what types of businesses are legal in your area and which clients you can serve. Then, get ready to do your market research, which may sound like a daunting task, but really is a simple process that helps you better understand your competition, customers, and local market.

Try using websites like Weedmaps and similar sites to estimate how many marijuana delivery services and brick-and-mortar dispensaries are in your area. Research articles in local newspapers and industry magazines, and collect data you can find on revenues, customers, and related information. Determine the average amount of cannabis consumed by each patient, and calculate the number of growers and manufacturers that are needed to serve them. If you want to start an edibles business, for example, you need to determine how many similar products are currently readily available, how well they sell, and how your products will stand apart.

One of the best ways to conduct market research is hands-on research. So visit dispensaries located in your area. Take notes, talk to the staff about products you are interested in, and ask managers about how they choose new suppliers. Go online and study menus at local marijuana dispensaries and delivery services and see which products are featured and what they cost. This process of researching and collecting market information will not only help you provide an analysis of the local business environment, but it will also help you develop strategies to beat the competition.

Writing Your Executive Summary

The most important section in your business plan is the executive summary. It acts as a stand-alone document that you can give to potential investors who want a quick snapshot of your business and its likelihood of success. This summary should provide an overview of the company's vision, the management team, and why you are poised for success. It should introduce a problem in the industry and explain how you plan to solve it. In addition, it should have an overview of the projected profits and losses, the summary of the offering, and an analysis of the expected returns.

Keep in mind that the executive summary is a tool for you to articulate your vision and future company plans. When you put your ideas and strategies in this format, they'll act as a guide for you to track your business's progress and stay on point as it evolves. Because it's a condensed, focused version of the larger business plan, it makes sense to write it after you have completed all the other sections.

Developing the Narrative

You can hire writers and editors to help write the business plan, or if you have writing experience or the drive to try, you can do it yourself. You can read other business plans or look at templates for ideas about how to organize and write your own. Even if you only get through a rough draft, it will be a valuable exercise and good source material for an experienced writer to take to the next level. Your primary goal is to present a clear and convincing case for your business, with an overview of the industry, details on the market and customers you'll serve, and how you will execute your goals and vision.

Being creative is a critical skill in running a marijuana business, so don't feel constrained by the traditional components found in other business plans. As you develop your outline and start writing, think strategically about what information you need to include and how to present it in a compelling fashion. If you're passionate about the ideas that led you down this path, make sure that commitment and enthusiasm comes across in your business plan.

Long business plans are out of fashion. Investors want densely packed packets that express your vision and the offer in less than 15 pages. Within these pages, you should separate your data into parts, including the deal structure, the company's history, a description of its services, and its marketing strategy. Discuss your organizational structure, staffing plans, and the forward-thinking ideas you have for the future. Make sure your corporate lawyer reviews this plan and includes all the proper disclaimers necessary.

Drafting Your Cannabusiness Financials

Potential investors will look at your financial projections carefully to establish the company's likelihood of success. Building your spreadsheets based on well-researched projections is critical to conveying a convincing message. Substantiating these projections is especially crucial for marijuana businesses, as such businesses run into challenges with banking access and limits to allowable deductions under *Section 280e* of the Federal Income Tax Code. Before any investors agree that you are likely to succeed, you need to demonstrate that you understand and have plans to mitigate the risks of cash handling, tax audits, loan repayment, and any other local conditions placed on marijuana businesses. All of these factors have implications that should show up in your financial projections.

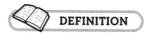 **DEFINITION**

> **Section 280e** is a section of the Federal Income Tax Code that restricts tax deductions for any business involved in trafficking a controlled substance. Marijuana businesses generally pay 25 percent or more than other companies in federal taxes.

Getting into the marijuana industry is a gamble. In most cases, there are a limited number of licenses available and a large number of applicants. For example, Arizona offered an additional 31 marijuana licenses in 2016 and received over 700 applications. With this cutthroat competition, funders will want to know the plan if your team doesn't receive a license. You should consider how much you want to spend in order to submit a competitive application, which is an expensive process normally conducted by experienced consultants and professionals.

After you draft your financials, review the remainder of your business plan. When you make promises in your plan, they must be reflected in the financials. Continue to revisit and revise your financials as your business vision changes. This should be an ever-evolving document even after you become operational.

Uses and Sources of Income

In order to prepare your financials, you must identify what you need to spend money on and where that money will come from. You need to prepare a report on your estimated start-up and operating costs and projected revenue. After that, you must determine how much up-front investment is required, and decide how much ownership in your company you are willing to give away to investors in exchange for this money. Together these elements will inform your financial pro forma, which are the core spreadsheets that forecast the future shape of your business.

Investors generally want to see financial projections going forward for three years and at least one past year's information if are an existing operation. Your profit-and-loss statement should show your gross income and expenses, along with any net income that will be generated over those years. After preparing the detailed spreadsheets, sum up how much of an investment you're asking for. Your cash-flow statement will help you determine how much outside investment is necessary. Create an overview that shows where that money will go and when it will be paid back—either as a direct return on a loan or as profits for equity investors. Funders must be convinced that the company can service the debt or that it has the shares to cover debt set aside.

Build these spreadsheets based on well-researched assumptions in order to come across as reasonable and reliable. Take care to document your assumptions so that when you uncover new information, you can easily make the appropriate adjustments and demonstrate to investors that your projections are based on the best and most up-to-date information. Once you begin operations, regularly review and update these documents to help you predict future changes and to make better business decisions now.

HASHING IT OUT

Hire a Certified Public Accountant (CPA) to review or assist with your financial documents—but note that finding one willing to work with a marijuana business can be difficult. CPAs may be putting their certification at risk in states where their local board of accountancy has not specifically authorized service to this type of business. If you can find one, a cannabis-specific CPA may help you find cannabis-friendly service providers, including merchant processing, payroll, insurance, and even a financial institute where you can open a business account.

Creating Your Growth Timeline

Set up a spreadsheet to estimate your sales over a three-year timeline. In states with an existing market, this should reflect available information on patient numbers and annual sales, and it should be supported by a data-driven marketing plan explaining how your new business will capture market share. In newly legalized states, your projections will likely take more work.

In your spreadsheet, include a basic calculation for the cost of goods sold (COGS). Subtracting this from revenues gives you your gross margin—the money left to cover costs, debts, and profits. Depending on the specific business model, COGS also represents the bulk of the tax deductions available under IRS ruling 280e in the marijuana industry.

Everyone knows projections are based on assumptions and estimates, but being realistic shows you understand the business. Unending growth without a clear and compelling rationale comes across as a red flag. Plus, once funded, you'll have to justify your projections to your investors, and you don't want to be explaining wide differences in your initial assumptions.

Setting Up Capital and Operational Budgets

Set up another spreadsheet to estimate the costs required in order to make the sales you are projecting. Any claims made in the business plan should be represented in these budgets, such as the provision of benefits for full-time employees or the remodeling of the proposed site. Substantiate your assumptions with the best available data, including local rates for real estate, wages, and taxes. Don't forget estimated legal costs, and consider how you yourself will be paid.

When structuring this section and any accompanying documentation, it helps to consider who will review your business plan. For government officials, highlight local job growth, tax payments, and any community benefit or charitable donations described in your business plan. For investors, clearly lay out justifications for costs.

Once you have your projected revenue, start-up costs, and operational budget, you can calculate how much investment you need. Use this information to ensure that the amount of money you are raising is sufficient for your business to be sustainable. Find your break-even point and estimate how long the business will take to become profitable and when it will be able to repay its investors.

 **HIGH ALERT**

Typically, all owners must submit fingerprints for a background check. In addition, many states also have a residency requirement. Consider your state's requirements before soliciting investment, or you may compromise your business's ability to seek a cannabis business license. Note, these strict requirements continue to apply after you win a license. Hire a lawyer to draft clear ownership language for the business, with mandatory buy-sell or termination clauses for owners or operators who fall outside the state's qualifications.

Determine what you are offering in exchange for the money you need. If your state requires that you operate a nonprofit, selling shares is not an option. You can only secure loans. Think about how much control you are willing to relinquish to investors and what terms you can afford to offer. Interest and principle payments will affect your bottom line, while offering shares sets up expectations of profit sharing that you may be held accountable for in the future.

If you are offering shares of ownership, summarize your proposal in a capitalization table, which is a document that simply summarizes the ownership of the company. The form of the table may vary, but it will always show the investment, shares, and percent ownership for each individual, including the founders. While seeking investment, this table should also include unissued shares and the value of the shares that are being offered to new investors.

Capturing Your Investors' Attention

Before investors read your extensive business plan, you need to sell them on your idea. That's where the *pitch deck* comes in. Build a concise but strong presentation that communicates your ideas quickly and effectively. The strongest pitch decks reduce complex business strategies, market statistics, operational details, and financials into a unified and compelling plan that readers can quickly and easily digest.

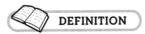 **DEFINITION**

> A **pitch deck** is a succinct slide show presentation about your funding opportunity. It includes a problem statement, your solutions, team biographies, and a brief description of the investment and its expected payoff.

You and the other founders have to pitch the deck, selling the idea to investors with your dynamic presentation. People are investing in you as much as in the company, so presenting and proving yourself capable is essential. Get ready to explain how your plan and your team for implementing it are worth the investment. Live and breathe your financials and the assumptions behind them. Be ready for tough questions, and don't get caught without answers. You might only have one chance with your funders, so be ready to impress!

Basic Pitch Deck Components

Create a PowerPoint-based pitch deck to market your offering to potential funders. Your deck should highlight three important factors: your current opportunity, a problem facing the cannabis industry, and your solution to that problem. With these components, it explains why you started the company, what you plan to do, and how you will become successful. Include a simple market analysis establishing the demand for your company or its products, a summary of your business plan and what makes you unique, and an overview of your marketing plan and branding strategies.

Complete your pitch deck by demonstrating that you are the person who should be addressing the industry problem you've described. There is no one right way to do this—use whatever means possible to play up your strengths. You can provide an organizational chart that demonstrates how you'll structure the executive and management-level employees, which is particularly useful if your strength lies in creating super-efficient *Standard Operating Procedures (SOPS)*. Or, you can provide a series of biographies of your key team players if their experience is a unique winning feature. Your goal is to assure potential investors that you will succeed.

 **DEFINITION**

Standard Operating Procedures (SOPs) describe and detail all of the operations that each of your employees will be performing during their regular work shifts. SOPs are the step-by-step instructions that guide each role or activity and ensure that all tasks are completed in a uniform manner. SOPs are critical to compliant cannabis operations and in many states must be submitted prior to receiving a cannabis license.

Tell a Compelling Story

Your pitch deck will be one of the most crucial factors for investors to consider when deciding whether or not to fund your brand. Like any good story, the deck should have a clear beginning, middle, and end. It should reveal a compelling plot that leaves the reader wanting more—which the business plan will provide!

Not all investors are alike. Depending on their individual background and professional training, investors may want to see a wide array of information presented to them in equally diverse ways. Investors experienced in the marijuana market will want you to demonstrate that you have the skillset and experience required to succeed, while an investor from another sector may be more interested in seeing your financial model and potential exit strategies. Research your prospective investors and tailor your pitch deck to tell the right story.

Making Your Pitch Deck Stand Out

Having a unique visual image makes a critical first impression about your company, conveying your professional aesthetic, target market, and potentially your values. Use a professional graphic designer to create your logo and the themes that form the foundation for your company's brand identity. Your logo should encapsulate everything that you and your business represent in regard to business ethics and practices. Creating a logo takes a lot of time, and working with a branding professional can help make sure you get it right.

If used correctly, your theme will leave a lasting impression in your readers' minds. Keep it simple. While working on the layout and design, it's easy to get carried away with the use of animation, transitions, and complex visual elements. This can be fun, but you don't want to have a *distracting* pitch deck. Your deck should have a simple aesthetic and be rendered into a simple PDF file. Using this generic format will prevent unauthorized changes to the file and allow potential investors to view it on most digital devices.

The Elevator Pitch

When it comes to pitches, less is more. This may seem counterproductive to the highly nuanced business strategies and operational practices described in your business plan, but keep in mind that an elevator pitch is a description of your company in the broadest terms possible. It's an invitation to see the bigger picture and the finer details in the future. Use this short time to present the ideal vision of your company and the services it offers.

You'll want to include enough details in the pitch to intrigue potential funders, but you don't want to overwhelm them with the details of an industry that they may not know much about. Leave room for questions, which can be answered in the pitch deck and business plan. This is the first impression that your potential investors will hear. Be sure that your pitch is as clear and concise as possible.

 HASHING IT OUT

An elevator pitch should cover these questions in two or fewer sentences each:

- What industry are you working in?
- What is wrong with the current industry you are working in?
- What is the name of your company?
- How does your company intend to fix what's wrong with the industry?

Example: I run a licensed medical marijuana dispensary. This segment of the industry is increasingly competitive, and we have to lower our cost of goods sold to increase profits. Our company, Dispensary X, is expanding into the manufacturing space next door, where we will produce marijuana products for much cheaper than we pay now on the wholesale market. We need funding for this expansion and can offer competitive returns to investors.

Your public-speaking abilities will help determine your likelihood of success and in finding investors. Your ability to pitch the plan does not equate to your capability to form, manage, and operate a company, but it will directly affect how people perceive your idea and the purpose of your company. If you can't confidently communicate the mission, vision, and values of your company, you're unlikely to inspire enough confidence in investors for them to fund your cannabis business.

The Least You Need to Know

- A thoughtful, convincing business plan is the first step to creating a successful business.
- Thorough research and analysis of your competition and customers will go a long way toward proving the validity of your business idea.
- For your spreadsheets to be convincing, they must be based on well-researched projections.
- A compelling pitch deck and elevator pitch will be your best bets for interesting investors in your business plan.

Securing Your Start-Up Funds

You won't get anywhere without the funds to start your marijuana business. It costs money to incorporate, and initial expenses like rent, remodeling, equipment, and staffing start hitting way before your first dollar ever comes in. Your founding team has to be able to pay these costs themselves or must raise funds quickly. Otherwise, you won't have a marijuana business to run.

Raising funds is hard, as marijuana businesses are still high-risk. Federal laws prevent bank loans, so you'll have to find other sources. There are still plenty of options, once you know where to look. Make sure you have a solid plan, a competent founders' group, and an impressive pitch team. The marketplace is increasingly crowded and competitive, and you need to stand out.

In This Chapter

- Learn why you have to put in your own money
- Review ways to raise outside funding
- Find out the key components of funding proposal
- Compare loans to equity deals

Securing Your Funding Source

There are a few ways to fund a cannabis startup, but none more important than bringing your own money to the table. If you don't need it, don't raise money. Despite the glamour of Silicon Valley and early stage investing, the best founders avoid raising capital to maintain control of their company. Marijuana businesses often have high gross incomes, so you might not need outside investment to reach profitability.

Think carefully before taking funding from others. It places an enormous responsibility on your early-stage company, adding financial pressures and bringing other stakeholders into decision making. Make sure to review your state medical marijuana laws for your state's rules on investor qualifications. This could include disqualifying or limiting out-of-state funders and people with criminal records.

Besides using your own money, there are three main ways to fund your cannabusiness. Approach your friends and family for support. They might be interested in getting into the industry, providing you with camaraderie in addition to funds. Pitch traditional outside investors, including private lenders and venture capitalists. Smart investors who're looking for equity positions in promising startups surround the marijuana field. And, finally, take a look at new-age funding sources, such as incubators and crowdfunding.

 HIGH ALERT

> *Lifestyle* can be a bad word when raising funds. A lifestyle business is one that is optimized for the founder or team's lifestyle rather than for scale or growth. Much of the economy is driven by small businesses that provide tremendous value to communities and great pride to their owners, but simply aren't investable. Ask yourself, "Could this be a billion-dollar business?"

Your Own Funds

Don't expect anyone to believe in your company more than you do. In fact, almost all founders, cannabis or not, are thought of as crazy when they start their own businesses. It's only after companies become profitable that others become convinced. Cannabusiness founders have to work even harder to be taken seriously after years of Cheech and Chong jokes and the specter of prohibition looming around.

When it comes to fundraising, if you aren't willing to invest your own money into the start-up, no one else will want to, either. Founders who don't put money in first come across as not fully committed to their vision. Funders wonder why, and they're rightly concerned that the reason could be personal debts or fear of risk. So unless you have a wealthy family member who can help with seed capital, plan to put your own money in first. Doing so sends a signal to investors, letting them know that you have adequately prepared to start this company. Nothing says that better than funding the first few steps yourself.

You can loan funds to the businesses, provide money in exchange for ownership shares, or loan money on a *convertible loan* that offers the chance for future shares. Make sure your corporate attorney creates a contract for these funds, and that the other founders, the board, and any officers with authority sign off on the terms. It's essential to avoid any future confusion about your ownership stake or the payback terms.

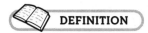 **DEFINITION**

> **Convertible loans,** or convertible notes, allow the holder to convert monies owed into company stock at a future date. The terms are established from the start, including the timeframe of the potential conversion and the value of the shares to be exchanged.

Family and Friends

After you tap out your own savings and investment money, it's time to call, email, text, and private message your family and friends. These are the people who believe in you regardless of your previous business experience. They are also likely willing to accept friendlier loan terms than your typical outside investor.

When you approach friends and family, your business pitch doesn't have to be as refined, cohesive, or finished as when you approach outside investors. Think of it as great practice for your pitch to outside investors, should you need to expand your funding search. Ask your friends and family for feedback on the pitch itself. Specifically ask them about your body language, your timing, and your overall presence when you pitch. The details and terms don't matter as much for them, so make sure they provide constructive criticism in other areas.

A typical family-and-friends funding round features either a convertible loan or an equity investment deal that's favorable to you. It's easier to create these documents than you might think, as long as you hire an experienced lawyer. Such documents both allow you to continue raising money and building your business, without setting a real price or value on it. It's hard to determine a startup's worth and, without it, outside investors will be hard pressed to see a valuable investment. Your friends and family believe way more in you than your projected numbers.

Traditional Outside Investors

If you're lucky, your company will be fully funded by the end of your friends-and-family round. However, either now or in the future, you'll need to be ready to pitch to real outside investors. They will ask the tough questions, demand financials, perform due diligence, and hopefully write you the type of checks to give your startup a chance to succeed. That's what you are really asking for from investors: a chance to build your dream company and for everyone to succeed.

I can't stress this enough: You must come prepared. No one who'll write you a check for $100,000 or more is going to do it without serious due diligence. They'll want at least a few meetings to talk through the project, and some time to think about it. Be prepared for this part of the fundraising experience to take twice as long as you expect and be twice as hard as you anticipate. Make sure you and your other founders can cover the company's bottom line while you wait.

To start, get your financial projections tight, and be ready to explain any assumptions made during the modeling. Potential investors will ask a lot of questions, and you must know the numbers, inside and out. If your company has shareholders, you'll need a capitalization table to show the breakdown of their current and planned distribution. Investors will want to know who owns the company, how much they each own, and what is committed to convertible note holders.

 HIGH ALERT

Once after flubbing a simple question during a mentoring session, a multi-millionaire funder said he could tell I was not "living and breathing" my company's numbers. It was a pivotal learning experience that struck hard. Now, I make sure to always know my financials, and am ready to pitch when the opportunity hits. Make sure you do the same!

Besides the financials, you need a business plan narrative, which describes the company, the deal, the market, and the potential earnings for any lender or investor. This business plan should be carefully reviewed by your lawyer, as it needs to have all of the right risk disclosures. Create a pitch deck to go along with your proposal. Your pitch deck should be no more than five to seven slides outlining your project and deal points. Funders do not want to wade through a volume of data. Boil the details down into tight financials, a short narrative, and a concise pitch deck. Then, start reaching out to potential investors.

Build your potential investor list by doing online research about cannabusiness funders and by asking colleagues in the industry for advice and ideas. Consider attending a few industry conferences and events, especially those geared towards business. Take time to think about the type of investor you want. Are you looking for someone with expertise that you don't have, or do you want money from a hands-off investor? Constantly build your list of potential investors, giving this list the same attention you give to building a client list. Provide these relationships with constant care and attention, so they are there when you need them.

There is much to consider at this stage, so take your time to create a fundraising plan. Write out the best- and worst-case scenarios for investors and your company's *runway* is paramount. Planning for the worst contingencies now will prepare you to manage big problems should they occur. When you start with a coherent, fact-based plan to raise money, you can easily adjust it as needed.

Angel investors are the lifeblood of the early stage start-up economy. An angel investor is characterized as an individual who invests their own personal funds into a company, not those of a fund. Professional angels write $50,000 to $150,000 checks a few times yearly to fund start-up companies. This widely varies, though, and yours might be invested only in you. These investors rely more on intuition and experience rather than on tangible metrics, and a strong founding team is frequently considered the number-one quality in a good investment.

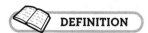 **DEFINITION**

> A **runway** is the amount of time your company can operate in start-up mode without going out of business. Your investors want to know that you have a plan to pay the bills and stay afloat until capital comes in and profits start to flow.
>
> An **angel investor** is someone who loans their own personal money to a company.

New Age Investing

Marijuana businesses struggle to get investment from traditional investors. Thankfully, a new wave of investing has given tools and options for founders to raise money. The first option is going into an accelerator or incubator. Accelerators offer mentoring and coaching programs to help existing companies get ahead, while incubators do the same for startups. There are now multiple cannabis-specific ones, including Gateway Incubator, Canopy, and Cannavator in the Bay Area.

There's a competitive application process for each one of these. They're hard to get into, but it can be valuable for first-time founders. Accelerators and incubators generally offer a 3- to 4-month experience, where you're immersed in the cannabis industry. Your company is given initial investment funds, generally between $20,000 and $50,000. You get to meet a host of mentors and attend classes in business management and operations, learning firsthand from experts in a variety of fields. You'll also get workspace, access to media opportunities, and a demo day where you can pitch to investors.

Being in a class of other start-up companies is inspiring. Starting a new business is a lonely proposition. Most of the time, you and your team are the only ones who believe in your vision. So having a few more people see your plans and help guide you through creating them is incredibly important.

You might consider presenting your business plan at one of the marijuana industry's pitch contests. Groups like WeedClub from San Francisco and ArcView from Oakland, California host regular round-robin competitions. Entrepreneurs apply to participate and winners are chosen to present based on the strength of their plans. The winners then get to pitch at specially planned events in front of crowds packed with accredited investors. Competition is tough, with mercilessly timed formulaic presentations before experienced investors. But, if you win or even just catch the eye of the right investor, funding can come quickly.

Marijuana businesses compete for funders' attention at pitch events such as San Francisco's WeedClub at Runway.

You might also try crowdfunding for your marijuana business if you can't find traditional investors or secure space in an incubator. You can now crowdfund through services like Indiegogo as the Evoke vaporizer company did for their start-up money. In fact, they raised way more than their initial asking amount. However, understand that taking early commitments means that you have to deliver on your amazing new concept. There are numerous examples of startups that took on a large number of pre-orders and then failed to deliver.

Potential Funding Mechanisms

There are several ways you can take on funds for your company. It could be in the form of loans, which come at high interest rates from institutional lenders and are capped by state usury laws from individuals. Loans from individuals also are a great way to raise funds, if you can get one, as the interest generally caps out at around 10 percent and the lender has zero control over your operations. You should beware of higher interest rates from exempt lenders, such as banks and mortgage brokers, as these deals can be too good to be true and the hidden costs can sink you.

Convertible loans are a good option; they allow you to take on the funds as a loan with the option to offer equity instead of payback in the future. It enables you to keep your regular payments low while you build the company, and it gives you maximum control during your startup phase. You might want to take on shareholders right now, giving common or preferred stock to people willing to risk the investment funds for it. You'd have decision makers on board, though, so expect to communicate regularly in order to keep them happy. Choose a method carefully, and consider the consequences and benefits of each with your team and its corporate attorney when making a decision.

Convertible Loans

Convertible loans, also called convertible notes, have become more and more popular over the past few years as the market for start-up investments has grown. These are basically short-term loans that can potentially be converted into equity on a set schedule. Meaning an investor who puts in funds for your seed round can choose to convert their loan to equity in a few years when they can weigh the true value of the loan interest versus the worth of the shares. Your company gets immediate access to the funds, generally with no interest or principal payment until the potential conversion date. The note holders don't have operational control as lenders, but they'll surely keep an eye on the company to gauge its success, way before the date they can choose to convert their funds.

The reason convertible loans are so founder-friendly is because you are essentially receiving money from investors without establishing a price for your company. Your company likely isn't of much value in the start-up phase anyway, so setting the maturity date for these loans a few years in advance gives you a chance to build it before the shares convert. The loan sets the maturity date and the interest rate. The interest itself will likely accumulate with the principal and be given back as extra shares. Noteholders benefit by setting the conversion price of their shares now. They're gambling that the company's future value will be higher than predicted and that the end payback will be larger.

Such deals are quicker and easier to put together than equity deals. Convertible loans don't require shareholder or subscription agreements, nor do they include pro forma financial disclosures. The deal is contracted more like a traditional loan with less hassle and lower legal fees.

Convertible loans also have tax advantages. Because they are loans, you don't need to price your funding round, giving value to your own shares. This is beneficial in the early days when money is tight and risk is high. You don't want a hefty tax bill as an early-stage founder as a result of a high early-stage valuation.

HIGH ALERT

Convertible loans are not without risks. Your company is either going to have to pay back loans in the future, or give out valuable shares at a discount. If your company ceases to exist by then, you might find yourself targeted by angry funders. They may come after your personal assets or those of any successor company to try and recoup their losses.

Equity Partners

We have already discussed that it's hard to value your company in its early stages before you have any meaningful income or savings. Because of this, issuing shares based on true value is hard at this point. However, taking on debt is also difficult for a startup. Your best seed-round equity partners are your friends and family. They are likely willing to accept fewer shares at a higher value than outside investors, and they'll hassle you less for decision-making power in those early years.

Make sure any outside investors you consider working with are accredited investors according to the U.S. Security and Exchange Commission (SEC). Unless your company is registered with the SEC, your equity investors must have a net value, not including their home, of more than $1 million and make at least $2,000,000 a year.

Your team must also decide what rights to offer shareholders, using either *preferred* or *common* shares. Preferred shares generally come with more protection and special rights than common stock shares. This includes the first right to dividends and to any funds at the time of corporate dissolution, but does not generally include voting rights. Common shareholders have voting rights, choosing the board of directors and making other decisions, and the worth of their ownership grows as the company gains value. Other shareholders' rights could include everything from liquidation preferences, anti-dilution protections, participation in future rounds, blocking rights on specific company actions, and more. Make sure to plan well when you establish your company and its operational documents, and be very cautious and thorough when negotiating equity shares with investors.

The Simple Agreement for Future Equity (SAFE) is another alternative way to take on funds for shares. Using this model, investors give money to the company now in exchange for the right to take shares totaling this amount during the company's next equity-funding round. These contracts are generally simple, about five pages long, and enable small businesses to take on investment funds quickly and easily. Designed by a Y Combinator accelerator co-founder, SAFE is imagined as the "positive evolution of the convertible note." Make sure everyone involved in any of these deals has lawyers involved to be sure they are properly transacted on both sides.

Getting a Loan

Marijuana businesses are highly unlikely to secure bank loans. Federal regulations set forth banking rules for it, which were established by the federal Financial Crimes Enforcement Network (FinCEN) in 2014. Banks that choose to work with marijuana businesses face extra rules and oversight, which are aimed at stopping organized crime and money laundering. All throughout the rules, FinCEN makes clear that banks engaged in offering services to state-legal marijuana businesses are violating federal conspiracy laws. It's an altogether unenticing proposal for nearly every bank around.

FinCEN advises that banks with marijuana businesses' accounts complete the following due diligence:

"(i)verifying with the appropriate state authorities whether the business is duly licensed and registered;

(ii)reviewing the license application (and related documentation) submitted by the business for obtaining a state license to operate its marijuana-related business;

(iii)requesting from state licensing and enforcement authorities available information about the business and related parties;

(iv)developing an understanding of the normal and expected activity for the business, including the types of products to be sold and the type of customers to be served (e.g., medical versus recreational customers);

(v)ongoing monitoring of publicly available sources for adverse information about the business and related parties;

(vi)ongoing monitoring for suspicious activity, including for any of the red flags [that indicate violations of law]; and

(vii)refreshing information obtained as part of customer due diligence on a periodic basis and commensurate with the risk."

—*FIN-2014-G001, Banking Secrecy Act Expectations Regarding Marijuana-Related Businesses, February 14, 2014*

This leaves two options: private loans and those from individuals. Individuals are your best bet, as this group likely contains your friends and family who'll give you a fair interest rate, hopefully below your state's established usury rate. They'll also be more willing to renegotiate terms if you need more time or lower monthly payments along the way. You might also find angel funds in the form of a loan. Keep in mind usury rates apply in this scenario as well, to help assure that small companies don't get taken advantage of with high-interest loans. Aim low and see if you can find an individual willing to provide you funds below 8 percent interest. If you have good credit and can back the loan with collateral, you might be able to reach this goal.

Beware of *toxic funding*, which can come your way from private lenders. Toxic funding is so expensive to borrow that your company won't survive the paybacks. The ruse is that these companies loan you money at high interest rates, causing you to forfeit company control or ownership to them when you can't make the payments. Private lenders are often not restricted in the interest rates they can charge on loans, although some states cap these at 36 percent. To cannabusinesses, with few choices for getting started, even high rates can look enticing. But, you can quickly get into a spiral of debt trying to pay high interest and principal loan payments, especially in your first couple of years in business. It's best to spend time finding supportive friends and family or waiting to meet fair-minded investors for your company.

 **DEFINITION**

> **Toxic funding** is funding with such a high interest rate that payoff will be impossible and default to the funder is imminent.

Negotiating Terms

If you are planning to start and run a marijuana business, get professionals involved. You'll need a stellar business lawyer and an accountant who understands the peculiarities of the marijuana industry. Negotiating these funding deals isn't easy, as each funding method comes with complications and concerns. The fallout from making mistakes could cripple your company, leading to personal and corporate liabilities. It's best to have professionals on hand to guard your interests.

Find a business lawyer who has worked with cannabusinesses before. Don't be the group that pays for one to learn how to negotiate for a cannabusiness for the first time. There are numerous complex laws that need to be evaluated and considered. Ask your colleagues in the marijuana industry for referrals, and find an attorney with a successful track record. If you can't find anyone, with cannabusiness experience, look for someone experienced in business formation and financial law. Your criminal defense attorney may be willing to help, but this isn't their specialty, so again, paying for them to navigate the learning curve will be expensive.

You also need an experienced accountant to review the deal. Lawyers know a bit about the accounting side of marijuana business transactions but not enough. Make sure your accountant investigates the tax implications of the fundraising method you plan to use. Figure out the hidden costs in taking and paying back loans in the future. Perform a complete analysis of the implications, and ensure you can pay them back before you take on funding. Review your personal finances, too, and understand how your founder's shares will be taxed and make sure you can afford it. Don't get caught by surprise by the cost of taking on funds; make a plan to cover them, and stick to it until you hit profitability.

General Terms to Secure

Negotiate smart, making sure that your proposal strikes a fair balance between your needs and the investors' wants. There will certainly be some back and forth discussions on terms. Know your boundaries, and think about what you can offer to sweeten the deal without giving away control or more ownership and income. For example, if the potential investor owns an edibles company, consider offering them premier shelf space in trade for keeping the loan's interest rate low.

You want unobtrusive funders who bring skills to the team, but don't force their ideas on you while you are building and scaling the company. The best terms allow your team to be in charge of decision making for at least three years or longer (if not forever), if possible. The first three years is crucial growth time for the business, and you'll need it to implement your company's vision without interference from concerned investors. Keep them informed and happy, after all you might require more funds, but inform on your terms and at a pace you can manage.

Carefully negotiate the loan's repayment terms and ensure that the company can afford them. Don't set yourself up to be in the red for years due to high loan payments. Read all the small print in every contract, and be sure to root out any clauses that could lead to a takeover. Your goals as founder should be to hold tightly to the voting rights instilled by your founder shares, to gain more shares over the years through sweat equity and by equity buys, and to secure a job contract that protects your role leading the company. If all goes well, you can hold a secure executive position for years to come, and eventually retire on the healthy sale of your shares.

Financial Traps to Avoid

Create a fundraising plan to prepare for your best- and worst-case scenarios. Outline what you want to raise, who your ideal investor is, and what deal points you hope to secure. Know where you will look for money, identify your deal breakers, and get ready to compromise to attract funders who fit.

Keep it real! Do not purposefully overestimate the value of your company. Your funders will hold you to these expectations. After all, this is why they invested. Place a fair value on the company—one that is realistic, accomplishable, and speaks to the successes ahead. Any variations from it will need to make sense when you explain them to your investors. Be sure your accountant tries to poke holes in your budget before you present it, therefore, if needed you can fix it by replacing more realistic numbers. You can't create a perfect budget, but take your time and get it as close as possible.

Don't give away too much ownership or control of your marijuana business too soon. You need time and unfettered control to start and scale the business. Outside investors, or even family with an interest, can take up time and energy that should be spent growing the company. If you can, keep at least 51 percent ownership for your founders, at least through year three. By then, the company should be stable, and you should be able to turn your attention to investor relations in a more dedicated manner.

Make sure you find investors you like. Do not go into business with overbearing or anti-social people, as you will be stuck dealing with them for years to come. Having an activist shareholder who constantly pushes their ideas over those in the real work plan can be an uncomfortable time drain. Make sure funders are coming on board to support the vision of your marijuana business and not their own ideals. You can take on shareholders like that later, when you have time for investor relations and when the company is ready to review forward-thinking strategies for growth.

The Least You Need to Know

- You and the other founders must invest in the company before anyone else will chip in.
- Friends and family funders, either lenders or equity shareholders, make the next best investors.
- Your pitch materials for outside funders must be concise and well presented.
- Sophisticated funders will grill you on your financials, and you must have ready answers.

Negotiating Your Lease

Negotiations of any kind require strategy and forethought, and leases are no different. These are multi-year, sometimes multi-million-dollar contracts that bind you and the landlord into an intense relationship fraught with viable concerns. After all, you are planning to run your marijuana business inside their asset property, which the landlord could lose to asset forfeiture if everything goes wrong.

With this in mind, be ready to be competent and charming. You need to help the landlord get over their fear, prove your competency to run the company, and show that you either have or can get a permit to operate a marijuana business there. Once the landlord agrees in concept, you still have to negotiate lease terms that work for both sides. Often, the best way to do this is to hire a real estate broker or lawyer to help.

It's important to negotiate a good lease, as you will be stuck with the terms for years to come. Pay attention to key components, including the length of the lease, the tenant improvements required, and the terms of your annual rent increases. Getting a good deal will ensure your company can function for years into the future, and a bad lease will drain it with high rents and costly repairs.

In This Chapter

* Learn why marijuana businesses pay high rents
* Find out how to negotiate your lease
* Understand how hiring a broker can save money
* Get prepared to ask for lower rent

Finding the Perfect Building and Location

Location really does matter. State laws generally let cities and counties ban marijuana licenses. Where allowed, municipal regulations limit where cannabusinesses can be located. These *green zones* can sometimes be only a few blocks long, with limited locations available within them. Building owners who rent to marijuana businesses charge higher than average rents; owners of buildings sell to them for more.

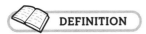 **DEFINITION**

A **green zone** is a municipal area in which marijuana businesses can be located and operate.

Vet the neighborhood carefully, as marijuana business licenses are often blocked by nearby property owners who have a fear of increased crime and suspicious traffic. The reality is that crime has been proven to go down near marijuana businesses, due to their increased security profile. However, regulators often simply choose another applicant if neighbors push back. Make sure you reach out to neighbors before renting or buying space. If you find organized local opposition, look for a different spot.

If you are in retail, make sure your location is near its customer base or their regular travel routes. It's hard to get people to walk, drive, bike, or take public transportation to places outside of their normal daily scope. If you're not located in it, they're not likely to visit often. For manufacturing, find discrete locations with security features like fencing, drive-in bays, and off-street parking. Many permit processes redact these locations from public view in order to lessen the targeted crime potential. Regardless, your goal is to protect your facility and keep its location on a discrete, need-to-know basis.

 HIGH POINTS

The City of Berkeley created zoning maps showing several combinations of potential exclusionary zones. They found that if dispensaries were required to locate in commercial zones and be more than 1,000 feet from preschools, home daycare centers, and K-12 schools, the remaining space would be so limited that no group could qualify for a permit. The final law establishes that dispensaries cannot locate closer than 600 feet to a K-12 school, with all other concerns excluded. Federal Drug-Free School Zone laws set these perimeters much higher at 1,000 feet, and they include colleges, universities, parks, public-housing facilities, youth centers, and pools.

Check your local zoning laws for other requirements you need to follow. This could include strict rules on allowable square footage for marijuana businesses. Some states and municipalities cap the size of cultivation and manufacturing facilities, and you will not be issued your permit if your space exceeds this rule. There are also likely parking requirements for your space, based on its square footage and your number of employees. Be sure to meet these requirements. Check for any rules about outside signage and make sure you don't exceed the regulations. Make sure to find a space that is fully qualified, and then stick to the rules to keep it.

The real estate market is tight in places where marijuana businesses are legal. Green zones are small, available spaces are few and far between within them. People who own buildings in these areas significantly raise the sale prices, and those renting charge the maximum the market will bear. Rental space can go for $10 per square foot or more, and sales prices can be double. If your goal is to purchase a building, you'll have to stand out from the crowd to get the space. Start with a high offer and be ready to sweeten the deal to compete with other potential buyers.

> **HASHING IT OUT**
>
> Before starting your location search, decide if your goal is to rent or buy a facility. If possible, position yourself to do either, as this expands your chances of finding the perfect space. Note, getting a real estate loan is not easy for marijuana businesses, so most cannabusinesses are limited to the rental market.

Hit the Pavement

In this tight rental market, you need to be organized in order to compete. Create a plan for your hunt to maximize your time. Start by developing a winning proposal to give potential landlords, selling your project as desirable for their space. You don't need to give them your entire business plan, but they need to understand your intentions and measure their risk. Explain the company's goals and the methods you will use to meet them. Landlords want to see that you are qualified for a permit and have the talent to launch the project, as well as compliant with state and municipal law. It helps to have notable board members and advisors on your team. Property owners want to see that your application has gravitas, and that the expertise is there for the company to thrive.

Get a city map, and clearly mark the green zones. You need to focus your hunt and not waste any time looking at great spaces with no chance of being permitted. Start by driving the neighborhoods. Look for areas that aren't suitable and cross them off the map. These might include high-crime areas, places near preschools or parks, or spots with nearby residential neighbors. Take down information on any space with a "for rent" or "for sale" sign, and record the address of any unoccupied buildings or places going out of business.

Go online to look for more leads. Search craigslist, Loopnet, and other sites that list commercial rentals. Record the details and contact information of any green zone spaces that meet your needs. At this point, you'll surely notice that a few brokers represent most of the region's rental listings. These are the people you need to impress. If you can get them on your side, they'll help sell your proposal to the owner. Unfortunately, it's more likely that they'll say no, fast. Numerous applicants contact brokers with green-zone locations, and they've already decided whether to say yes or no to industry uses.

Don't let rejections stop your progress. Make a list of potential spaces, and call each one to pitch your plans. Create your elevator pitch, as you will only have one minute to interest the property owners and brokers. Lead with your strengths and anticipate their concerns during your pitch. If you can back the lease with collateral, have VIP board members, or if you are already an experienced business owner, let them know right away. You have to be likeable and competent to open the door for further discussion.

 HIGH ALERT

Never operate a marijuana business without the permission of your landlord. You can only get a marijuana permit with their written approval and, without it, you are at risk of losing everything. Operating commercial marijuana businesses without a permit is generally a felony. Felons, under nearly every marijuana law in the country, are precluded from getting permits. Find a regulated city or county, locate a space in the green zone, tell your landlord what you do, and get a permit.

Working With a Real Estate Broker

Get a real estate broker if you plan to buy a space. The building owner will have one, negotiating for the best deal for their clients. Yours has to have the skills to go head to head with them, so your terms are met, too. Property owners are excited by the green rush, and they're looking to sell high. Make sure your broker knows enough about the industry to temper their expectations so you get a fair deal. Your broker will help craft the deal, making sure each step you take is legal and that your liabilities are limited.

Brokers will also help you find a space, either for purchase or for rent. They often have *pocket listings*, so you get the first look at freshly available spaces. This limits the competition's access to these spaces and increases your chances of securing a contract. Your broker will also help sell your idea to the building owner. Make sure to hire a reputable broker, as landlords trust them and are willing to listen to their pitches. Remember that brokers generally only get paid if you make a deal. You might have to sweeten the deal for them and pay a flat or hourly fee, too. They'll face a lot of rejection on your behalf, and you need them motivated and happy.

 **DEFINITION**

A **pocket listing** is a property that a broker is under contract to sell or rent and is not publically advertised.

Negotiating Your Lease

Marijuana businesses are high-risk and owners pay high rents for it. It's a tricky business for building owners. The federal government still considers medical cannabis to be a Schedule I drug. It's still federally illegal to cultivate, manufacture, and sell marijuana. The Drug Enforcement Administration (DEA) can arrest the owners of buildings, and the Department of Justice (DOJ) can seize the building.

Granted, the last three times the DEA and DOJ tried to forfeit licensed marijuana businesses—all California dispensaries—they failed in court. But, the effect is still chilling. In addition, banks can forfeit properties, too. Most commercial mortgages have clauses that enable the bank to cancel the mortgage and seize the property if they discover the landlord is using it to commit a federal crime. If this happens, you'll likely be asked to leave immediately.

Finding a rental space will be difficult. Multiple potential renters will have already contacted anyone with an available space. Owners know their asset is valuable, and that tenants can profit in the millions through its use. Yet, owners face a big potential loss by renting to you, with the police or banks able to forfeit the property based on federal laws. You will have to present an offer that balances this risk to make a deal. Expect to pay a high monthly rent and a large security deposit and plan to pay for your own tenant improvements. Most marijuana businesses feel lucky just to find a location, and they're willing to pay high rent in order to get their license.

Showing Proof of Income

Because your marijuana business is likely a startup and the industry has limited access to banking services, you are not going to have a great corporate financial profile to show the landlord. You may not even have a bank account, as many marijuana businesses use cash accounting systems. You also are not likely to have enough liquid assets to secure the lease.

Expect the landlord to ask for personal signers and guarantors for the lease. This means the board of directors or founders will be asked to provide personal proof of income and ability to pay. They will have to sign the lease as individuals and be willing to pay out the terms of the contract, even if the business fails. This may be the only way you can secure the lease to start. Note, you might be able to renegotiate in the future and put it in the company name.

Preparing to Negotiate

Commercial leases are generally *triple net*, meaning that you pay rent, plus all maintenance, insurance, and taxes on the space, which is the common lease for marijuana businesses. You are not likely to be offered a *percentage rent* agreement, where you pay a base rent, plus a percentage of retail sales. Landlords do not like the perception of sharing in marijuana profits. They will, however, use this standard to guide the base rent proposed, so expect to be asked to show your profit and loss statements to help them gauge their price. Landlords will also charge a security deposit, which can be used for items like unpaid rent, defaults, and repairs.

You want to get the best deal for your company in this complex negotiation. Go into talks with information about what you can afford to pay over the course of your entire lease term. Be confident in your numbers, and let them know you are a good risk. Get ready to push back on the landlord's demands, based on well-thought-out reasoning.

You should work with a real estate broker or a lawyer to get the best deal. They will talk to the landlord about the deal points and create a letter of intent outlining what will be included in the deal. From there, either the owner or your attorney will create the lease document for you and the building owner to review, finalize, and sign.

Securing Your Terms

Following is a table that highlights the major lease negotiation points. Study this list and always be prepared going into your discussions with your landlord.

Lease Terms	What You Want	What the Landlord Wants
Description of Premises (address, area, and condition)	The building address, parking lot, any easement agreements between multiple tenants listed, and a clear understanding of any existing problems with the space	To give you as few parking spaces as possible and as little access to shared space in the building as manageable. They will try to give you the space as-is, so you have to pay for the tenant improvements.
Tenant name	The lease to be in the company's name, and not in your own	The lease to be in the personal names of the board members or owners
Allowable Uses	To list all possible current and future intended uses of the space.	To know everything you intend to do in the space and to be given the right to approve any changes you make to the space, both now and in the future
Commencement and Termination Dates	A minimum of a 5-year lease, with at least two options to renew, for a total of 15 years	A 2-year lease, with one or two options to renew

Lease Terms	What You Want	What the Landlord Wants
Rent Amount and Annual Increases	To pay a similar amount by square foot as other dispensaries in your area, generally ranging from $4 to $10 a square foot Free rent for the first three months and lowered monthly rent during the time it takes to secure your building and marijuana permits	To charge you the equivalent of a percentage rent and triple net lease combined, or more
Security Deposit	To pay the equivalent of 2 months' rent	As much of a security deposit as they can get you to pay
Tenant Reimbursed Expenses	The landlord to pay for utilities, including garbage, water, electric, and gas, repairs in any shared areas of the building or parking lot, and regular wear and tear	You to pay for all utilities, maybe even those in the shared parking lot, and for all future repairs, after any initially negotiated upon move in
Tenant Parking Spaces and Parking Lot Maintenance	As many off-street parking spaces as possible, even if you have to pay more rent for them	Enough parking spaces to ensure your members do not park in the neighbors' spaces or create a nuisance on the street
Improvements to Be Made By Landlord	All aspects of the facility, inside and out, to be in working order and up to the standards required for marijuana businesses. Includes HVAC, windows, doors, ADA-accessible bathrooms, ceilings, floors, heating, sprinklers, and any other physical aspect of the facility	You to make as many of the needed repairs yourself, both now and in the future
Right of First Refusal to Purchase the Building	The right of first refusal to purchase the building, if they want to sell it, with a method for appraising the building built into the contract	To market the building to the highest bidder, if they decide to sell in the future

Once you agree on these terms, create a memo of understanding with the landlord, outlining all of the key points. Use this to write the lease, making sure it explicitly grants you the right to use the space for your marijuana businesses. You will need this clause in there to get your cannabusiness license. This also obligates the company, or you personally, to pay rent for the entire length of the contract, regardless of the company's success, so be sure to consider this long-term liability carefully before signing.

The Least You Need to Know

- Marijuana businesses are limited to locating in their municipality green zones.
- Your facility must meet all regulations regarding exclusionary zones and must be located at least 600 to 1,000 feet from a K-12 school.
- Property owners are wary of marijuana businesses, so create a package of information to sell them on your plans.
- Negotiating your real estate deal is complicated. You will get the best deal by having a broker involved to help.

Setting Up
Your Cultivation Facility

Marijuana cultivation is now legal in 28 states, but getting a permit is not always easy, and neither is growing the plants once you have one. In this section, learn how to choose the best marijuana genetics based on your location and your proposed method of cultivation. Read about indoor, outdoor, and greenhouse cultivation, and review the differences between growing in soil or hydroponically.

Read about how to secure your cultivation facility, control airflow, and prevent human contamination from entering the space. Keeping marijuana plants pest- and mold-free is hard work, but the market demands it. The plants also need the right medium, lighting, and fertilizer to grow. Learn more here about what it takes to be a top marijuana cultivator.

Choosing Your Genetics and Growing Method

There are thousands of marijuana strains available to cultivators, and finding the right ones to fit your needs is tricky. Where you are located, the size of your facility, and the proximity of neighbors will narrow the choices. The method you use to grow will limit the options, too, as some systems are unable to handle large sativas and others have wasted space unless they are filled with the same. Fast-growing indicas thrive indoors, while sativas like the natural sun and a long grow season. Hybrids are flexible and can move between both options with ease.

Cultivators grow from seeds or clones, depending on their preference. They also choose to produce for direct consumption by patients or for use by manufacturers, and they budget their expenses accordingly. Some grow methods are expensive, like ebb and flow hydroponics, while others are less so, such as outdoor soil cultivation. Greenhouse growing is cost intensive to start, but the long-term profit potential makes it attractive to committed cultivators. New cultivators have a steep learning curve, and the competition in the industry is ferocious. But with proper planning and execution, anyone can cultivate award-winning marijuana.

In This Chapter

- Review the difference between soil and hydroponic cultivation
- Compare outdoor, indoor, and greenhouse systems
- Study the importance of pH-balanced water
- Learn the nutrients needed for marijuana growth

Choosing the Best Genetics for Your Grow

Every cultivator has different needs. Indoor growers want strains that ripen fast, without sacrificing potency for speed. Outdoors, people propagate sativas and hybrids to get larger plants and bigger buds. Indicas are great for outdoor cultivation, too, as they can be forced to flower in midsummer resulting in two crops a year.

Cultivating for specific terpene profiles is also popular. Strains like Tangie and Sour Diesel are known for their attractive and distinctive smells. Patients can expect dependable effects from these easily identifiable strains. This level of consumer confidence means those strains sell fast at dispensaries. Growers consider smell to be a balancing act. Consumers choose their medicine based on aroma, but if your crop smells too strong, it could generate neighbor complaints and become vulnerable to theft.

HASHING IT OUT

The terpene craze hit the cannabis market about five years ago, when cannabis labs first started testing for these smell molecules. Cannabis terpenes group into several major smell profiles: pine, orange, musk, spice, floral, berry, skunk, and diesel. These organic compounds are partly responsible for the effects of marijuana. For example, orange-smelling plants contain linalool, which is good for anxiety and stress, and piney-smelling marijuana has pinene, which has anti-inflammatory effects.

There are several other basics to consider when choosing your strains. Are you cultivating for quality or quantity? Certain plants like Hindu Kush thrive when mass-produced, but others need care and attention to thrive. What sector of the market will you serve? Marijuana is grown to sell on dispensary shelves or for use in manufacturing processes. Products cultivated for extraction purposes do not require the same level of care that whole plant medicines need to be ready for sale.

For many cultivators, the most important criteria are to grow for speed and bulk. Luckily, breeders have created award-winning cannabis strains that cater directly to this market. Fast-growing plants, with high THC content and unique terpene profiles, are some of the most sought after in the industry. For example, Blue Dream is a favorite strain for cultivators and patients alike, known for its ease of growing, dependable growth cycle, and standardized quality and potency. Consider your needs and find the right strains for your goals and circumstances.

Location

Outdoor cultivators can find strains bred to grow well in almost any environment. It's important to understand the characteristics of each plant and find those that are a natural fit. Doing research ahead of time will help avoid wasting money on seeds or clones that are difficult to grow in your intended area. For example, long-flowering sativas cannot reach full maturity in regions with shorter than average fall sunlight hours. Indicas should be cultivated under these circumstances.

Indoor growers have to create an outdoor environment inside. Locating your cultivation facility in a hot, humid region will require constant effort to mitigate these unfavorable conditions. Instead, locate your grow where temperatures are moderate and where molds and mildews are not a general problem. If your location is less than ideal, choose your plants accordingly and grow indicas to limit their exposure to negative elements.

Indica and sativa strains evolved differently based on their indigenous locations. Sativas are equatorial, late-maturing plants that grow best in long hours of natural sunlight. Indicas are their dwarfed cousins, short and strong, who grew up in the mountainous regions of Asia. As each plant was carried around the globe, they retained their ancestral qualities, and they thrived in environments similar to that of their origin. Hybrids blend characteristics of each, and innovative breeders have created hybrids to grow well in almost any environment. Most cultivators choose to grow indicas, sativas, or hybrids based on their location or the peculiarities of their indoor grow facility.

Sativas vs. Indicas

Sativa Characteristics	Indica Characteristics
Plants grow over twenty feet tall.	The plants grow short and bushy.
The flowers are arm length.	The flowers are spaced along the stem in dense buds.
The stalks and stems are big like trees.	The stems are thinner and weigh less.
Their flowering cycle is 10 to 12 weeks long.	Their flowering cycle is 7 to 9 weeks long.
It's heat resistant.	It's cold resistant.
The plant's effects are more cerebral and less physical.	The plant's effects are less heady with more of a body high.

Grow Method

Cultivators choose whether to use indoor or outdoor facilities and which grow method to apply. Marijuana plants need a stable structure to live in and a method of delivery for well-balanced water and proper nutrients. The choice to grow in soil or in a *hydroponic* system is crucial, as it affects every step that happens afterward. Equipment needs, power requirements, and waste-disposal methods vary widely for each.

 **DEFINITION**

Hydroponics is a method of growing marijuana where water, rather than soil, delivers nutrients to the plants.

Planting in dirt is the standard method of cultivating marijuana. Growers either put the plants directly in the ground or in pots primed with specially designed soil mixtures. Ground planting can be problematic as nutrient uptake depends on the soil's alkalinity. Marijuana requires water that is between 6 and 6.5 on the pH scale, which measures alkalinity. The contents of your soil can increase this to a dangerous level. Growers need to test the runoff and lower the pH of their starting water accordingly to account for its pH. Soil cultivators tend to grow plants in pots for this reason, in addition to the ease of moving the plants, if necessary.

Outdoor soil growers have a lot of strain choices. With the right location, they can grow sativas, indicas, or hybrids successfully. Sativas have a slightly higher wholesale value, as do award-winning indica and hybrid strains. Outdoor Durban Poison, Jack Herer, and Cookies strains are all desired by wholesale buyers and are patient favorites. Growing organically can raise your crop's value by a $100 per pound, so it's worth learning and using these techniques.

Commercial growers can also choose to produce marijuana for sale to manufacturers. The shelf look of these flowers is less important than its ratio of potency to weight. Plants like Mowie Wowie, Big Bud, and Blue Dream are high THC plants that grow well unsupervised as long as they get the proper water and nutrients to meet their needs. Marijuana businesses that make edibles, tinctures, balms, and extracts such as hash, wax, oils, and shatters all depend on this supply to create their products. This cultivation method costs less and has a lower wholesale value, but it's less stressful to grow and the results are still prized. Slightly failed crops and the less compact lower buds from high-value outdoor cannabis are both sold to this market, too.

 HASHING IT OUT

Mowie Wowie is a Hawaiian sativa strain, which was popular in the 1970s. It was taken to California, and it spread globally from there. It can grow more than 10 feet tall with yard-long flowers. It has a mild effect, making it desirable to patients looking for a light and uplifting sativa. Unfortunately, it's rarely seen these days, as it's a lanky, long-growing sativa and most cultivators don't like to propagate it.

There are a variety of hydroponic methods used in cannabis cultivation. Certain strains of marijuana are well suited to indoor hydroponics, including indicas in the Kush and OG families. These grow small, dense plants with tight flowers. Cultivators can use the *sea of green* method with these strains where the plants are grown from seed or cuttings until they are around two feet tall. Then, the light cycle is altered to induce flowering, which creates a bonsai-style shrub with only a few branches and dense high-value buds. Each stalk only weighs around one ounce when dry, so the goal is to grow a large number of plants in the smallest possible space.

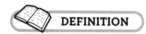 **DEFINITION**

The **sea of green** method is a type of cannabis cultivation that maximizes the use of indoor space and resources to grow high-quality cannabis in the smallest possible area. It's a Dutch concept that translated well to America during the 1980s, when it was a felony to grow even one marijuana plant. Knowledgeable growers moved indoors, using sea of green techniques to grow in small, hidden spaces.

Hydroponic gardeners cultivate in pots filled with Rockwool, rocks, coconut fiber, or other such grow mediums. Nutrients are delivered to the marijuana plants via carefully prepared water in controlled systems. Large sativas and big hybrid plants are not generally grown this way, as they require bigger pots, more space and infrastructure, and a higher quantity of nutrients and water. Sunset Sherbet and other indica-leaning hybrids are desirable indoor strains, as they grow small, with long, bud-covered stalks.

Indoor cultivators tend to pick strains that grow fast, flowering in seven to nine weeks. This trait is a genetic quality of indica plants and bred into indica-leaning hybrids. Sativa can be grown indoors, too, but they are often grown in soil pots, rather than hydroponically. These plants are top-watered with pH-tested and nutrient-enhanced fluids, rather than being flooded from below as in hydroponic systems. Conversely, outdoor cannabis can be grown hydroponically, either in greenhouses or in other simple water-fed systems.

Product Quality and Potency

Marijuana growers often choose strains for their expected cannabinoid and terpene content. Strains for smoking should taste and smell nice, such as Sour Diesel, with high terpene profiles and high THC. Because most of the THC is burned away when a plant is smoked, starting with a high content is important to the absorption rate. Cannabis grown for extractions should have a high trichome count with lots of visible oils. Hash Plant, OG Kush, and White Widow are covered in trichomes, and when handled carefully they're ideal for manufacturing uses.

Cultivation for cannabidiol (CBD) is a specialized field. Only a few plants like Cannatonic, AC/DC, and Harlequin have been identified as high producers. These plants grow best in outdoor environments, where they grow in bulk. The shelf-look of their buds is less important than creating the cannabinoid-infused plant matter for use in extractions. These strains do not grow dense buds, even in the best circumstances. Rather, CBD strains tend to have airy, leafy, stretched-out flowers.

Growing

Cannabis cultivation is quickly becoming a mainstream job just like being a farmer of food or any other product. Experienced people and companies are flocking to the industry, and access to knowledge and equipment is at an all-time high. Illicit cultivators are moving from grow houses and closets to large-scale warehouses and acre-sized plots. Farmers from other industries are learning to apply their skills to this field, where they're modifying their processes to work for marijuana cultivation. These innovations lower production costs, increase productivity, and maximize environmental safety. All of this combined increases the availability of high quality marijuana to manufacturers and dispensaries.

Mistakes are inevitable, and all cultivators run into problems along the way. Crop failure is a real risk. Bugs, molds, unseasonable weather, power failure, and theft can all affect the outcome. The best cultivators establish operating procedures to protect themselves, and they adapt quickly when problems do arise. Make sure to choose a grow method that suits your facility, indoors or out, and strains that are a proper fit. Mismatching these factors can doom your crop to failure.

Indoor cannabis plants are grown fast and kept small to limit the opportunity for contamination by bugs, molds, and mildews.

From Seeds

There is a long-standing argument among growers about whether it's better to grow from seeds or clones. Both have benefits and can produce great results. However, both grow methods come with problems. Seeds can be hard to sprout, requiring extra care to get them ready for vegetative growth. They might be male plants, so growers have to watch them closely during their flowering to ensure only the females survive. Males pollinate the females, turning a high quality crop into low-potency, seedy marijuana with hermaphroditic flowers that are turned away at dispensaries.

Marijuana grown from seeds is often heartier than when cloned, starting life with the vigor of a first-generation, disease-free plant. These plants are more bug-resistant when kept healthy and maintained with care. But, it's hard to find seeds. They are mostly limited to a few seed banks in America, such as DNA Genetics, Crocket Farms, and Cali Connection in California. Most other legal states don't allow home cultivation, so sales are limited to business-to-business transactions.

Where home cultivation is legal, seeds are available in packs of 10 at reputable dispensaries. Often these are feminized seeds, which are created when a normal female plant is bred with a hermaphroditic female plant that shows male flowers. These seeds sprout female plants, but they are more likely to turn hermaphroditic. Growers using feminized seeds have to watch closely for male flowers on their plants, as they can mature and pollinate the crop. This can ruin the entire crop, making the buds seedy and lowering the cannabinoid content.

From Clones

Cultivators often prefer to grow from clones. These small cuttings are clipped from strong mother plants. They create their own root systems before being planted in soil or grown hydroponically. Growing from clones is easier than growing from seeds, as the plants are hearty and less likely to die in their first month of life. They are also guaranteed to be females, except in cases where weakened mother plants lead to clones that drift into hermaphroditic expression.

 HASHING IT OUT

Marijuana plants are cloned by using sanitized scissors or razor blades to clip off the tips of its branches. These tips are then dipped in a root-stimulating chemical bath or are simply planted naturally into mediums like Rockwool or dirt. The cuttings are kept under fluorescent lights in watering trays, often in terrarium-style units to retain humidity. New root growth starts within 7 days, and the plants are ready to move into their vegetative growth cycle in 2 to 3 weeks.

Clone makers grow mother plants from seeds, flowering cuttings from the plant to understand its attributes. After assuring a plant creates marijuana with high cannabinoid contents and pleasing terpene counts, they designate it as a *mother*. Mother plants can live for 20 years if they are kept in stable environments free from bugs and contaminants. Mothers can also be grown from clones. However, clones cut from these plants are more likely to drift from their mother's genetic traits, sprouting male flowers and exhibiting characteristics like stunting or stretching.

Commercial cultivators carefully maintain mother plants to keep them bug and contaminant-free. They supply these clones to dispensaries, sell them to other cultivation businesses, and use them for their own flowering crops. Passing along a contaminated clone has negative consequences, as some of these problems are difficult to solve. Spider mites and root aphids can infest a crop quickly, killing the crop or making it unsalable to dispensaries. Problems like white powder mildew can destroy the entire grow space, requiring cultivators to gut the space and decontaminate it before replanting.

Dispensaries have a hard time finding a stable supply of clones for their patients. Only a few companies produce them for the resale market, mostly due to the consequences of growing so many plants in one space. Federal laws still mandate a 5-year prison sentence for possession of more than 100 marijuana plants and a 10-year sentence for more than 1,000. Clone producers must have thousands of plants growing at any given time, which is a risk most cultivators are unwilling to take. Even dispensaries are at risk, as a healthy clone department must be stocked with hundreds of clones to meet the needs of the patient clientele.

Tissue Culture

Tissue culture is the test-tube propagation of cannabis plants. Much like cutting up a potato and growing new plants from each eye, the idea of tissue culture is that cultivators can chop up marijuana and grow new plants from each chunk. It can only be accomplished using a specific mix of nutrients and hormones applied under the correct lighting and environmental circumstances.

Tissue culture is the legendary Holy Grail of cannabis cultivation. Growers talk about it and search for the ability. But, almost no one has successfully done it, and no clones are available that have been produced this way. The race to succeed is on, though, as clones produced by tissue-culture propagation are currently being grown in lab settings, free of the molds, mildews, and bugs plaguing the clone industry. When available, tissue culture is sure to become the method of choice for procuring clean genetics for home or industrial cultivation.

Tissue-culture plants are grown in vertical tray-storage systems, which contain multiple shelves in a single tower. Producers can grow a large number of starter cultures in a small amount of space. These plant pieces live in nutrient-specific formulas created to feed their cells and can live as sprouts for an indefinite time period as long as the environment is clean and stable. The plants start to grow and flower when placed in a grow medium under stronger lights. Marijuana-specific tissue-culture systems do exist in the marketplace, but they are only successful if used in sterile environments by trained staff.

Choosing Your Cultivation Type

Choosing the right type of cultivation for you will depend on several main factors. First, check your local laws to see if cultivation is even allowed. If so, find out if they allow outdoor and indoor growing or if one or the other is outlawed. Always choose the legal option, as violating cultivation regulations can lead to large fines and possible jail time.

After learning the laws, you'll need to find a properly located facility and obtain permission from the landlord. Growing unapproved marijuana can lead to your lease being cancelled and the police called to eradicate the crop. These risks are too costly and dangerous to chance. Finding a municipality with favorable laws and a landlord willing to approve such property use isn't easy, so you should expect to have narrow choices where cultivation methods are likely determined by your location's physical limits.

Outdoor growers need a space with access to water and sunlight and security features that discourage human invasions. Fields that are set back from main roads and fenced with a flat area for planting are most desirable. Indoor growers need space without close neighbors, who may be easily bothered by the noise and smell caused by cannabis cultivation.

Outdoor cultivation is limited in cold northern regions. The shorter sunlight of these regions have a negative effect on vegetative growth and flower formation. In these areas, indoor cultivation is preferred. Conversely, maintaining a cool indoor environment can be too costly in hot, arid places, so outdoor or greenhouse cultivation is best. Choosing your type of grow method is one of the first choices you'll have to make when starting a marijuana cultivation business, so you should take plenty of time to decide. Once you get started, it's costly and time consuming to switch between the three methods.

Indoor Cultivation

Indoor cultivation allows people the greatest control over all plant growth factors, because they build the entire system from scratch, creating every element found outside. Lean management is key, with just enough light, space, and airflow given to each plant. Nutrients are provided by the cultivator through the soil and by nourishing the plants using pH-balanced, nutrient-enhanced water. This cultivation method is a complex daily exercise, requiring the cultivator to change the lighting and nutrients at different times in the growth cycle.

Growing indoors enables producers to control plant size. Most choose to grow bonsai-style, sea of green crops, but it's possible to propagate large plants inside as well. Marijuana grows well in standardized systems. It can be cultivated on a set schedule with predictable results, and talented growers should be able to manage four crops annually.

Indoor marijuana crops produce plants with similarly sized, easy to trim flowers.

There are a smaller range of pests that can prey on your indoor plants. With that said, cultivators must keep a constant vigil for the worst of them—spider mites, white flies, and aphids. Yes, you won't have deer or rats eating your marijuana, but bugs can wiggle indoors and devastate your entire crop. Spider-mite infestations can last forever, even if your infected grow room is scrubbed from top to bottom. Growers often introduce *beneficial insects* to their grow rooms to help combat these plagues.

 **DEFINITION**

> **Beneficial insects** pollinate plants or help control invasive insects of other species. In the marijuana industry, ladybugs are used in grow rooms to fight spider-mite infestations.

Indoor cannabis is highly sought after by dispensaries and individual users. These plants are grown with fewer large leaves, so most of its power is put into flower production. The buds grow dense and covered in trichomes. Cultivators have to budget carefully when comparing the benefits of growing indoors, where the costs are higher but the marijuana sells for more, verses outdoors where production expenses are lower as are the sale prices.

Outdoor Cultivation

Many people believe that indoor cannabis is better than anything grown outdoors, but that opinion is quickly changing. At today's dispensaries, quality outdoor organic cannabis sells faster than any other product on the shelf. Buyers compete to find the best sun-grown marijuana, and they're willing to pay for it. The cost for these carefully maintained and manicured products is up to a $1,000 more per pound than for regular outdoor-grown flowers.

Users prefer sun-grown organic marijuana because of the purity of the processes and for the effects natural sunlight has on them. Cultivators spend extra time on these primo plants, maximizing its cannabinoid content through proper watering and trimming techniques. In the end, these plants grow big, dense, trichome-covered flowers, which trim down nicely into quarter-sized buds for the retail market.

Sun-grown organic cannabis is exceptional, though, and most outdoor growers produce commercial crops instead of connoisseur-grade flowers. Normal outdoor marijuana plants grow big and airy with less naturally occurring THC. These crops are produced with less intensive procedures than those used for sun-grown organic plants. The goal is to grow a commercially viable crop, that is cultivated for the lowest cost in the shortest amount of time. These plants are then sold at discounted prices to dispensaries or manufacturers, for use in baking or extracting rather than primarily for smoking.

Outdoor cannabis can be planted in the ground or in pots. Because marijuana requires a specific pH content to grow, planting directly into the ground outdoors only works if the soil is tested and then properly balanced with added nutrients. It's much easier to grow in pots, where the run-off water can be tested and adjusted based on the results. Outdoor marijuana can also be grown using several popular hydroponic methods. Aquaponics systems, where the plants' roots dangle into fish-tank ecosystems, thrive outside, as do plants grown using the Wick system. In the Wick system, plants are simply placed on a pallet in a kiddie pool, with a rope wick carrying water from the pool to the pot.

Growing marijuana outdoors is not without its problems. Wind can damage the trichomes growing on the outside of the flowers, lowering the potency of the plants. Rain can attract molds and mildews, which can attack the tight flowers and the nodes of the branches, ruining the crop. Pests also have unfettered access to outdoor marijuana, and cultivators must protect their plants from bugs and other predators. Theft is also a concern, with the distinctive smell sometimes drawing the wrong kind of attention. Random hikers, local teens, and criminal gangs have all been known to steal marijuana plants. Outdoor growers certainly face increasing risk levels as the plants mature and their value rises.

Greenhouses Cultivation

Greenhouse growing can be done high or low tech. Commercial crops are produced in giant facilities in glass buildings that come complete with *HVAC systems*, force-flowering covers, and spaces ready for installation of stand-alone or connected grow trays and watering systems. The largest known interconnected marijuana-growing greenhouse facility is around 350,000 square feet in size.

DEFINITION

Heating, ventilation, and air-conditioning systems, known as **HVAC systems,** are essential for all indoor and greenhouse marijuana growers. Greenhouse plants require a stable temperature—not too hot or too cold—and fresh, pure air to thrive.

A small, simple greenhouse costs around $1,000 off the shelf, can be easily built using the manufacturer's instructions, and is a less expensive alternative to growing marijuana indoors. Larger self-installed versions can cost up to $25,000 for spaces 30 feet deep. Greenhouses bigger than that require professional installation, to assure that the building, its HVAC, and other included systems are properly built. These spaces can be up to 70 feet long and 50 feet wide, and they can be joined together in modular units to fit any sized property.

Greenhouses allow for year-round marijuana cultivation. HVAC systems keep the spaces warm or cool so plants can thrive despite changing outside temperatures. Forced-flowering covers and supplemental lights trick plants into following artificial grow cycles. This creates the right circumstances for out-of-season vegetative growth and flowering, and experienced cultivators can get two to four crops a year in greenhouses. Greenhouse-grown cannabis is stronger than commercial outdoor marijuana, and the buds looks close enough to indoor-grown that even experienced buyers can have a hard time telling them apart.

Popular Growing Methods

Cannabis can be cultivated in many different ways, but each starts with the basic choice of growing hydroponically or in soil. Both methods deliver nutrients and water to the plants, and either can be done indoors or outdoors. Some systems are plug-in, so access to power is required. Others are passive, requiring little oversight other than occasional watering.

Hydroponic and dirt cultivation will each yield good results for a dedicated grower. The success of each crop depends on the time and effort put into it. It's easy to grow cannabis outdoors in a state of benign neglect, watering it, and doing nothing more, but these plants will have little resale value. Put a fence around that same plant and feed it specialized nutrients and pH-balanced water, and it will produce shelf-ready buds. Grow it indoors in a finely tuned hydroponics system, and the value of each pound could double. Take time to familiarize yourself with the costs and benefits of each method, and chose one that works for you.

Hydroponic Growing

Hydroponic cannabis growing is a popular method for people seeking high yields without the mess of growing in dirt. The plants grow in gravel, Rockwool, or another medium, and the pots are kept on raised tables. In most hydroponic systems, watering is set on a timer and the tables flood with pH-balanced water and nutrients throughout the day. Equipment failures can quickly ruin a crop. For this reason, hydroponic cultivators keep a constant watch over their systems, including the timers, lights, and fans, and repair any problems immediately.

You can use a variety of hydroponic systems for marijuana cultivation. They break into six main categories, and each cultivator adapts these basic systems to their space and the attributes of their strains.

Hydroponic Cultivation Systems

Name of Method	Brief Description
Ebb and Flow	Marijuana is planted in pots stored on trays that are flooded with nutrient-dense water several times a day. This water drains after each feeding and is reused throughout the cycle. This method is the most common form of hydroponics used by marijuana cultivators.
Aeroponics	The plant's roots are suspended in a dark, temperature-controlled environment and are misted with nutritional water on a continuous schedule. This method is efficient at delivering plant nutrients; however, salt buildup can sometime clog the sprayers.
Aquaponics	Plants are suspended above a large fish tank complete with actual fish. The plant's roots dangle in the water, which is a nutrient-rich environment for growth. These systems can be expensive to establish and difficult to maintain.
Wick System	Plants are placed with a rope wick dangling from the bottom of their tray or pot into nutrient-rich water below. Capillary action draws water to the plants' roots. This method is low-tech and easy, but may require use of an air pump to prevent the nutrients from stagnating.

continues

Hydroponic Cultivation Systems (continued)

Name of Method	Brief Description
Deep Water Culture	The marijuana is grown in baskets hovering above a water source with its roots constantly submerged. This method requires properly oxygenated water to prevent the plants from suffocating, along with carefully prepared water to provide nutrients.
Nutrient Film Growing	Plants are grown in baskets or net pots above troughs or channels, which have a continuous flow of nutritious, pH-stable water flowing over the roots. This method uses both gravity and pumps to prevent the pooling of stagnant water.

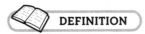

DEFINITION

Capillary action is the process that causes liquids such as water to move through another substance, even defying gravity to travel upwards.

Dirt Growing

Cannabis plants thrive in nutrient-dense, pH-balanced soil. They can be grown in pots using a planting mix bought from your local plant store and set outside to grow in natural light. Growing in dirt is the simplest method of cultivation, as the plants need nothing more than water and an occasional trim to keep them healthy. Growing in dirt is also the most forgiving cultivation method; you can make an occasional mistake, such as forgetting to water or using the wrong nutrients, and it will not immediately kill the plants. Hobby and home cultivators often grow this way, growing a few plants on their patio or in the backyard to get a small fall harvest.

Proper water drainage is important when growing in soil. Drainage prevents root rot, where the roots strangle in stagnant water and algae and molds can harm the plants. Growers sometimes use coconut fiber, along with perlite and vermiculite, to lighten and aerate the potting mix. Bugs can also hide in the soil. Some are so damaging that they can kill the plant before the grower even notices the infestation. Outdoor growers cannot get complacent, or their plants will suffer the consequences.

Soil generally produces a better flavor in the marijuana flowers. Even when the buds look less appealing, patients report that the flavor and high are superior. This is especially true with organically grown marijuana, where nutrient materials like earthworm castings were used to improve the overall plant health. Buyers at dispensaries are always on the lookout for top-quality dirt-grown cannabis. Patients are suspicious of the chemicals used in hydroponic cultivation and want naturally grown choices.

Necessary General Equipment

You can easily procure cannabis cultivation equipment once you choose your garden type. Indoor, outdoor, and greenhouse cultivation, and soil and hydroponic methodology, all have some of the same needs and other more specialized requirements.

Each method needs the basics: digital pH and ppm-testing meters, pH Up and pH Down fluids to balance your water's pH, plant nutrients, and measuring cups and spoons to assure accurate dosing. Each method requires vessels for the plants to grow in and water systems that gather run off for testing and reuse. You will also need shelves, tables, storage bins, and garbage cans to keep your space clean and free of places to harbor pests.

Indoor- and greenhouse-grown cannabis need HVAC systems and possibly the services of a HVAC engineer to get your temperature and odor levels under control. Fans, vents, carbon filters, and negative ion generators are also needed to limit odors and protect the plants.

Indoor cultivation of marijuana requires two types of grow lights. Plants start their cycle under Metal Halide (MH) bulbs, which mimic summer light, and then switch to fall-like High Pressure Sodium (HPS) lights for flowering. These bulbs need to be replaced at least annually, as the light's potency diminishes over time. Greenhouse growers also use supplemental lighting to extend their grow season, so when fall days get shorter, they can still vegetate and flower at will.

Each method also requires a watering system, but these vary for each practice. You'll need hoses and water reservoirs when dealing with outdoor cannabis, and you'll need the same plus growing tables, timers, and pumps for indoor ebb-and-flow and nutrient film growing systems. Every method also requires water storage and preparation systems.

Fish, tanks, water plants, and filtration equipment are all on the list for aquaponic cultivators. Aeroponics requires electronic plant misters and grow tubes, so water can be regularly sprayed across the roots.

Regardless of your cultivation type and grow method, take time to research your necessary equipment list and find a system that's most productive and affordable for you.

The Least You Need to Know

- Cultivators choose strains based on the type of cultivation and growing method they plan to use.
- Indica and sativa strains thrive under different environmental circumstances. Hybrids plants are more adaptable and combine the best characteristics of each.
- Plants grown in dirt get their nutrients from the contents of the soil, while hydroponic plants get them from the water.
- Hydroponic plants are generally grown indoors, but can grow outdoors, too. Soil-grown plants are adaptable to either indoor or outdoor cultivation.

Designing Your Grow Space

Growing cannabis commercially requires much more than just sticking a few plants in the ground. In order to prevent contamination and ensure a healthy harvest, indoor growers must follow stringent clean-room procedures. In order to protect that harvest, they must follow stringent security procedures as well. Manufacturing facilities are no different. The security of the facility and safety of the procedures are of maximum importance. Marijuana businesses have an obligation to their employees to provide safe workplaces and to the end consumers to product pure products.

Compliance with law enforcement and regulatory agencies is crucial to the well-being of both your business and your employees. Take time to think through each of your facilities' weaknesses and design a system to prevent these problems. Going above and beyond basic safety and security requirements never hurts. In fact, it can prevent threats from becoming disasters.

In This Chapter

- Learn the components of marijuana facility design
- Discover how to build your space for later expansion
- Find out how safe entryways prevent contamination
- Study security and safety procedures

Creating the Floor Design

When cultivating cannabis, everything you do has consequences that affect your final product. Your grow-room floor design is one of the determining factors in the success of your harvest. Plan the entryways, passageways, and administrative offices to create a design that promotes smooth workflow and causes no harm. Leave room to move around and care for the plants as they grow. Don't place them so close together that you can't move around without damaging them—you shouldn't have to crawl around on the floor when your plants get bigger.

The grow room itself is the top priority. Design your facility to maximize light so that none is wasted, and pay special attention to how the light hits the plant canopy. Your goal is to maximize how much reaches every part of each individual plant. Use a light meter to measure brightness throughout the room, and make sure light is evenly distributed across the grow space. Consider installing light movers to evenly convey the lamps across your grow tables throughout the day.

Think long-term when planning your space. Create a design that enables you to expand your operations in the future. For example, if you eventually want to make other products from your cannabis flowers, you might need to grow more plants. Make sure to find a space that has room for expansion. Plan at least two years into the future, and if you want to go into cloning, extracting, or making ingestible marijuana products, keep this in mind as you map out your space.

Entryway, Staff Locker Room, and Offices

The entryway to your facility is one of its most important features. Plan the space carefully to prevent pest and contaminant intrusion. Impurities are all around us; in fact, we ourselves are one of the biggest sources of contamination—stray hair, clothing particulates and debris, and flaking skin can all pollute your facility. Construction materials, spills, leaks, dust, and brooms and mops can also introduce problems. Ideally, your entryway leads directly to a staff locker room, where all outside belongings are stored, and a staff uniform is put on. Contaminants like spider mites and E. coli can be easily transmitted from your staff to the plants.

Safety is a huge concern. Licensed cultivation centers are generally required to have cameras, lights, alarms, and sometimes guards, to protect the employees from harm and the marijuana from theft. The entryway should be impenetrable to anyone other than staff and pre-approved guests. Consider installing biometric locks where entry is permitted by fingerprint scans only. The entryway should be set up as a safety lock, with a second secured entrance to pass through before gaining access to the facility. This door should also have video surveillance and an alarm system to assist in preventing unauthorized entrance. The door to your grow room should never open right off the street.

Your facility needs a management office, where basic tasks like marketing and bookkeeping happen. This space should be kept separate from the cultivation space, so that the staff does not need to dress in full safety gear. It's best located off the entry hall or directly inside the second entry door. If the administrative staff has to pass through the cultivation areas to get to work, they will need full body coverings, head to foot, like everyone else. The office should be kept clean, and all documents should be stored in locked file cabinets. If the facility has a cash safe, it should be located here, meaning the office will need to be alarmed and under video surveillance.

Grow Space

Treat your grow space as a *clean-room* environment, just as you would in a lab. Have *HEPA filters* installed in your HVAC system to filter intake air against particulate contamination. Follow all clean room and *clean-zone* procedures and protocols and implement required compliance training for all necessary staff and employees.

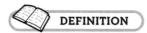 **DEFINITION**

A **clean-room** or **clean-zone environment** is a contamination-free space, where outside particulates are eliminated through use of protocols for entry and exit, airflow, clothing, and product handling.

A **HEPA filter** is a High Efficiency Air Particulate filter. These are used in grow rooms to purify the smell of marijuana from the air and to eliminate incoming airborne matter that could contaminate the plants.

Sterile zones between the internal passageways and grow room are essential. These zones require an area in which to change from street clothes to clean-room garments. Gloves, face-masks, hairnets, and beard nets are standard. Wear a smock, or a full body suit, and place clean booties over your street shoes. Aim to achieve the same clean-room standards as required by hospitals.

Clean-room maintenance and cleaning must be carefully planned to ensure contamination containment. Employees must adhere to well-written standard operating procedures (SOPs). Take special precautions when using outside contractors; they might not be used to such strict standards. Employee behavior can also lead to contamination of the clean room. Even moving quickly can lead to contamination—the speed at which you walk determines how many particulates per minute your body casts off. All personal items such as keys, jewelry, and cellphones should be stored in a locker outside the clean room. No eating or drinking should ever be allowed, and employees should never wear cosmetics, lotions and creams, or perfumes in the clean room. This includes fake tans, nail polish, gel nails, and powders.

Chemical and Tool Storage

It's essential to use only pre-approved chemicals and tools in the clean room and clean zones. Your local fire department will probably require you to provide a list of all the chemicals and materials used in your facility. They need to approve the materials so they know what to expect when responding to an emergency. Tools are a major source of contamination. Clean your tools with the same products and procedures as other clean-room surfaces. Never leave tools on the floors or surface areas of equipment. Instead, place them on a sterile tray to keep them clean during use and for ease of cleaning after. Store chemicals and tools in clean-room-approved storage cabinets, preferably made of stainless steel.

You must have SOPS for tools and equipment used in production, cleaning, or maintenance that address best-practice contamination protocols. Any chemical waste generated in the clean room must be properly handled and stored or disposed of in accordance with state, federal, and best-practice standards. Properly training your staff helps ensure compliance and minimizes the risk of contamination.

 HASHING IT OUT

Always use and store hazardous materials in accordance with federal, state, and local guidelines. Train personnel using these materials in the correct response protocols in case of spillage or other accidents. Some states require personnel applying fertilizers and chemicals in cultivation operations be licensed by the state to do so.

Bathrooms, Aisles, and Other Features

When building your facility, think about the layout of break rooms, restrooms, and offices. A sensible, efficient floor plan contributes to your clean-room standards rather than hindering them. Consider the path by which you will distribute materials and supplies. Group office space, storage space, mailrooms, workrooms, copier areas, and the break room together when planning your building layout. It's essential that staff does not enter the cultivation rooms in street clothes, so keep this in mind if these functions are spread throughout the building. Staff will need to put on clean gear each time they re-enter the grow space.

Place bathrooms as far away from your clean areas as possible, as they can easily produce contaminants. Make sure the bathrooms have hot water, soap, and towels, as employees must use restaurant-safe standards for handwashing. This means they need to run their hands under warm water for at least 20 seconds and dry them thoroughly after. Damp hands spread contaminants. Install separate, localized exhaust systems for bathrooms, offices, and non-growing spaces; do not use the same ventilation system you use for your clean rooms.

Don't neglect the hallways of your facility. They need to be kept clean from floor to ceiling, should be well lit, and under video surveillance at all times. Every door should have a purpose, either to function as a safety lock or to be the entrance into a room with a specific function. Each room must have a dress code, which could be street clothes in the administrative offices and lab gear for the cultivation facilities, and every person needs to understand what is required beyond each door.

Aisles can often be neglected in a grow-room design. You need plenty of space to maneuver around throughout the grow cycle. To start, you need to be able to reach each plant for grooming branches, plucking yellowing leaves, and rearranging them under lights to achieve optimal light spread. Later in the plants' grow cycle, you'll need space to reach each for watering and to monitor for contamination. If you can't fit down the aisles, you won't be able to care for the plants. Picture them grown when you determine where to place your walkways and how wide to make them.

Drying Room

The drying room is one of the most important rooms in the facility, and you must take special care when designing it. The room should be designed and sized for wet product. Design the room to accommodate as much freshly cut marijuana as you believe you will ever grow. It must be equipped with the correctly sized dehumidifier and ventilation system to prevent the growth of mold. To avoid crop loss, build redundancy into your design. Install a backup dehumidifier and a generator to run equipment in the event of electrical failure.

Adequate airflow and circulation help prevent mold and fungi outbreaks. Drying rooms should be temperature-controlled, *positive-pressure* spaces, and you must keep them dry and dark to prevent the growth of unwanted fungi. Your goal is to keep outside air out by creating an isolated clean room and using HEPA filters to clean the airflow system. To maximize the use of space, build stacked drying racks rather than spreading harvested plants around the room on screens. Plants need to cure here for a minimum of two weeks to dry—likely longer—so it's important that the environment stays pure or your crop could be ruined.

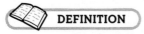 **DEFINITION**

Positive-pressure rooms are sealed areas with airflow systems that exchange the air at least 12 times per hour, using HEPA filters for purification. These rooms generally have an antechamber, beyond which street clothing is not allowed.

Trimming and Packaging Room

Trimming rooms should also be positive-pressure rooms. They must not allow unwanted air to enter, even when the door is opened. You can monitor positive pressure by installing an airflow-control system with a differential pressure transmitter. Trimming rooms should be windowless to keep potentially harmful sunlight off of dry flowers.

Always clean and sterilize your trimming room before bringing product in for final processing and packaging. In addition, you must clean and sterilize the room at the end of every work shift. Do all of your trimming and processing on stainless-steel surfaces. Don't allow wood into the drying or trimming rooms, because it can harbor bacteria and can't be disinfected. Keep all equipment and supplies coming into your trimming room clean and sterilized.

 HASHING IT OUT

You can either trim cannabis by hand or use trimming machines. Some growers do both. Trimming by hand means more chance of human contaminants, while machine trimming requires you to spend more time maintaining and sanitizing equipment.

Trimmers must wear protective gloves, hairnets, and smocks that meet all clean-room requirements. You can even require badges that set off an alarm if employees do not wash their hands after using the restroom. No restroom door should never open directly into the trimming room.

Your trimming room should be cleaned before and after each use, as should all equipment. No dust should be allowed to gather in this space, and staff should never bring outside materials in, not even food or water. You may want to install an internal facing window in the trimming rooms, along with cameras, so that all activities inside can be monitored at any time to encourage workers to comply with best practices.

Early packaging is necessary to prevent contamination of the final product. Staff should package all product in accordance with your process-control SOPs, which includes labeling and assigning batch numbers and clearly stating potency and lab-test results. As soon as the marijuana is trimmed and fully dried, it should be vacuum sealed into storage containers like lightproof plastic bags or jars. Each packaged unit should have a security seal. Some cultivation centers have storage bags nitrogen-purged to extend freshness.

Production Kitchen

In Washington state, kitchens producing marijuana-infused edibles must be entirely enclosed with no openings. All walls, ceilings, and doors must have smooth surfaces that are durable and easy to clean. Washington also has special material and height requirements for splash walls. No restroom doors are allowed to open directly into the kitchen. All edible and topical manufacturing, processing, and packaging must be done in the same room.

Proper ventilation is always required to exhaust smoke, vapors, and other airborne contaminants. Generally, local fire officials determine what safety equipment is needed and the protocols required for their safe implementation and operation. They also mandate the frequency of equipment inspections. Fire-safe hoods are required over all major equipment used for cooking, including ovens, stovetops, and fryers.

You must install a separate handwashing sink a specific distance away from utensil- and food-storage areas to prevent accidental contamination. The staff must have a locker room for their street gear, and where they can dress in kitchen wear. Some production kitchens require aprons, while others require full chef coats and pants. Either way, the goal is to prevent any contaminants from reaching the food-based marijuana products, be that pet hair or human waste.

Your production kitchen will have to meet all of the local health codes, even if you do not fall under the supervision of a health department. California treats edibles manufacturing as light manufacturing, and not as food production, but each kitchen still needs to establish internal governance that brings the kitchen to code. This means using safe equipment, storing and cooking food at the proper temperatures, and teaching staff how to safely handle food. At least one supervisor in each kitchen should be health-department trained in safe food handling and able to implement and teach the rest of the staff on these processes.

Manufacturing Space

Marijuana manufacturing spaces can be tailored for cold-water extraction, extraction of cannabis oils and waxes, or production of other items like balms. Different products require different environments, though all production requires adequate ventilation. Facilities that produce oils and waxes use specialized equipment with specific electrical, fire hazard, vapor, and noise-abatement requirements.

Butane extraction is the most cost-effective method of producing cannabis oils, but it's also the most hazardous and therefore has the most stringent safety and processing requirements. In Colorado, the open extraction of oils and waxes using butane is prohibited. Other states like New Mexico allow it under strict regulations, and California will soon license this use. All butane extraction must be done using closed-loop systems, preventing any gas from escaping into the atmosphere.

Any facility using butane extraction processes must install a hazardous exhaust system and a local hydrocarbon detector to ensure compliance and to alert the operator of any leaks during operation. All equipment for extraction must be inspected to ensure it's properly built with adequate protection against explosions. CO_2 extraction, another popular method of making oils and waxes, must be done in a dedicated room that's equipped with a CO_2 monitor and alarm in case of leaks. These machines run at high pressure and must be well built and inspected regularly to assure proper function.

HIGH POINTS

Marijuana extracts are produced in five different manners:

- Keif and hash are made by dry-sifting marijuana to break off the trichome crystals.
- Water hash is made when agitated ice water is used to float the plant matter and sink the trichomes, which are then collected to make hash.
- Pure extract cannabis oils are made using alcohol to extract the active plant ingredients. After evaporation, a cannabinoid-rich paste is left for consumption.
- Butane extractions are created when butane is blasted through marijuana, catching the trichomes. The butane evaporates, leaving a pure, strong extract behind.
- CO_2 extracts are created the same way as butane, but unlike butane, they are non-volatile and will not explode. Vape pens use CO2 extracts combined with a liquid solvent like polypropylene glycol.

No matter what kind of manufacturing you have planned, the basics are the same. Create a safe entryway, have a staff breakroom for donning protective clothing, create clean hallways and aisles, make sure airflow is filtered and flows well, and have space for sanitizing and storing equipment. Beyond that, each type of manufacturing has specific equipment and different production processes. Some use organic materials and low-tech processes like making rolled joints, and others use hazardous materials under strict safety protocols like production of butane wax. Your facility's design must fit the needs of your processes and follow the laws and regulations that govern them. Creating a safe workplace and pure products is the goal.

Maximizing Security and Safety

Municipals create building, fire, and environmental health codes, along with other safety protocols, that marijuana businesses have to meet. Local and state marijuana laws add to these, and the conditions of your marijuana license spell out these requirements. At the very least, your facility will be required to have an alarm, a monitoring system, and video cameras in adequate numbers and locations. This video security system also serves as a compliance-verification tool. In Oregon, if your cameras are down for more than 30 minutes, the state must be notified of the outage. Many states require marijuana businesses to keep stored video for 30 days, while others may require you keep it for longer periods.

You will also need to build in a fire-protection system with alarms and sprinklers that respond to and report fire hazards. Your building must have adequate, well-lit, fire exit signage, as well as clear passageways for fire and safety egress. Egress doors should be well marked and kept free of obstructions. If you are in an area prone to earthquakes, any items in those fire pathways must be tethered to the wall to prevent them from tipping during emergencies.

It's a good idea to hire a security consulting firm to help you develop an adequate security plan for your particular situation. Don't be afraid to call in the experts. Try to poke holes in your own security plan. Any potential intrusion points must be mitigated. Leave room to expand your security protocols and system in the future to meet unexpected needs or new requirements.

Elements of a Comprehensive Security Plan

Marijuana facilities should have top-of-the-line security systems. Don't scrimp on security; invest in your safety. Put in a comprehensive alarm system. This includes alarms on every external door, shatter guards on the windows, and motion sensors in the facility. Use video cameras throughout the facility and all around the perimeter, especially above all external entry points. Make sure they record at night, so either use night-vision cameras or keep internal lights on at all times. Put bars on your skylights and build your vault with steel walls. Install fences around your perimeter, and make sure the parking lot and other external areas are well lit.

Dispensaries and other marijuana businesses often employ an outside security firm to provide 24-hour guards to keep their facilities safe. If you plan to have security guards, make sure they are licensed by the state, especially for any weapons they carry. Their main job is to observe and report, seeing crime before it happens and notifying the police. Marijuana facilities need to keep good police relations, as the police are responsible for stopping a crime in progress and should be called in emergencies.

Make sure your security plan is visible. Post *No Trespassing* signs around the facility, put the security company's stickers on the windows, have uniformed guards at the doors, and obvious cameras recording around grounds. Use walkie-talkies and computer chat windows to easily communicate with staff in limited-access controlled areas. Use manned and electronically controlled gates and doors for entry, buzzing people into the facility after ensuring it's safe to do so.

Make sure you have adequate and secure storage for your marijuana products. Using fire- and theft-proof safes and vaults is common practice. You must control access to all marijuana products and cash, and only pre-screened personnel should have access. State and local authorities often require employee background checks, screening out people with criminal records for theft, fraud, or violent crimes. Some marijuana companies implement whistleblower programs, which encourage employees to report incidents of theft or suspected wrongdoing.

What to Do in a Worst-Case Scenario

Even the best security precautions don't guarantee that you will never face a worst-case scenario such as burglary, robbery, or theft. Preparation for these types of situations before they happen must be a primary focus of your security and training plans.

A good, ongoing relationship between your business, your security company, and the local police department is essential in the event of criminal interaction. Your ability to quickly and effectively relay information to law enforcement authorities is paramount to quick resolution. There are many different threats that you must be prepared for. Armed robbery is obviously very dangerous, yet while something like employee theft can be less hazardous, it's also a significant concern.

Having a plan and knowing how to react before an emergency situation occurs enables you to respond and react effectively. Role-playing exercises must be an integral part of your company's training and security culture. Consider implementing training programs for situations such as armed robbery; active shooter encounters; fire, medical, and natural emergencies; employee theft; and gross negligence.

The Least You Need to Know

- Design your grow facility with future expansion in mind.
- Grow rooms and manufacturing facilities require meticulous clean-room procedures to prevent contamination.
- Different facilities have different safety requirements depending on the products they produce.
- Go beyond state and local security requirements to better protect your facility from intrusion and theft.

Elements for Growth

Growing marijuana indoors has many benefits, such as controlling every aspect of the environment and maximizing yield. However, it can be significantly more expensive than growing outside. Indoor growers must replicate the sun using marijuana grow lights, meaning they must carefully measure light, temperature, water, soil, and air circulation.

The conservation of light, water, and soil helps keep indoor-growing costs under control. Incorporating reflective surfaces helps to efficiently use your light sources, while recycling water and soil help conserve both environmental and financial resources. Striking the right balance can be challenging at first, but it definitely pays off at harvest time.

In This Chapter

- Discover the essential components of a grow room
- Learn the units of measure for light, nutrients, and water
- Study different growing techniques to maximize yield
- Consider money-saving ways to conserve water and maximize light

Lighting

You'll frequently hear the words *lumens* and *kelvin* when growers talk about lights. *Lumens* is the measure of visible light and refers to brightness, while *kelvin*, which is a measure of color temperature, refers to warmth. Light can be measured as a frequency composed of color bands with each color promoting different types of growth throughout the season. Different stages of growth require different kinds of light.

 **DEFINITION**

Lumen is a unit of measure for the brightness of a light source. **Kelvin** is the measure of a color's temperature in a light band.

During vegetative growth, your plants need the light of the midday sun. If you're growing indoors, this requires Metal Halide (MH) bulbs that emit light from the blue end of the spectrum. The flowering stage requires High Pressure Sodium (HPS) bulbs, which are on the red end of the spectrum and replicate autumn light. LED lights are another option for indoor growing, as long as cultivators choose the correct color spectrum for both vegetative and flowering stages.

The higher the wattage, the more surface area your lights will cover. A 1,000-watt bulb lights a larger area than a 400-watt bulb. The type of light you use and the dimensions of your grow space will also affect the amount of wattage you need.

A good horizontal reflector hood can increase a plant's yield. Reflector hoods will help your bulb be more efficient, as the hoods reflect light toward the plant. The closer the hood is to the bulb, the more light it reflects. It also generates more heat, so cultivators need to be careful not to burn their plants. Aiming a fan into the hood helps circulate the air around the bulb and keeps the temperature down. Some lamp systems actually hook the ventilation system to the bulb itself to draw off excess heat.

You can also incorporate reflective walls into your grow rooms to maximize the brightness of the room. Some people use Mylar sheets for this, though most growers prefer a reflective white paint.

Your Lighting Needs

Metal Halide (MH) bulbs are currently the most efficient source of artificial light for vegetative growth. These bulbs come in a wide range of wattages with 400 to 1,000 watts being the most popular. During vegetative growth, MH bulbs are used to grow the plants tall and wide, without the occurrence of flower development.

High Pressure Sodium (HPS) bulbs are a high-efficiency bulb that mimics the autumn sun. Like MH bulbs, HPS bulbs come in a variety of different wattages with 600 to 1,000 watts being the most popular among indoor growers for flowering. In nature, marijuana plants grow in the summer with natural light that is similar to the light of MH bulbs. In the fall, the natural light cycle shortens and shifts to the red end of the spectrum, causing plants to flower and grow buds. Marijuana growers recreate this scenario inside, forcing plants to flower by changing the ratio of light to dark and through use of HPS lights.

HIGH POINTS

High Intensity Discharge (HID) lamps are the most common type used for indoor growing, and are arguably one of the most efficient ways of producing high yields. HID lamps include MH and HPS bulbs. HID lamps produce the best light spectrum for the vegetative and flowering cycles of marijuana growth.

Cultivators must ensure an equal amount of light across their entire garden canopy to get the most out of these lamps. Light meters can detect hidden spots with low light, and plants can then be reorganized to minimize this problem.

Keep the light pattern in mind when planning any lighting layout. Cultivators must understand how it travels, reflects, and bounces around the grow room. Sophisticated growers use light movers to ensure more even distribution. Light movers are set on tracks and move constantly across paths during peak hours. It's important to remember the importance of equal light distribution when using more than one lamp. Plants that receive the same amount of light will grow very similarly.

The amount of necessary light is the subject of much debate in the cannabis industry. Many growers believe that the correct answer is, "as much as you can get without burning your plants." A basic guideline is to get between 2,500 and 7,500 lumens per square foot to the plants. This requires bulbs with wattages that divide into 30 to 80 watts per square foot.

Proper Lighting Design

Design your grow room to maximize all your available resources. Ensure that as much light as possible is actually hitting the plant canopy rather than the walls or walkways of your grow room. Wasted light is wasted money. Also, keep in mind that seedlings and plants in the vegetative stage require longer periods of light. Additional grow lights make it possible to grow in the winter, when days are short. Turning the lights on just before dark allows you to extend the growing season.

Commercial cultivators use a variety of lighting strategies. The most popular are Screen of Green (SCROG) and Sea of Green (SOG) methods. The Sea of Green method, as mentioned previously, allows for a larger number of plants under each light. The Screen of Green method, on the other hand, trains the plant to optimize flower production. In this method, growers tie plants to a screen as they grow, creating more flowering sites and therefore multiple stems and buds per plant. While SCROG requires a bit of extra work during the flowering cycle, it yields more product per plant.

Many growers incorporate vertical lighting into their grow room because it can greatly increase the amount of direct light to each plant. During flowering, cannabis plants can be trellised, which encourages them to grow laterally as well as horizontally. This drastically increases the plant canopy by expanding it to three sides rather than one, ultimately leading to more buds per plant.

Summertime Light Savings

Greenhouses are structures with a clear covering, such as glass or a special plastic that enables sunlight to pass through. Greenhouse use has skyrocketed in the growing industry where cultivating is legal because they save cultivators money and benefit the environment by reducing the carbon footprint of a large growing operation. Greenhouses combine the best part of growing outdoors—natural sunlight—to the added environmental control of growing indoors.

Depending on a greenhouse's design, cultivators can control temperature, humidity, soil, air circulation, and light. Many large-scale greenhouses are equipped with supplemental lighting, enabling them to be used throughout the year.

Water

In Lake County, California, the average yield of an outdoor cannabis plant is two to four pounds. It's estimated that growing 50 two-pound plants on one-eighth an acre of land requires about 24,000 gallons of water. Each plant needs 480 gallons. Water quality is as big of a concern as usage. The kind of water growers use can either help their plants thrive or spell disaster.

Finding a Water Source

Sourcing water and maintaining water quality is top priority for cannabis-cultivation facilities. Cannabis is a very resilient plant, and most strains can tolerate feeding and watering mistakes to some degree. Consistently delivering water and nutrients in the wrong concentrations or quantities, however, can harm or even kill your crop. Lucky cultivators find indoor grow spaces with perfect water right out of the tap. However, most need to treat the tap water to lower contaminants or adjust its pH before use.

Some cultivation sites have a well onsite, while other locations will need to have water trucked in and stored in a tank. Buying water in bulk can get expensive, but it's sometimes the only way to ensure a quality water source. Cultivators must never steal or divert water from a natural source. It's a surefire way to find yourself outside of regulatory compliance, and you can end up paying large fines or losing your permits this way.

Cleaning and Repurposing Waste Water

Water recycling, also known as *water reclamation*, is not a new idea. Non-potable water-recycling systems have been in place for many years. In arid states like California, Texas, and Nevada, municipal wastewater is often collected and treated to the extent that it doesn't meet drinking-water standards but can be used for agriculture, landscaping, and lawn irrigation.

 HASHING IT OUT

The Environmental Protection Agency (EPA) is partially responsible for regulating wastewater treatment and drinking water quality. A majority of states have also established guidelines for the use of recycled water. Refer to your local water quality control board and/or department of agriculture for more information on these regulations.

Due mainly to increasing drought conditions in some states and groundwater depletion, the use of non-potable water is currently expanding. Recycled water can satisfy most water demands, as long as it's correctly treated to ensure water quality appropriate for its intended use. In an effort to reduce costs and make better use of natural resources, you may need to purchase reclaimed water or have a water-reclamation system installed in your facility. It's a very common practice and well worth the investment.

Saving Water Year-Round

Water conservation should be part of any cannabis cultivator's everyday operations and therefore their business model. Among the methods of conserving water are covering tanks and using drip irrigation systems, which deliver water directly to a plant's roots. Drip irrigation eliminates the evaporation inherent in spray watering. Using timers to schedule watering for the cooler parts of the day can also help conserve water.

Some growers have even built their own holding ponds to capture and store rainfall for use throughout the year. Properly managed ponds not only reduce water costs, but create a habitat for local wildlife—and give you a place to go fishing!

Compost increases the water-holding capacity of your soil and can be used to fertilize your crops. Spreading *mulch* made of straw or wood chips around plants also helps retain water.

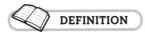

DEFINITION

> **Mulch** is material placed on top of the soil or added around the stem of a plant to protect and improve the plant's health. It helps the soil retain water and prevents the growth of weeds.

Soil Nutrients

Groundwater is never pure; it picks up naturally occurring minerals and human contaminants as it travels through the earth.

Pure water doesn't conduct electricity. However, when you have conductive water, it indicates a high mineral content present in the water. *Total Dissolved Solids/Electrical Conductivity* (TDS/EC) meters have two electrical conductors; when you place them in water, voltage passes between them. The amount of current that passes through the liquid indicates the conductivity of the water. The meter converts the current into a readable display of TDS and EC in parts per million (ppm).

DEFINITION

> **Total Dissolved Solids (TDS)** is the measurement of minerals and contaminant solids in water that cannot be removed with standard filtering.
>
> **Electrical Conductivity (EC)** is the measure of a liquid's ability to conduct electrical current.

By determining the baseline ppm of your water, you can calibrate the strength of the nutrient solution to add. If, for example, your tap water starts with a TDS of 600 ppm, and the fertilizer suggests dosage strength of 1,000 ppm, the total ppm of the runoff water will be 1,600 ppm. This is the maximum recommended ppm for a full flowering plant, so your water will need to be purified or your nutrients will need to be lowered if the plant is in vegetative growth. The only real way to lessen ppm is to filter the water using a system strong enough to clean out the minerals.

Choosing Your Soil Mix

Choosing the right soil mix also helps ensure you grow a high-quality final product. Many growers use commercially produced soil mixtures, while others make their own hoping to achieve better results. Both methods have their pros and cons.

Commercial soils generally have built-in nutrients that will last for a short time before cultivators have to add in more. Nutrient-rich potting soil is available at local garden supply centers. It's important to grow in soil that retains water well so the marijuana plants can soak in as much as they need. Too much water retention promotes fungal growth. Potting soils with *vermiculite* or *perlite* increase water retention.

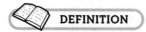 **DEFINITION**

> **Vermiculite** is lightweight, highly absorbent, magnesium- and aluminum-based material used in soil mixtures.
>
> **Perlite** is a form of obsidian (volcanic glass) that allows proper drainage when used as a plant-growth medium.

The problem with these pre-mixed soils is that they could come with bugs, molds, or mildews that could be catastrophic to your crop. Use only reputable brands when using store-bought potting soil. Keep close watch on the plants for early warning signs of any problems. You may be able to control a pest infestation in its early stages, whereas waiting could doom your entire grow room.

You can also easily make your own potting soil. Successful cultivators create proprietary mixes, blending dirt, additives like perlite and vermiculite, and nutrients like those found in compost or worm castings. Any grower can do the same; just pay attention to these ingredients and the ratios that will suit the plants best in your environment. Regardless, a balanced pH level—not too alkaline, not too acidic—is essential to the plant's ability to take up nutrients. If your soil is too acidic or alkaline, use pH-up or pH-down solutions which are readily available at gardening stores to fix it.

A happy marijuana plant growing strong in natural light

Soil Nutrients for Happy Plants

Marijuana plants need access to proper light, a lukewarm environment, plenty of pH- and ppm-balanced water, and the correct nutrients to grow healthy. Cultivators must work hard to make sure that all of these factors work together. But it's not easy, which is why the majority of marijuana users get their supply from a dealer or dispensary, leaving cultivation to experienced growers.

You'll need pH up and down fluids, proper nutrients, and the tools to measure each. Cannabis plants have many different requirements during their growth cycle, requiring mineral and non-mineral elements to thrive. It's easy to spend more money than necessary on soil and nutrients, so do your homework before going shopping.

Every fertilizer package has three numbers on the label, which refer to the main elements used for plant growth: nitrogen, phosphorus, and potassium (NPK). If the label says *10-4-4*, it means that the fertilizer is 10 percent nitrogen, 4 percent phosphorus, and 4 percent potassium. Marijuana's need for NPK changes throughout its grow cycle. During vegetative growth, the plant needs high nitrogen, so a nutrient like FoxFarms Grow Big 6-4-4 solution works well.

Flowering also changes the plant's needs, so phosphorus takes the lead. Solutions for flowering have moderate nitrogen levels, high phosphorus levels, and lower levels of potassium. General Hydroponics FloraNova Bloom is an example of a flowering nutrient, with a ratio of 4-8-7.

Cultivators generally choose one product line to use for nutrients, using their various solutions for every growth phase and to provide micronutrients to the plants.

Nutrients Needed for Marijuana Growth

Macroelements	Nitrogen (N), Phosphorous (P), Potassium (K), Sulfur, Magnesium, Calcium
Microelements	Iron, Manganese, Zinc, Copper, Boron, Molybdenum
Beneficial elements	Sodium, Silicon, Cobalt, Iodine, Vanadium

"Mineral Nutrition for Cannabis—Macroelements." https://sensiseeds.com/en/blog/mineral-nutrition-for-cannabis-macroelements/

Cleaning and Reusing Soil

Cultivators can reuse their soil, but they must check its nutrient content first. This is done by watering each individual plant and testing the run off using pH and ppm meters. If the water has a pH balance between 5.5 and 6.5 and if the ppm is in the right range, the soil is good to use. However, the previous plants likely consumed most of the nutrients during their flowering cycle, so growers have to reinvigorate their soil's ability to feed the plants. Mixing something like bat guano or worm castings into the mix can do this.

Real-world commercial farming operations only reuse soil after it has been steam pasteurized. The process cleans out all bugs, molds, and mildews, but at the cost of washing the nutrients from the soil. Growers who pasteurize their dirt must create a mix that adds these nutrients back in. Steam pasteurization equipment is costly and out of reach to all but the largest scale cannabis cultivators. For these larger growers, it's worth the time and expense, but small farmers usually buy new soil for each crop.

Using Pesticides

The idea of using pesticides on marijuana plants is controversial. One on hand, marijuana attracts a host of bugs that ruin harvests and kill plants. On the other, cannabis is inhaled and ingested, and no one really knows the effects pesticides have on humans when they do so. It is possible to look at the tobacco industry and to commercial farming, though, and make assumptions about what can be safely used, or not.

In Maine, the state's first medical marijuana law contained a prohibition on use of pesticides. It also mandated that dispensaries grow their own marijuana, leaving the retail and medical experts given the permits struggling to meet demand. When the Wellness Connection of Maine's crop got bugs, they applied pesticides, despite the rules. In the ensuing scandal, they were penalized for the violation. But the laws also changed, and the state put out a list of approved pesticides. Most other states have done the same, establishing allowable pesticides based on the practices of other like industries.

Dangers of Pesticides and Fertilizers

Experts warn that unwelcome chemicals, including pesticides, may bind with the THC and other cannabinoids and threaten the health of marijuana users. Medical marijuana samples collected randomly in California and Colorado have both tested positive for dangerous pesticides. The results in California showed pesticide content at 1,600 times the safely ingestible amounts, albeit tested by an unaccredited lab selling tests to dispensaries. The findings are startling, and cultivators have to take note. Marijuana users do not want poisonous medicines.

The best way to avoid contamination is to not use pesticides at all. They can stick to the walls and hang out in the ventilation systems, making it impossible to purify future crops. Insecticides, fungicides, and herbicides all compromise the purity of the marijuana. These toxins are inhaled when cannabis is smoked and ingested when it's eaten, leaving patients to face unknown hazards from this practice. If the pesticide can damage the nervous system of bugs, they can certainly affect ours.

Colorado, Maine, and Washington State Regulations

Pesticides are easy to spot in today's lab tests, which evaluate marijuana for large families of contaminants rather than for specific products. Most dispensaries screen for pesticides, either by choice or as mandated by law, and they reject any products that test positive. In Colorado, increased cultivation facility inspections uncovered more than 100,000 contaminated plants, and the use of banned pesticides has caused the recall of several major brands of edible medicines.

Lab testing keeps the system honest. Tests are performed by cultivators, manufacturers, and dispensaries, and by regulators and the media. There have been several investigations into cannabis pesticides in Colorado where the media acted as whistleblowers, exposing top-brand producers using banned substances, and their product was then recalled.

Maine requires any cultivator using an approved pesticide to obtain a license from the Board of Pesticides Control. This agency is tasked with assuring the chemicals are used safely and that the public is protected. Maine used to ban all pesticides, which was a problem for cultivators. Even nontoxic substances and food-safe products were banned.

States like Colorado, Maine, and Washington have written guidelines under which pesticides are allowed and set rules about testing for those that are not. Banned products must never be used, and allowable pesticides must be dosed in accordance with the manufacturers' instructions.

There are no exceptions, and violations can result in costly product recalls, fines, and license forfeiture. Following such rules, dispensaries and users can be sure that products from licensed facilities are safe to consume.

HVAC

The importance of the HVAC system you choose cannot be overstated. An undersized system can result in long downtimes and expensive renovations, and too large of a system can be a costly waste both up-front and in power usage. Before contracting with an HVAC company, make sure they have experience with cannabis-cultivation installation. Most companies base their design calculations on comfort heating and cooling systems rather than environmental control systems. The heat created by the lights, ballasts, and other grow equipment quickly becomes a strain on a typical HVAC system.

Although it's not officially part of the HVAC system, cultivators sometimes use airflow to pump CO_2 to their marijuana crop. Plant growth increases when CO_2 is added to the environment. It's essential for photosynthesis and can make your plants more heat resistant. The downside of supplying additional CO_2 to plants is the expense. If you choose to add it, carefully calculate exactly how much you need for improved growth.

Proper Temperatures

Your HVAC system's job is to maintain the correct temperatures for successful cannabis cultivation. Proper temperature is important for photosynthesis, so you'll need to monitor the temperature in your grow room. Place monitors in several locations to ensure consistent temperatures throughout the room.

Low temperatures reduce evaporation through the leaves, which cuts the suction force required for roots to take up nutrients. Maintaining a low temperature enables the plant to take only what it needs, leaving behind unnecessary nutrients. With your grow lights on, an ideal temperature for your plants is 68° to 77° Fahrenheit (20° to 25° Celsius). With the lights off, the temperature should be between 62° and 72° Fahrenheit (17° to 22° Celsius). There shouldn't be a big temperature difference between day and night.

Necessary Ventilation

A properly working HVAC system brings in fresh air and exhausts warm air. Inadequate airflow can mean the difference between a healthy garden and a dead one. During the lights-on period, the plants will take up CO_2 very quickly. The right amount of airflow provides the correct amount of CO_2 to your garden.

During the lights-out period, plants take in oxygen and expel CO_2 and moisture, which can raise humidity levels. Poor ventilation leads to powdery mildew, fungus gnats, and spider mites taking hold of the crop. Cultivators need to use fresh-air intake systems to prevent the intake of pests and other contaminants with the outside air.

Odor control is important, too, as the smell of marijuana is distinct. Most laws require the smell to be self-contained within the cultivation facility. Violations of this rule can result in costly repairs or facility closure. Cultivators use carbon filters to scrub marijuana particulates from the air and negative ion generators to weight the smell molecules, causing them to drop to the ground. Sophisticated HVAC systems will route air out the facility's roof, lessoning the possibility that it will reach the public.

The Least You Need to Know

- Plants require different light levels and nutrients at different growth stages.
- Contaminants in water and soil can damage or kill a crop, so growers must be vigilant when recycling water.
- HVAC systems should only be installed by technicians familiar with cannabis-growing requirements.

Dispensary Operations and Management

This part is fun! Buying and selling marijuana are both joyous experiences. Producers have pride in their product, and buyers will have fun exploring the offerings in your marketplace. Patients and adult users are happy to be a part of the legal system and grateful to dispensaries for the various offerings and service. If it weren't for the lingering problem of federal prohibition, this would be a perfect business for anyone.

This part of the industry is very competitive, though, and only well-prepared, connected, and hard-working entrepreneurs survive. You need a beautiful facility and a one-of-a-kind selection to stand out in the crowd. Learn here how to hire the best buyer and find out what marijuana products you need on your shelves to be top notch. Learn how to sell these products to your clients here, too, with tips you won't find anywhere else to help you provide the best service and to make the most sales.

Designing Your Facility

When designing your dispensary floor plan, you must consider more than just appearance. The goal is to effectively serve as many patients as possible, which requires a careful assessment of available space. Hiring design professionals to help map out and implement your vision can be expensive, but it will pay off when your visitors return again and again.

To run a successful dispensary, you must carefully orchestrate the patient's entire experience, from pulling into the parking lot to walking out the door with their cannabis products. Because you must also keep your staff and patients safe, hiring the right security company is even more important than hiring the right design company.

In This Chapter

- Learn how facility layout maximizes throughput
- Understand how to design your space to showcase top brands
- Discover which professionals you'll need to hire
- Consider your facility-wide security plan

Layout of the Public Areas

The layout of your dispensary dictates the flow of your patients' transactions. Purchasing cannabis should be safe, pleasant, and efficient for them. For you, it needs to be carefully orchestrated to assure that only qualified people have access and that each transaction is traceable as required by law. It's a careful balance of pleasant customer service and transaction monitoring and safety controls.

Your front-door security guard is generally the first person patients encounter upon entering your dispensary. Because nervous first-timers sometimes confuse security guards with police officers, the guard should greet them with a smile and put them at ease. Competition is tough in the marijuana industry. Patients have numerous choices of where to spend their time and money, and you want them to choose your dispensary. Create a floor plan that showcases your medicines in beautiful cases and where staff can serve members with kindness and efficiency. Patients are looking for the best medicines, served by the nicest people, and sold at the fairest prices. Wow them with a beautiful environment, too, and you will win their loyalty.

Parking Area

A customer's experience begins in the parking lot, which should be convenient and easily accessible. A location near a main thoroughfare or freeway on- and off-ramps encourages more visitors. Having adequate parking is also a plus and will keep them coming back. Placing surveillance cameras in your parking lot and ensuring your lot is well lit at night provides another layer of safety. Having regular security patrols and providing staff to escort patients to their cars will also make your dispensary safer.

Not every dispensary has an off-street parking lot. Many depend on street parking or nearby paid lots for their patients' use. Marijuana businesses generally have to prove that enough parking exists nearby to meet the needs of their daily visitors, and that these spaces are safe before they are granted permits. Providing security for patients parking on nearby streets or in paid lots is tricky, as your guard's area of supervision is limited. Your guards need to be focused on protecting the dispensary, not the entire block, so have other staff available to escort patients to their cars. Consider asking the city to limit parking times to 30 minutes near your dispensary to help create more turnover in these spaces.

Entrances and Fire Exits

Entrances and exits should be well marked and well lit. Fire exit signs must be properly posted, displayed, and illuminated according to local building-code requirements. Make sure all fire lanes are always clear of debris and that any fixtures along them are affixed to the wall. Your staff must know where all fire lanes and exits are located, and they must be trained and ready to escort clients outside in case of emergency.

All doors and fire exits should be alarmed and monitored at all times. Most cities and states require a buzz-through-only door leading into the dispensary area. In most dispensaries, these doors lead directly from the reception or waiting area into the service area. Many dispensaries also use buzz-through doors from the outside into the waiting room. During open hours, video cameras and guards should monitor all doors. One guard should be stationed at the front door, and one more should perform continual rounds to look for problems on the grounds. During off hours, a remote security company should monitor all dispensary doors and windows. The police should also be immediately notified of any breech and dispatched.

Accessibility

Municipal zoning regulations and federal laws require businesses to maintain a certain number of accessible parking spaces as defined by the Americans with Disabilities Act (ADA). Your city or county dispensary permit ordinance may require that you have more than normal businesses. Check with your local regulations to find out the rules in your area.

The Americans with Disabilities Act (ADA) is a federal law that guarantees disabled people the right to enjoy life the same as everyone else. This includes the right to purchase goods and services, and no business is allowed to discriminate against any person with a disability. Instead, businesses are required to accommodate access, including allowing service animals in all public locations of a facility. Other accommodations include maintenance of accessible features such as counters, doors, restrooms, and parking spaces.

Reception Area

Your dispensary's reception area is your most visible public space and your first chance to really impress your visitors. Dispensary waiting rooms often resemble those in doctor's offices; most include a selection of magazines and literature and frequently offer a tea or coffee bar. Your reception area should be immaculately clean and elegant in addition to warm and welcoming. Design this space utilizing as much natural light as possible.

The role of this space is to provide room for patient registration and check-in. New members will need room to sit as they review and complete your registration materials. Your receptionist will need a desk with an ergonomic setup for the chair and computer. He or she will be doing data entry all day, and they'll need the tools to be quick and efficient. Their desk will also need room for a printer/scanner, a phone, and for any literature you want members to receive during registration. Returning members will need space to line up and be checked in quickly. Make sure this space is ADA accessible with plenty of room for each person to enter and exit safely.

Dispensary Area

Patients should enter the facility's dispensary area through a reception area so access can be monitored and limited to approved members. Very few dispensaries allow direct access to their sales counter from the street with no reception room in between. Such facilities require members to register at a side reception desk on their first visit, and then each sales clerk performs a membership verification process before beginning to provide services.

Your dispensary should be carefully monitored for safety, with video cameras and panic buttons in place, and loss-prevention staff monitoring the sales floor. The marijuana products, along with their potency and prices, should be displayed for people to view, and staff should be ready to answer questions about each. The space should have plenty of room to handle varying degrees of traffic flow, from accommodating lunch rushes efficiently to managing the needs of one or two people during slow times without losing its charm.

Patients are at your dispensary for high-quality medicines and services by a knowledgeable staff to help guide their choices. Make sure your best products are displayed for easy view. Put your marijuana flowers in a well-lit case, so the crystal covered buds shine like jewels. Display your edibles in bakery cases on cake platters or in their own branded packages. Display the vape pens by strain, potency, and company, so people can easily view the available choices. Keep additional products near the registers for impulse buys, like infused honey sticks, rolling papers, or lighters. Patients are looking to be impressed by your offerings, so make sure not to disappoint them.

HIGH POINTS

Many dispensary operators hire high-end retail design consultants to help plan their layout and choose colors, lighting, furniture, and fixtures. Patients enjoy shopping at these designer dispensaries, which are kept conspicuously clean and organized. They are often staffed by uniformed budtenders and are well stocked with high-end marijuana. Such dispensaries have been featured in high-end magazines and have won architectural awards, and they're credited with decreasing crime and increasing retail sales at nearby businesses.

Create memorable displays to help ensure that your customers return and bring their friends. Many dispensaries today look like high-end art galleries or boutiques—a look that does not have to cost millions to achieve. IKEA sells colorful display cases with good internal lighting, or you could buy used equipment to refurnish at low cost elsewhere. Old wooden display cases are easy to come by on the secondhand market, and they can look stunning with a simple coat of finish.

Community Services

The adjunct services you provide are even more important than the design of your dispensary. Offering patients valuable services in addition to cannabis products helps distinguish your dispensary from the rest. Make space for a chair-massage station, for occasional events like tea parties, and for peer-counseling groups. You can offer these services on a sliding scale or at a discounted fee to members. Such services will attract members who shop while they attend, both encouraging loyalty and making sales.

True patient-wellness centers offer services such as acupuncture, yoga classes, and cannabis cooking and cultivation classes. Some, such as Magnolia Wellness of Oakland, provide onsite health practitioners, including a nurse and chiropractor, to provide additional services to members. Get creative with the wellness services you offer and watch your business grow. Patients appreciate community wellness services; even those who don't partake of them will still be more inclined to visit a business that supports the community.

You can also partner with local community-service organizations for even more exposure. Donate to your local senior center, library, or park to make sure the holistic needs of your members are met. Serving the community feels good and provides great publicity for your dispensary as well. Get out in the community and show people what your dispensary can offer to them.

Deciding on the Layout and Décor

When employing consultants to develop your facility and your brand, you'll likely work with a general contractor; retail, graphic, and lighting designers; and perhaps even a landscape designer. The space they create is as psychological as it is physical, and it needs to announce your brand. These professionals will work together to create ideas that are buildable and fit into your overall vision for your company, all the while meeting budgetary and regulatory requirements.

As you work with your design team, remember that your goals are to maximize revenue, *throughput*, comfort, and employee efficiency. The more attractive your space, the more likely it is that the clients will like it and your neighbors will look favorably upon it. Of course, you can do the design work yourself, especially if you have a strong vision and the time to source materials and book and supervise contractors. You will save money in design work, but it might take more of you and your staff's time to manage. Consider your skills and your budget seriously before getting into a DIY design scenario.

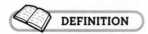 **DEFINITION**

Throughput is the maximum number of customers you can serve in a given amount of time.

Today's dispensaries increasingly seek to avoid negative social stereotypes associated with cannabis users. They avoid use of the marijuana leaf in their logos and hippie imagery in their design work. Rather than displays reminiscent of pipe shops or convenience stores, today's dispensaries prefer well-lit displays designed to feature high-end retail items such as jewelry.

Bringing the Outside In

Make your dispensary feels warmer and more inviting by bringing in lots of natural light. You don't want to have any cannabis visible from the street, so it can be tempting to forgo window space. However, more windows mean more available ambient lighting. Some dispensary designers solve this problem by using lots of flowers and foliage outside of the windows, which also beautifies the indoor space, or by glazing the windows or using one-way glass.

High ceilings and the use of skylights also help to bring the outside lighting in. You might even decide to install an indoor patio area with an open ceiling where customers can socialize. Take a look at your region and neighborhood. It reflects the tastes of your customers and should guide your interior design. If your neighborhood has a lot of murals, consider doing one inside your building. If trees and water surround your facility, use natural woods and blue colors in your design. If your facility is historic, spin the design from there; if it is modern, make sure the interior matches the outside. Having a beautiful design that suits the tenor of your neighborhood will help you stand out.

Using Recycled Items

Using recycled items in your design saves money and helps make your facility unique. Consider using recycled fixtures or build floors and/or counters using salvaged wood. Old windows can be reused in a number of visually interesting ways, from painting them with mirror paint and hanging them in the waiting area to using them to build displays or office partitions. Think about unique ways to use other building materials such as doors, pallets, and shelves. You can build your own display counters with these reclaimed items, adding charm and appeal to your dispensary.

Be thrifty and do your research. Restaurants and stores remodel and go out of business every day. Check craigslist, Etsy, and eBay for used equipment, and search online for liquidation stores selling fixtures. Some communities have building-material thrift stores in which you can find vintage fixtures at a steep discount. You can easily find used jewelry and bookcases, couches, and refurbish them with a good cleaning. Restaurant supply stores often sell used furniture and supplies, so check them for tables and chairs and for items like coffee pots and tea service stations. These types of fixtures are a small design element that can make a big difference in your space, so seize this inexpensive opportunity to accent your image.

Working with Contractors and Securing Building Permits

Inevitably you will use contractors in the process of building or remodeling your facility. Expect to spend a minimum of $40,000 in build-out costs, and closer to $100,000, including electrical work, parking-lot improvements, wall building and removal, and construction of ADA-accessible features. The cost of paint, counters, fixtures, and décor are not included in this amount.

Trying to do the work yourself instead of hiring professionals can end up costing more in the long run. You need to hire a contractor familiar with regulatory requirements. Make sure to understand all municipal regulations before beginning any work that may require permits. You don't want the added expense of explaining to the city why you are not in compliance with the codes, nor do you want to jeopardize your facility's conditional-use permit. Your contractor will usually pull the required permits as a matter of course, but it would behoove you to verify they are issued before starting any work.

 HIGH ALERT

Permits are required for any work done on your facility that is larger than one sheet of particleboard. No walls can be put up or taken down without the permission of the city. You will be responsible for paying any fines incurred if these permits are not in order, and the building or fire inspector who discovers the unpermitted work will not be amused. They could shut you down until the proper permits are secured, and the work is inspected. Don't risk it!

Using Behind-the-Scenes Space Wisely

Keeping administrative offices neat and spare also helps maximize your dispensary's throughput. If you don't use an item at least weekly, it has no place in your office. Organize your offices in such a way that administrative employees can do their jobs with maximum efficiency. This will be reflected on the sales floor and in the safety record of your company.

Your dispensary's behind-the-scenes space will be near equal in size to its public areas. There are many different functions to accommodate, some of which require privacy or extra security. You need room for administrative desks, storage areas, a buying office, space for the packaging team, and a staff break room. Each of these has aisles, needs fire exits, and has special requirements that take up square footage. Dispensary owners often spend all their time and money on constructing the entryway and sales floor, and they forget the importance of a well-functioning back of the house.

Administrative Offices

Your senior and administrative staff need room to do their jobs. This means providing computers and desk space for your chief executive officer, general manager, financial director, human resources director, and bookkeeper. These people use and store sensitive information in their offices, so organization and safety are important. Purchase locking file cabinets and desks, install video cameras in these offices to monitor activity, and restrict key access to these areas. Many dispensaries have limited office space, so shared work areas are common. Make sure each person has room to move around so each can do their work without impeding the other.

Many dispensaries set up a money-counting station in one of their administrative offices for sales staff to use at the end of each shift. Your money-counting office should be next to or near the vault room so that cash never has to travel far unsecured. Cash-counting stations need an efficient bill counter, a coin counter, and space for staff to complete recordkeeping forms. Counting cash should always be done under the supervision of the senior staff, and these areas should always be under camera surveillance with working panic buttons.

You'll also need to create storage areas in these offices. You'll need room for office and cleaning supplies, staff uniforms, equipment, and promotional materials. Important office records and confidential patient information will also need to be securely stored in locking cabinets behind locked doors. Make sure to include this in your planning so you don't end up trying to squeeze in supply cabinets later.

The Buying Room

Each purchasing agent needs their own office in which to negotiate product transactions with vendors. This office, like the one in which you count money, should be next to or near the vault room. The cannabis they purchase needs to be placed directly into safe storage. In most instances, purchasing agents' offices do not have any outside windows. Vendors and dispensaries alike are looking for anonymity during these negotiations. As with all parts of the dispensary, this office should be video-monitored; video allows you to easily resolve any disputes about how much money or product changed hands during any given transaction.

Your purchasing agent's office should include a large scale for weighing product and a microscope for inspecting the marijuana for visible contaminants. They'll need a sturdy desk, three office chairs, a computer and printer, and locking file cabinets for record storage. Many dispensaries keep vacuum sealers in purchasing offices so that all incoming flowers can be sealed for freshness. Decorate the office with thought. Your buyer will be negotiating deals in there, trying to get the lowest price for the highest quality products. Create a stimulating yet relaxing environment for the discussion—one that the seller wants to be a part of, even if it means lowering their cost.

Vaults and Safes

Vault rooms, which store both money and cannabis, must be well planned and constructed to ensure safety and regulatory compliance. Key features of a well-planned vault include floor-to-ceiling and wall-to-wall steel encasing, biometric keyless entry systems, security video cameras with offsite storage, and offsite alarm monitoring and motion sensors. Some have time-lock features, digital dialers with cellphone backup, and intercom systems and distress alarms. Vaults are often built to withstand theft, earthquake, fire, and other disasters.

HIGH POINTS

Your vault should not be built against an outside wall of the building. Keep the vault well inside your facility; every wall is an additional layer of security.

The vault area, access to which should be as restricted as possible, should contain shelves and storage bins large enough to store all of your cannabis at night. The cost to install a vault may seem a bit intimidating. Many companies charge you according to the thickness of the vault walls. The thicker the wall, the more expensive it is to build. However, keep in mind you stand to lose hundreds of thousands of dollars if you get robbed, and your cannabis insurance company will give you a better rate if you install a well-built vault.

Some dispensaries do not use vaults, using large safes instead. These safes need to be large enough to secure all of the flowers, concentrates, and cash on hand each night. It might require multiple safes, depending on your stock. Dispensaries generally keep safes in other areas, too. It's a good idea to have a drop-safe for employees to deposit cash into during their shift and after when they count out their drawer at the end of each shift. Some dispensaries keep their marijuana in a vault and their cash in a separate area, as the staff that need access to each can differ. Regardless, make sure to bolt all safes to the ground, so they cannot be dragged off by thieves.

Packaging and Manufacturing

Your packaging area is where staff will break pounds of marijuana into individual salable units. This area must follow clean-room procedures, if possible, meaning they need to be windowless, environmentally controlled rooms with positive air pressure. When the door opens, air should rush out to prevent contaminants coming in. Staff working in this area should wear lab coats, gloves, and hairnets. The packaging area should contain stainless steel tables, comfortable stools, scales, stainless steel bins, and well-organized packaging materials like bags and labels. These rooms generally have a supervisor's table with a computer and label printer.

Manufacturing rooms within dispensaries are similar, although they are more tightly controlled by state and local regulations. These rooms must be built to the same clean-room standards required in stand-alone facilities and meet any rules stipulated by local and state laws. Dispensaries generally do not make CO_2 or butane extracts onsite, but sometimes they'll make sifted hash and edibles, produce gift bags, or even cultivate cannabis in the same facility. It's important to follow all codes and regulations when designing and building out such spaces and to secure any permits before beginning work.

Staff Areas

Employees need easy access to the time clock when they arrive for work. Put your staff locker room or break room near the front door, if possible. This way, staff can clock in and drop their belongings into a bin or locker immediately upon arrival. Each person should have a mailbox in the break room, where they can receive company memos. Put a bulletin board on the wall for all postings required by law, as well as any other information you want to pass along to staff.

Staff also need space to take their breaks and eat lunch. Therefore, consider putting counters and stools around two walls and a thin table and chairs in the area. You should also provide a mini-fridge with a microwave. The staff cubbies will fill up the fourth wall, along with coat racks for staff to use. If you need more space, hang cabinets above the lunch counters and use that for storing serving utensils, cups, plates, and miscellaneous items. These areas should also be video-monitored and inaccessible to the public.

Waste Management

Your dispensary will have three forms of waste to manage: general trash, marijuana waste, and confidential paperwork. Each requires a different strategy to manage safe disposal. Your general trash should be sorted and recycled. Any non-confidential paperwork, cans, plastics, and glass should be separated for curbside recycling. If your area doesn't have curbside recycling, plan regular trips to the recycling center to maintain this green practice. Your regular garbage should be removed every day to keep the facility clean and orderly, and prevent attracting any pests.

For the marijuana waste, dispensary permits often dictate its waste requirements in great detail. Marijuana and marijuana-production byproducts are often considered dangerous waste that requires special handling protocols. The fear is that marijuana waste will be dug out of a dispensary's garbage and sold or that it could be accidentally ingested. In order to prevent these problems, dispensaries must follow their state and local regulations for waste disposal. Many simply require pulverizing the marijuana waste and composting it with coffee grounds or another substance to render it useless.

For confidential paperwork, such as patient data or financial records older than seven years, you should shred all documents before recycling them. Small desk-side shredders are fine for a small volume of paperwork, and the shredded materials can be put in the normal recycling or compost afterwards. For larger amounts, find a local company that specializes in shredding documents. They can handle the task for you by providing secure containers and guaranteeing safe and secure disposal.

Maximizing Your Security Plan

Nothing is more important than keeping the product, staff, patients, and premises safe and secure. Maximizing security will require you to go above and beyond state and local regulations.

For example, many state and local regulations require security guards during normal hours of operation, but employing an after-hours security guard is never a bad idea. Security guards are state-regulated, and they have strict laws governing their licensing and use of weapons. If you want armed security guards, they must have the required training and be licensed by your state to carry the type of weapon you are requesting they carry. Hiring a professional, licensed, security company is always a wise choice. You don't need weapons to have a safe facility, though, as that sometimes encourages robbers to use bigger weapons. Instead, create a comprehensive plan that uses a variety of mediums to secure your facility. Buzz-though doors, layered security, and limited-access areas all help keep a facility secure without weapons.

Monitored Alarm Systems and Video Surveillance

Having a monitored alarm system extends your security boundary and adds additional layers to your security plan. Components of a monitored system include silent panic alarm buttons installed at key points around the facility, shatter alarms on the windows, motion sensors, and door alarms. The system should also come with long range key fob alarms, which your security staff can wear while patrolling the area. Choose an alarm company that provides 24-hour monitoring, who will notify the police and management, anytime an alarm is triggered.

Your entire facility should be monitored using surveillance cameras inside and out. Use a system that allows you to watch operations in real time from your phone or laptop. Ensure that your video surveillance system has adequate storage space to contain at least 30 days of good quality, recorded video. Be sure that it can record at night, or plan to keep your lights on 24 hours a day. Consider having offsite video storage in case a smart criminal decides to take the video storage device to avoid being identified.

Having an Internal Security Plan

You must have an internal security plan and reinforce it with regular training drills. This plan should include training for and rehearsal of every possible scenario, including active shooter, robbery, physical assault, fire, and natural disasters. Be prepared before you are faced with an actual emergency. Don't skimp on training for these emergencies, and hire professional trainers to train your staff if you are not skilled to do so yourself. Consider implementing an emergency code system. When other employees hear a code over your public address system or walkie-talkies, they'll be better prepared to respond.

Your local police department is often willing to consult on your security plan. They can help you punch holes in it and advise you on its strengths and weaknesses. This is generally a free service, but they may charge a fee. Chances are that your police beat coordinator will manage this inspection. He knows the crime statistics and most common problems in your area. He'll also likely be in charge of investigating and solving any problems that occur at your facility, and he can be a good ally to your company. You may want to join your neighborhood crime-prevention council, in order to meet the neighbors and to form joint solutions to issues of concern.

The Least You Need to Know

- Building a successful dispensary requires careful consideration of the flow of patients through the facility and the appearance of the space.
- Design-consulting companies can help you design your dispensary's brand from packaging to light fixtures.
- Organization of a dispensary's behind-the-scenes workspace helps keep patient areas moving smoothly.
- Video monitoring, armed guards, buzz-through doors, and biometric locks are among the security measures that can help protect your dispensary from theft.

Building Your Dispensary's Menu

The menu is the main thing that sets your dispensary apart from the competition. Customers will reward you with repeat visits if it outshines all others. In order to have the best dispensary, you must offer the finest product at the most competitive price. Developing good relationships with vendors can help ensure the lowest wholesale rates, and it will give you access to new cannabis products before your competitors see them. The best thing for sales is to stock the newest products first. Making exclusive deals with suppliers and distributors is key to staying ahead of the competition.

Offering wellness services and hosting education programs is another way medical marijuana businesses attract and keep customers. Many popular dispensaries provide adjunct services for free or at sliding scale prices. This ranges from having practitioners provide treatments such as massage therapy and acupuncture to hosting onsite special events and member support groups. California's medical marijuana law initially required that dispensaries act as caregivers for their members, helping provide for the health, safety, and housing of each. Laws have since changed, but municipal laws can still require these services, and many of the original and newer dispensaries continue to provide them.

In This Chapter

- Study keystone pricing
- Discover the importance of exclusive products
- Learn about pricing structure
- Understand how wellness services attract patients

Building a Competitive Marijuana Menu

You can have a great marketing strategy, the most beautiful dispensary, and a friendly helpful staff, but if you don't have the best quality marijuana, patients will go elsewhere. They are looking for two factors: a dependable supply of cannabis and access to the newest freshest products in the marketplace. This means filling your shelves with medicines to suit each potential client from the novice to experienced user. You need to stock a variety of price points and potencies and have every possible form of the medicine available.

The experience of visiting your dispensary should be an experience that the customer cannot soon forget. You need a comprehensive branding and marketing strategy to get them in the door, including an online presence, plenty of creative development, and a good graphic design. Backing up all this will be the marijuana products themselves, showcased in your dispensary for best effect. Having competent and charming sales staff to assist each member is the final key to creating return clients.

Patients are looking for safe and clearly labeled cannabis flowers and products, and you must be able to keep up with demand in both quality and variety. You need to continually introduce new products and user technologies to your shelves to stay relevant and ahead of the competition. Negotiate with suppliers to co-brand products with your company logo, giving additional exposure to your brand and the appearance of a proprietary product line.

Becoming the Best

Your buyer will need to have excellent negotiating skills to ensure that you are always getting the best possible deals and exclusive offers for your inventory. They have to know how to build and use personal relationships to find these offers, and they must be fearless enough to negotiate good deals. They will have to closely monitor the competition, viewing their online menus, and asking your customers what they like about other places. They might even consider sending secret shoppers to do price and service comparisons.

You have to build your brand and reputation on having the very best cannabis products available in every category from flowers and edibles to oils and waxes, and everything in between. Be continuously aware of what the other dispensaries are doing so that you don't miss a current trend or a new product line.

For simplicity's sake, compare your cannabis flower menu to that of a grocery store's salsa shelf. There's never just one kind; there are a number of choices to fit each shoppers' palate and price range. Like salsa, you'll need cannabis that is mild, medium, and potent. You'll need low-, medium-, and high-priced brands, and a variety of flavors. This means stocking sativas, indicas, and hybrids in at least 3 potencies and 3 price points, or 18 strains minimum. And, your members want choices at every level, so popular dispensaries stock 25 to 30 strains at a time. And that's just the flower menu!

 HIGH POINTS

A competitive marijuana menu needs to contain all the major product lines: flowers, concentrates, extracts, edibles, and topicals. Use these minimum guidelines to set up your menu:

- 25 marijuana flowers
- 5 water hashes or keifs
- 15 waxes and shatters
- 5 brands of vape pens
- 5 tincture blends
- 15 types of edibles
- 5 kinds of topicals or balms
- 1 high CBD and 1 THC cannabis oil extract

You should also supply accessories like rolling papers, small pipes, and lighters. Cultivation books sell well at dispensaries, too, so stock a supply of ancillary items to ensure the needs of patients are met.

Your buyer will need to build a competitive menu of ingestible medicines, including edibles, tinctures, and other items available in your marketplace. Patients depend on these medicines, and once you choose your brands, make sure to keep them stocked at all times. Nothing loses clients faster than being regularly out of stock of in-demand items. The most popular edible items are chocolate bars. They package nicely, have a long shelf life, and the flavor is well suited to combining with cannabis. Cookies and brownies are the next most popular, but it's important to have a nearby source to keep fresh products on the shelves. Marijuana pills, tinctures, lollipops, and breath mint strips are all popular items at dispensaries. Of course, the same principle applies: you need every price point and potency, and old standby products and new ones with the "wow" factor.

You'll need waxes, shatters, oils, hashes, and keifs. You will also need to stock a variety of vape pens, both well-known brands and local, small-batch varieties that interest patients. Bath balms, lotions, and patches are all of interest to your members, and if they are available, you should carry them. Always search out specialty products to suit clients with exact needs, like CBD, pure terpene, and THCA raw cannabis products.

Sprig Soda is a unique product that attracts buyers with its fresh look.

Setting Marijuana Flower Potency and Price Points

Most dispensaries break their marijuana flowers down into categories according to size. Customers are willing to pay more for larger buds. If a bud is dense, trimmed, and about the size of a quarter, it is deemed grade *A*. These flowers, if they test at more than 15 percent THC, are the best-selling items in any dispensary. The smaller buds in each unit are graded *B*. These are often fluffier than A-grade flowers. They have more leaf matter left on, and they sell for less. The broken bits of shaky leaf and buds in the bottom of the bag make up the final product in each unit, the *C*-grade marijuana. This is usually sold by the ounce at dispensaries, as opposed to being sold by the gram or eighth of an ounce that the higher grades are sold in.

Patients can tell the general potency of a marijuana flower just by looking at it. Dense, crystal-covered A buds generally rate between 15 to 18 percent THC. Leafy B buds are less potent. Having been starved of sunlight on the plants' lower branches, they developed fewer trichomes. Patients know that these buds are less strong, generally below 10 percent THC, and the leaf is even less potent. Trichomes generally proliferate on the buds, and although the leaves do contain some of the cannabinoid content, it can be as low as 3 percent.

A-, B-, and C-grade marijuana flowers.

Make sure your products are packaged in a standardized manner. Only package A buds together for your top-shelf products. No matter what the variety, your top-shelf products should only contain these larger buds. Save the B and C buds for mixes, so members can have access to clean medicines in a variety of price and potency points. A mid-grade mix is the product of choice for members with less to spend, but who still want the flavors and effects of the top-shelf buds. Often members purchase a mix of all three products, so they can blend them together at home for potency, flavor, and effect.

A-grade buds with less distinct smells or other slight flaws like low moisture content are often marketed at lower prices. Outdoor cannabis grows less densely, and the natural light variations can mean less trichome content. They are less potent and sell for lower prices because of it. Your buyer should look for high-quality, lower-cost A buds to fill each price point on your menu. Take the B buds out of these, too, and add them to the mix. Dispensaries generally have a B-bud mix on the menu and a "Baker's Mix" of C-grade product.

Grouping Your Other Products for Pricing

For hashes, waxes, shatters, and other concentrates, try to match the price point to potency. Products with similar THC contents should be priced near the same. For vape pens, price by weight of the product, with each half gram and gram device falling within the same reasonable pricing guidelines. The exception is for award-winning or limited-edition extracts from well-known producers. Exclusive brands demand higher prices, and patients are willing to pay them.

HIGH POINTS

The High Times Cannabis Cup is the holy grail of marijuana judging events. The value of your brand skyrockets if you win this cup. Champion strains sell at hundreds of dollars more per pound, as long as cultivation standards are kept constant. Cannabis Cup events are regional, taking place in legal states like California, Oregon, Michigan, and Colorado. The original event was held annually in the Netherlands, but as laws there have worsened, and those here have gotten better, the focus has become American-grown cannabis.

The manufacturer generally prices edibles, so consumers find similar price points no matter where they shop. The potency of these products varies widely, and higher potency doesn't always mean more cost. Some edibles contain a high dose in a small item and are priced by the extra cost of the marijuana. Others have high-quality ingredients and more expensive packaging, but they have a lower dose of marijuana. The price in these cases is for the ingredients and packaging. A $12 edible can contain 25 percent THC or 180 percent, depending on the goal of its manufacturer. When selling these items to patients, it's important for dispensary staff to always point out the item's potency and dosage. People buying high-dose, low-volume medicines should always be warned to eat only a small amount and wait an hour or two to gauge its effect before trying more. If your state has a dosage limit, always follow that to assure legal compliance.

Other products can be grouped for pricing by intended use. Your balms, creams, and bath soaks should be listed similarly to each other. If one lip balm is $2 and another is $7, your clients will be confused. They won't know whether to choose the lower cost one to save money or the high-priced one for better quality. A variance of $3 is better suited, with less potent products priced lower and those with more potency and finer packaging priced more. Whatever rating and pricing system you use, listen to customer feedback. Be willing to adjust and make changes that work better for your team and its clients.

HASHING IT OUT

Marijuana dispensaries will soon be able to categorize cannabis products according to their terpene content. With more research, we'll understand how terpenes interact with the cannabinoids, THC, and CBD, to provide medical benefits for the user. Patients will benefit greatly from the ability to read an ingredients label on their marijuana products in order to find out its active ingredients exist within each product and learn the expected effects thereof.

Determining Wholesale and Retail Prices for Medical Marijuana

Many factors determine retail price, starting with the wholesale price, which is itself determined by supply and demand. As production exceeds customer use, price drops. Both Washington and Colorado have experienced periods in which oversupply drives wholesale price down as much as one-third. For example, in early 2011, Denver wholesale prices dropped from $1,800 per pound to less than $1,000.

Although retailers often double the wholesale price to get the retail price—a strategy called *keystone pricing*—this doesn't work for every product. Dispensaries often price top-shelf strains the same, even if they paid different wholesale prices. In this case, across-the-board pricing makes more sense to customers than a keystone markup. The same idea applies to concentrates, where a sale price is structured based on potency, rather than just on the wholesale cost.

 **DEFINITION**

> **Keystone pricing** means that the retail price of an item has been increased by 100 percent from its wholesale cost, so that 50 percent of the sale price is profit.

With marijuana flowers, try setting a top price for your best strains, say $60 for an eighth of an ounce. Sell all of your top-shelf strains for this amount, regardless of what you pay for them. For mid-grade strains, use keystone pricing, rounded to the nearest increment of five. If you pay $20 per eighth, sell it for $40. For lower-grade cannabis, use a potency and quality rating to sell it for the highest possible amount. Your buyer might get a great deal on outdoor marijuana for $15 an eighth, but the market bears sales at $40. Mark it accordingly and make up for some of the income lost on your high-grade markups. For higher-grade marijuana, volume sales are important to balance the smaller profits. So if anything is not selling, price it to move, and use the proceeds to purchase better medicines.

Keystone pricing is the norm for edibles and topical marijuana products. Simply put, if a brownie costs you $4 wholesale, the dispensary should sell it for $8. Use this same markup with rolling papers, pipes, books, and other ancillary items. All of these items should be sold at double or more the cost to your dispensary.

Any edible, topical, or ancillary product that sells slowly should be marked down to move. Edibles have a short shelf life, and you don't want to lose the wholesale value due to expired overstock. Put it on special until it's gone, and buy less next time. For ancillary items, make sure your purchasing power is not locked up in books and t-shirts. Any item you purchase must move quickly or go on sale. The idea is to keep money flowing through your purchasing agent, so you can turn products into profit to pay the bills.

If you have a product that you make yourself, your cost is likely below the normal wholesale price. You have several choices in this case. You can mark the product up beyond keystone to match the shelf price of competing products, or you can sell it for a lower price than the others, going for both volume sales and a healthy markup. If you have an exclusive deal on a special or limited edition product, or one that is celebrity-endorsed, keystone pricing may be too low. Certainly price the item higher if the market will bear it. Marijuana retail businesses traditionally have high expenses and low profits, so use your markups wisely to sell the most products for the highest profits.

 HASHING IT OUT

Marijuana businesses have not yet tried the Costco model, offering paid memberships and huge discounts in return. In this case, customers might only be allowed to buy cannabis in increments higher than a quarter ounce, and hashes and concentrates in 5- or 10-gram lots.

Providing Complementary Care

Today's dispensaries offer a wide range of benefits beyond just supplying medical marijuana. This often includes providing life-enhancing services such as massage therapy, acupuncture or acupressure, chiropractic care, and yoga at sliding scale rates. They hold classes to teach cultivation and cooking with cannabis to help members develop self-sufficiency. And they sponsor condition-based patient support groups, and peer groups for veterans, caregivers, and seniors. People who access these services bring along qualified friends, and therefore, more business.

Dispensaries are community-based resource centers, and they become social hubs for their members. The more exciting and active your dispensary is, the more people will be drawn to it to buy their medicines. This makes dispensaries endearing to the public, rather than frightening, and helps assure that dispensaries are allowed to flourish, even during prohibition.

Using Outside Service Providers

Contract with professionals to offer adjunct care for your patients. Consider leasing floor space to a massage therapist once a week, especially if they are willing to offer sliding scale massages to your members. Make a deal with a local chiropractor to offer low-cost care to your members at their office. If you have room, invite them in to use your space for treatments. Host a monthly acupuncture clinic by screening off part of your sales floor and inviting clinicians in to do treatments. Chip in on their fees, if you can, so your members can get these services at a discount. Some dispensaries offer treatments for free, but these expenses are high, so providing them on a sliding scale is the norm.

You might consider bringing other professionals in to work with your patients. Some dispensaries offer Q&A sessions with local attorneys well versed in marijuana laws. These attorneys are often willing to do this for free in order meet potential clients or just to help out. You might ask a doctor to host an information night to educate members about medical marijuana, or ponder hiring a part-time nurse to work at the dispensary to handle any onsite concerns. Provide routine wellness checks, where patients receive blood pressure checks, flu shots, and an opportunity to ask health-related questions free of charge or on a sliding scale.

Offering Classes and Courses

Great dispensaries care about their patients enough to help them become self-sufficient. By doing this, they create dedicated clients who use the dispensary for their supplies. Teach your customers how to grow and process their own cannabis, and you can sell them grow books, clones, seeds, and trimming supplies. They also often return the benefits from their surplus crops back to the dispensary for resale.

Cooking classes are another fun way to bring people in the door, as patients enjoy learning to make their own edibles. The essentials of infusing marijuana into foods can be taught using a few plug-in appliances like a slow cooker and electric frying pan. Your staff can choose the recipes and even rotate the job of teaching. After class, patients can buy their cannabis Baker's Mix from the dispensary or pick up an infused butter to make their own home goodies. Make sure to stock a few cooking with cannabis books, as this is the time to sell them.

You might also offer classes in hash making, creating infusing body products, or how to make tinctures. Consider hosting entrepreneur nights, where interested patients can learn more about cannabusiness. Invite local experts or authors in to talk, sharing information about marijuana and other interesting topics straight from the primary sources. Each class will draw people to your facility, and they'll generally purchase while there.

Hosting Your Own Social Service Programs

Many dispensaries sponsor compassion programs offering free or discounted cannabis medicines to veterans, low-income patients, and seriously ill people with conditions like cancer and HIV/ AIDS. The dispensary and its vendors who donate funds and products generally fund these programs. Some dispensaries also have food pantries, holiday gift programs, and school supply drives. Make sure to create a giving community around your dispensary, where members can contribute to each other's well-being and that of the larger community.

If you have space, consider creating a meeting place for peer counseling and care groups to meet. Host PTSD monthly gatherings for veterans, seniors, new patients, and any other specialized group that needs attention. Give attendees a 20 percent discount on goods and services that day.

Make sure to get the word out about these programs to help recruit new members who might be interested and help develop good will around your community.

There are numerous ways to get involved in your community. Consider hosting an ice cream social with proceeds benefiting a local charity. Join garbage pick-up days around the neighborhood, host educational booths at local events, or donate to a mural project. You are only limited by your willingness to participate.

The Least You Should Know

- Most dispensaries offer standard pricing across a product category.
- Making friends with vendors pays off in wholesale discounts and exclusive products.
- Different cannabis products have different mark-up rates.
- Offering wellness and educational services keeps clients coming back.

Supply Purchasing

Your dispensary needs a stellar purchasing department to attract and retain clients. Patients are seeking fairly priced, effective, dependable medicines, so your purchasing agent, or buyer, must be well connected and in tune with the market. Your buyer also has to be a charming negotiator. Getting the best medicines and exclusive deals depends on their ability to establish these connections and to be the first stop for wholesale suppliers.

A buyer's position is highly skilled. A trained buyer can spend just a few minutes with any product and determine its expected purity, potency, effect, and value to your dispensary. The purchasing department is the first barrier for quality assurance. The buyer performs initial quality assurance inspections, providing the first line of defense against inferior product.

In This Chapter

- Learn the importance of having the best buyer you can find
- Review the skills you need to successfully negotiate for cannabis
- Discover how to manage vendors and suppliers
- See how experienced buyers screen suppliers

Having an Excellent Buyer

Your buyer should have more knowledge about cannabis and cannabis products than anyone else on the staff. They must understand the effects of sativa, indicas, and hybrids, and they should know how each strain's terpenes and potency create certain expected effects. They also have to be well connected and purchase the best brands for each type of medicine, and they must stock your dispensary with marijuana flowers, edibles, topicals, extracts, and concentrates across all potencies and price points.

Purchasing agents have to cultivate and maintain vendor relationships, making sure suppliers are happy with their treatment and that the accounts are up to date. They have to know how to budget so that new products can be purchased and consignment accounts are managed in real time. In addition, your buyer has to track inventory and establish reorder points to ensure that best-selling products never go out of stock. Don't overlook this side of the job. Make sure your purchasing agent understands budgeting in equal measure to their knowledge of marijuana medicines.

HIGH POINTS

Be sure your buyer is not a technophobe! Provide them with a point-of-purchase tracking and inventory-management system to access daily sales data. This information will help guide their purchasing strategies. They need to watch sales closely to use available funds for trending items. And, they need regular information in order to restock best-selling items before they sell out.

Getting the Best Medicine Takes Work

Buyers must cultivate special, long-term relationships to ensure access to the newest products and technologies. Vendors often roll out new products in limited amounts; you want to be the first dispensary they choose. Their desires are simple. They want to be comfortable during the transaction, and they want to get paid without hassle. Vendors like to work with efficient and friendly buyers who appreciate the effort that goes into creating top products.

Your buyer must do constant market analysis and comparison shopping to ensure customer access to the best, most sought-after products. They cannot be shy; picking up the phone, cold-calling suppliers, and meeting with numerous walk-in vendors is a big part of the job. A good buyer will balance their time to allow space for both meeting with regular suppliers and seeking out new ones.

Your buyer should be a great negotiator so vendors leave feeling like the transaction was mutually beneficial. It takes finesse to push for the best deal without offending the supplier by undervaluing their product and hard work. Your buyer has to know what the market will bear and must be sure that you have shelf space for the product. Your buyer should be looking for exclusive deals on top products, which often require contracts with large up-front payments—but this will certainly be worth it if you can secure an entire high-grade crop from a well-known producer. Patients are drawn to award-winning brands, and you will celebrate a healthier bottom line for it.

The Art of the Deal

The success of your dispensary depends on your purchasing agent's quick negotiating skills. Your buyer should go into each transaction knowing the general wholesale value and sales price for each item. Their goal is to negotiate a cost for each item that will enable you to mark it up for a reasonable profit. Their strategy should be flexible, as goals and priorities can change during negotiations based on new information or changing conditions.

 HASHING IT OUT

Good negotiating skills require the following:

- Preparedness: Know what you want and create a winning environment.
- Strategy: Get ready to explain your needs and how everyone will benefit.
- Compromise: Be willing to give something to get something.
- Leverage: Promote your strengths and show the added benefits of the deal.
- Agreement: Both parties should leave feeling good and looking forward to meeting next time.

It takes preparation, discipline, street smarts, and a level head to be a top negotiator. Your buyer should stay focused on the end users in order to negotiate the best deal. This marijuana is designated for patients, and the goal is to enhance the life of those it reaches. Purity, price, and the product's safety matters, and your buyer should be passionate about always providing the best marijuana available. Stay focused on the mission of your dispensary, and you'll find that vendors are very receptive to providing lower prices.

Finding Vendors and Cultivating Relationships

Finding vendors is not a problem, but finding the right ones takes work. You want those with consistent products: Do they have a high success rate, or does their product tend to fail third party lab testing? Do your staff report positive results from trying it at home, and do patients like it? Do they replace damaged products without question, or will your buyer be arguing for returns? Partnering with dependable suppliers to build sales is essential.

Your buyer will have to get out in the field, attending marijuana festivals and meeting suppliers at various industry events. Developing a good reputation is essential, as word will get around about their personality and about the dependability of your payments. Bad reviews will keep suppliers away, and good ones will have them knocking on your door for appointments. Networking with vendors is necessary in order to build a comprehensive supply network.

Screening Suppliers

State laws often strictly regulate the medical marijuana supply chain. Producers cultivate and manufacture under this supervision, and transportation is monitored for safe handling. *Seed-to-sale* tracking is required, so regulators can see the chain of control from cultivator to patient. Medical marijuana products are tested for safety before a sale is allowed, and dispensaries are mandated to track each item until it's transferred to a member.

DEFINITION

> **Seed-to-sale** tracking means that each marijuana plant is documented and traced from the moment the cultivator acquires and plants the seeds, through its harvest and any manufacturing processes, and until the final product is sold at a licensed retail facility.

Buyers have access to marijuana direct from the farm and manufacturer or through distributors who amalgamate supply from multiple sources. There are many choices, and your buyer has to find the highest quality items at the best prices. This means they have to understand the needs of your members, and proactively go into the field and find products to match.

Most dispensaries have unsolicited vendors ask for buyer appointments. Make sure you have a method to screen those calls and visitors to eliminate the ones that don't offer the products or prices you need. Your buyer's limited hours need to be spent maximizing deals, not coaching suppliers with substandard products. Dispensaries often require drop-in vendors to leave a sample. This way, the buyer can review each item and set up meetings with potential new suppliers, while kindly rejecting the others.

Check the reputation of any potential new supplier. Look at their online reviews to be sure there are no complaints or concerns. Review their online marketing strategy, and make sure it fits your values. Check their website and social media sites, and see if they promote partner dispensaries to drive sales. Choose your suppliers by the purity, price, and potency of their products, but also on the companies' ability to draw patients to your dispensary. Make sure they have plenty of point-of-sale literature and displays to help with in-house marketing, and see if they will commit to product sampling booths to drive sales. Buyers have a lot of choices in today's marketplace, so make sure to fully maximize your vendor relationships.

HIGH POINTS

Your buyer should ask new medical marijuana product suppliers to do in-house training for your dispensary staff. Fifteen minutes is generally plenty of time to educate your clerks so they can answer questions about the medicine from interested patients. Suppliers should also be asked to do pop-up educational booths in the dispensary. Patients like meeting the producers and learning about the production processes first-hand. It drives sales and creates committed fans.

Managing Vendor Appointments

Your buyer will likely have more vendors trying to make appointments than there are hours in the day since supply outpaces demand in most places. This doesn't mean you don't need to actively source products out in the field. You need to stay ahead of the competitors on finding great deals and securing contracts for high-grade, limited supply products. But expect a large number of walk-in suppliers at your dispensary, who arrive just like pharmaceutical reps, with brochures, free samples, and a sophisticated sales pitches.

Set up an appointment calendar for your buyer and have a receptionist to help keep the appointments moving on time. Invariably, vendors will show up late, setting back your buyer's entire schedule. Late vendors are at a disadvantage when it comes to negotiating because your buyer's time is worth money, and the cost of wasting it can be subtracted from the cost of the product. If time permits, meet with walk-in suppliers, or have the receptionist take the samples for later review.

Dispensaries often post their purchasing rules online. If not, vendors generally phone ahead to learn more, rather than dropping by for unsolicited visits. Some dispensaries only meet suppliers by appointment, and others take drop-off samples for review. One dispensary might refuse all unsolicited supply calls, while others like reviewing all new products, no matter the source. Vendors should do their research, and they should approach each potential client on their terms.

Negotiating Prices

Setting a product's price too high results in fewer sales; setting them too low means less profit. You need to find the happy spot that moves them off the shelf while making enough money to support your company. Your buyer must purchase products that meet three pricing criteria:

- Superior products that sell high and fast.

- Low-cost products that move quick at bargain prices.

- Mid-priced items that can be marked up 100 percent for retail. This last category should make up the majority of your stock.

Set prices according to purity, potency, freshness, availability, and current market trends. Your buyer should closely judge marijuana flowers on feel and aroma, and they must consider the trim job and overall visual appeal when setting its value. The best-looking, best-smelling, and strongest cannabis commands the highest price. Rare marijuana flowers and exclusive or limited-availability products have higher wholesale and retail values. Dispensaries rarely mark these up 100 percent, instead settling for a lower markup in exchange for the volume sales and clout that come with carrying exclusive brands.

HASHING IT OUT

Products that are hard to come by or in high demand will always command higher prices. Local producers make the best marijuana flowers, hashes, and extracts in small batches, and dispensaries compete to secure them. Word gets around to patients, who will happily travel to your dispensary for exclusive offers on unique products. Showcase these products in your marketing campaigns and make sure the supplier helps spread the word to their followers.

Contracts and Paperwork

Make sure your purchasing department stays up to date on paperwork. This means always tracking purchases and consignment accounts, and continually reviewing inventory and adjusting prices to keep inventory moving. All products coming into the dispensary inventory must be recorded, traced, and stored. Make sure you use a cash-management system to track and record transactions, and a point-of-sale (POS) inventory system, QuickBooks, or another internal tracking system.

Each product acquisition should include a purchase order or invoice and proof of payment. Your dispensary should assign a tracking number to each item and use it to follow the marijuana product from purchase to sale. Keep track of all monies paid to suppliers for tax purposes, as your product costs are deductible. Make sure your invoice and payment slips contain places for your buyer and the seller to sign, as these signatures are essential in proving the transactions occurred.

Dispensaries often have contracts with suppliers in exchange for exclusive offers or special rates. This comes in return for selling a certain amount of product over the terms of the deal. These contracts are legally binding once signed and must be maintained. Be sure to have your corporate lawyer review any contracts that lock you into expensive, long-term deals.

Cash on Delivery vs. Consignment

Traditionally, when a vendor drops off a pound of cannabis to a dealer, they expect to be paid in cash on the spot. Retail dispensaries are different, though, with brick-and-mortar locations and clear chains of responsibility. Consignment is more the norm these days, where dispensaries pay for each unit after it's sold.

Suppliers with the finest products can demand up-front payment. Their product sells fast, and the producers feel confident asking for high prices and payments on delivery. Dispensaries save funds for these, making sure to have payments ready to secure these premier products. The market is flooded with every other product, so dispensaries can demand better terms. It's standard in the industry to secure your marijuana products on 30-day net terms with no cash down and no interest on late payments.

Receiving cannabis before you pay for it has advantages and disadvantages. One advantage is the ability to get it lab-tested at an outside facility, and pay only if it passes a secondary safety screening. If the cannabinoid content comes back lower, you can then negotiate for a better price. If it comes back contaminated, you can return it to the vendor without worrying about collecting a refund.

One disadvantage to buying product on consignment is that dispensaries can fall into the trap of spending the funds before paying them back to the vendor. The inability to manage money can leave buyers with a cash-flow shortage. Vendors do not want to hear that you sold their marijuana and spent the funds without paying them. Word gets out quickly, and you could find yourself unable to secure new accounts, which can kill your business if it gets out of control.

 HIGH ALERT

Marijuana dispensaries are notorious for getting behind in their consignment accounts. Many end up owing hundreds of thousands of dollars to their suppliers and have no inventory left to show for it. Don't fall into this trap; set aside the funds from each day's consignment sales and have them ready for each supplier on demand.

Only large dispensaries can afford to purchase all of their cannabis in cash up-front. Remember, you need current stock and at least 10 days' backstock, which could add up to hundreds of thousands of dollars in inventory. Unless you started with a healthy budget and kept consistent profits, your dispensary is likely running consignment accounts. Often flowers and high-priced concentrates and hashes are received on consignment, and edibles and other small batch products are paid cash on delivery.

Arranging Safe Product Deliveries

Your dispensary must have a protocol for safely receiving delivery of medical marijuana products. Robbery and burglary are certainly concerns. You must protect your suppliers and staff and secure the assets of your dispensary. Limiting walk-in vendors and meeting suppliers by appointment is helpful, as you'll know when to ramp up security. Insisting that sellers make deliveries during daylight hours is also helpful. Providing sellers with an escort into the facility from the parking area is a good idea, too. Work together with your suppliers to develop safety protocols and implement them to the maximum during every visit.

Develop Security Procedures

Vendors travel from dispensary to dispensary, carrying marijuana products and cash, which makes them easy targets if they're not careful. Suppliers must be aware of their surroundings at all times, watching their rearview mirrors, changing their driving patterns, and using an unpredictable delivery schedule. Your dispensary can implement every possible security protocol, but if your vendors are not safe on the way to and from your facility, they could get in trouble during the delivery.

Vendors must always follow the rules of the road to keep from drawing attention from law enforcement. Insist that your suppliers store products and cash in lockboxes or locked trunks. Do not allow them to drive into your parking area with product or cash that is not properly stored in the vehicle. Vendors should never leave marijuana products or money on the seat of their vehicle and or in plain sight of the public. This is an invitation to a smash-and-grab.

Ask your vendors to check in with your receptionist when they arrive, before bringing in their product. This way, security can be notified to provide an escort or can at least be alert while the cannabis is transported from their vehicles. Dispensaries should have trained security officers on duty during all open hours to prevent problems and to effectively report any crimes to the police. Make sure you have working video cameras and panic buttons, so police can be notified quickly in case of emergency and can review the tapes upon arrival.

Vendor Check-In and Waiting Room

Requiring vendors to check in before their appointments enables them to feel safe and secure while they wait for your buyer. Many states require that all vendors be medical cannabis patients themselves and members of each dispensary they supply. If this is the case in your area, vendors should register through the regular patient intake system. If not, create a separate vendor tracking process, likely within your inventory management and bookkeeping systems.

If your dispensary has space, create a separate waiting area just for vendors. This way they can relax and prepare for their meeting outside of the public space. You can offer coffee, tea, and snacks to start creating a positive relationship. Use this space to help encourage participation in various marketing and training opportunities by putting out information announcing your campaigns. Make sure vendors feel safe and cared for at your facility so they'll be more likely to return.

Vertical Integration and Growing Your Own Supply

Most dispensaries choose to supply at least some of their own products in order to increase their profit margins. *Vertical integration* has its pros and cons. One pro is the ability to lower the cost of goods and to create unique branding opportunities. A con is that you might not have the production capacity to consistently supply your customers.

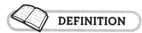 **DEFINITION**

> **Vertical integration** generally means that your dispensary plays some role in the manufacture of certain goods it retails. This lowers the cost of these items, increases quality control, and improves their profitability.

Small-Scale Production at Your Dispensary

Your local regulations may allow you to produce small batches of products that require little processing. This could include pre-rolling joints or making cookies in a small kitchen. There's nothing like the aroma of fresh-baked cookies to entice your customers. You can also make topicals with a small stove or hot plate and marshmallow treats with only a microwave. Make sure to check the local regulations before you get started, as some of these processes may require fire, building, or health department approval first.

Consider making gift bags to set near the registers as impulse buys. Group products together and offer discounts for buying the pack versus purchasing each item individually. Consider grouping edibles, topicals, or multiple items from a single product line. Many dispensaries offer gift packs with a lighter, a pack of papers, and a pack of rolling tips. These can be easily assembled by your staff during their downtime, and sold for $5 at the register. Add a flyer or a small sticker to the packet to turn it into a marketing tool, reminding patients to return again soon.

Vertically Integrating Cultivation

Retail sales and marijuana cultivation are two totally different skill sets. Most people specialize in one or the other, but there are two likely reasons to vertically integrate. First, dispensaries need to lower their cost of goods sold, and growing even part of their own supply can boost profits significantly. This plan comes with problems, though, as dispensaries rarely have space to cultivate a meaningful amount of marijuana, and the cost of maintaining a secondary facility can be prohibitive. Dispensaries do better negotiating fair prices from expert cultivators.

Second, cultivators get into retail to assure they have a dedicated outlet for their marijuana products. Succeeding in the dispensary industry is hard. Obtaining a permit and capturing a market share is a full-time job, and patients have choices in most areas. Cultivators mostly contract with existing dispensaries to sell their products, rather than trying their hand at retail.

Dispensaries sometimes try producing clones onsite. The lighting, water, and airflow needs for this are far less than what's required by a full-flowering cultivation facility. Mother plants and clones can be kept in the same room, and one staff member can maintain both. This space must have positive pressure airflow and be kept clean-room safe to assure that no bugs or contaminants are introduced into the space. Producing clones on sight makes sense, as these are difficult to transport due to each unit's size. However, clone rooms fail regularly as it's easy to pick up contaminants.

Dealing with Pricing Issues and Loss

Your business will never be perfect, so prepare in advance to solve the most common problems in a calm manner. Losses are to be expected, but make sure to analyze each to see that it fits within expected boundaries. Your shrinkage should fall into averages, and if not, find out why. Employee theft, system failures, and bad data entry can all lead to problems with inventory management and loss. Your job as the owner and operator of a marijuana business is to make sure this doesn't happen. You have to run tightly supervised systems and perform regular audits to prevent problems from exacerbating.

Price Discrepancies

It's important to keep the dispensary's menu accurate, as members depend on it to decide where to go. If they drive over and your menu proves wrong, they may not come back. If you discover a price discrepancy, find out why and eliminate it. Technology isn't foolproof and occasional glitches can destroy the functionality of your online menu. Keep a close eye on it, and make sure your team checks it throughout the day for mistakes. Human error plays a role in these problems; it's easy for staff to make data-entry mistakes.

If your menu says an item is $5 but your point-of-sale system says $10, you must sell the item to the customer at the menu price. If not, they will tell other patients and be unlikely to come back. Correct the discrepancy and move on correctly with the next client.

If your customers tell you competitors are selling a product for less, find out how and why. Are they selling it as a *loss leader*? Are they getting a low wholesale price because they buy in bulk or have a special deal? If your competitors are getting a better price, figure out how you can get the same.

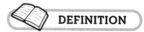 **DEFINITION**

A **loss leader** is a product you advertise and sell at a loss in order to lure customers in to buy more profitable items.

Watching Shelf Life

All marijuana-infused food items have a finite shelf life. Do not let these products sit on the shelf so long that you have to throw them away. Discount these items or bundle them with other products and sell them at discount well before their expiration dates. Make sure your inventory and floor managers keep a close eye on these products, and notify your general manager when it's time to put them on special. Items that get stagnant or sit on the shelf too long cost you money! Evaluate products that are not selling, and if you decide to continue carrying them, order less or price them lower.

Cannabis flowers also have a shelf life, so take care to store and handle them properly. Avoid exposure to heat, light, and air, which degrade THC and dry out the flowers. Store your marijuana in a cool, dark space, such as in a vault or safe. Any marijuana that moves slowly should be marked down and priced to sell faster. If you have a low-income or veterans' relief program, you can discount these items towards the end of their shelf life for patients in need. Make sure they don't go to waste, and that you always secure your investment and a small profit in return.

Product Loss

All marijuana businesses must account for losses of undamaged products. Flowers shrink due to water loss as they sit in storage. Shrinkage also occurs when you remove the stems from flowers or break down large buds to package them into grams and eighths. Make sure your inventory-management systems track these losses, and that all abnormal problems are investigated and solved.

Moldy and expired products need proper disposal, and each type of loss needs carefully documented. Product can become contaminated during handling at your dispensary. If it drops on the floor, is damaged due to a force of nature, or from mishandling, it must be accounted for and removed from inventory. These losses are inevitable in small increments, but any variance from the norm needs to be researched and documented. This could be from theft or from mistakes that you can prevent in the future.

The Least You Need to Know

- Your buyer is one of the most important people at your dispensary.
- Most dispensaries do at least small-scale production in-house.
- Product that is not moving well does not have to go to waste.
- Inventory costs you more the longer it sits on the shelf.

Providing Medical Marijuana to Patients

Providing medical marijuana to patients is not quite as straightforward as it seems. Before you can dispense cannabis, you must have standard operating procedures in place. You also need a well-trained staff that understands the importance of patient care. Finally, you need to decide if you're going to provide secure delivery or not.

In This Chapter

- Learn how to develop a management and operations plan
- Discuss tracking inventory and sales
- Learn cannabis customer service
- Review the legalities and stay in bounds

Developing Management and Operational Procedures

One of the first steps in starting your business is creating its Management and Operations Plan, which establishes each procedure and the responsibilities of each member of its chain of command. Many municipalities make this step part of the application process. Before they give you a permit, they want to see that you have a workable plan to operate your business. This means envisioning your procedures based on your facility's layout, expected daily visits, and the types of marijuana products you will be providing to patients.

Your chief executive officer (CEO) and chief operations officer (COO) are responsible for creating this manual. Their job is to envision and implement each process and to train supervisors to fulfill their respective roles. The supervisors are then responsible for training other staff members, making sure they each have the skills, ability, and knowledge to complete any assigned tasks. Having a strong human resources (HR) department in your company is important, as well. You must make sure your job descriptions and hiring processes work together to find candidates that match each position's exact requirements. Your company will thrive with a well-trained staff and tight management and operational procedures, especially when partnered with talented supervisors who understand these procedures.

Like the simple instructions provided with board games, your Management and Operating Plan must be clear enough that anyone can pick it up and understand how to perform their job.

Creating Your Plan

Part of your Management and Operational Plan will be the creation of Standard Operating Procedures (SOPs). SOPs dictate how you will structure your company and achieve its operational goals. They list each detail of your general operations, member registration, inventory management, point of sale, security, and staffing. They express the technology you use, key positions within your business, and how those positions relate to one another.

SOPs dictate how you and your team should perform everything from opening the store every day to interacting with customers and dispensing cannabis. They define your set expectations and how to maintain efficiency, while reducing errors and complying with regulations.

It's not easy to create these manuals from scratch, so you should try to have at least one team member experienced in the dispensary industry help in its creation. Look online for templates and examples that fit your style, and split the writing tasks between your in-house experts. Otherwise, you might want to hire a mentor or professional adviser to help create your manual. Marijuana licensing processes are often competitive, and having the best operations plan will help you stand out.

Keeping your procedures and policies up-to-date is a big, but necessary, job. As your company grows and you learn from experience, update the written SOPs to reflect procedural changes. Be sure to maintain regulatory compliance along the way and to get approval from state or local regulators, if required, before implementing them.

Empowering Supervisors and Inspiring the Team

It's hard for new business owners to delegate authority, but you cannot do everything yourself. It's essential to create a well-balanced team who embraces the company's goals, vision, and values. You need supervisors who arrive with knowledge, skills, and abilities, and who are not afraid to implement new systems. Starting a marijuana business is not easy; mistakes will happen. Your supervisors need to be able to make intelligent decisions fearlessly, and they must be able to handle failure and pivot to workable solutions.

Create clearly defined job descriptions for your supervisors and support their independence. Your leadership role is to make sure they each understand their role in meeting the company's goals, and that they have the tools and training necessary to succeed. As the company's leader, you must track progress, provide guidance and assistance, and make sure that each person knows that their contributions and efforts are appreciated.

You must also demand accountability when empowering your supervisors. Your initial expectations will be laid out in their job descriptions. The SOPs go deeper, detailing each procedure they supervise and which staff members they manage complete them. Empowering supervisors requires good communication at all organizational levels so everyone stays focused on the same goals. Recognize your staff's desire for self-improvement, and foster a culture of growth and continued education. Offer regular staff trainings for supervisors and all team members to build skills and encourage teamwork.

HASHING IT OUT

Encourage employees to further their education by offering to reimburse them for classes and outside training courses. Consider offering a tiered reimbursement schedule. For example, you could reimburse 100 percent of the costs for A grades and perfect attendance, 90 percent for Bs, and so on.

Tracking Inventory and Point of Sale

Your inventory comprises much of your company's capital investment; most of your funds are tied up in products, and you have to be careful with them. Therefore, you must track sales, expenditures, and all products coming in and going out. Most marijuana companies use a point of sale (POS) system that assists in tracking inventory and sales. These systems commonly use United Product Codes (UPC) or barcodes, a scanner, and a computer-based POS system to maintain data.

Your POS system needs a simple interface to speed up sales and limit mistakes.

A variety of companies have created marijuana industry-specific POS and inventory management systems. In Colorado, the law requires marijuana businesses to use seed-to-sale tracking systems that use Radio Frequency Identification (RFI) tags to follow each unit. Other states have less stringent rules where companies can choose which system to use. However, all of them come with strict audit regulations where operators have to regularly prove that their marijuana was carefully controlled and both cultivated and sold with strict adherence to regulations and laws. Some systems use a simple tag to track and follow inventory, but the systems are more cumbersome and less automated than RFI tracking. Make sure to complete a review of several available systems, both cannabis-specific and from the regular retail world, before choosing one for your marijuana business.

Using a Point-of-Sale System

You have to manage two kinds of marijuana product tracking—inventory management and point of sale. Inventory management starts right at the point of purchase. Marijuana companies must carefully record each item into inventory and account for it as it is processed from large wholesale units into smaller retail units. They also track *shrinkage*, which comes from loss of water weight as the product dries and when the stems and leaves are removed during processing. You need a system that can track *active stock*, which is out on the sales floor, and *back stock*, which is stored for future use.

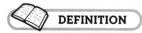

DEFINITION

Shrinkage is an accounting term describing the difference between what your inventory-management system reports and what is actually on hand. It stems from problems like lost items, theft, and human error. Businesses expect, and can predict, average shrinkage and investigate when losses exceed these amounts.

Active stock is the stock available for purchase on the sales floor, while **back stock** is the stock that is stored for later purchase.

Your point-of-sale system tracks cash register transactions, making sure that each item sold is recorded and removed from inventory. The POS system is used to substantiate each sale, showing money coming in and product going out, all to a verified patient. Ideally, you'll find a unified system that does both inventory management and point-of-sale tracking. Such a system allows you to monitor and report key data in real time, thus increasing accountability and efficiency. A well-managed system also enables government agencies to track your dispensing efficiently, without any unnecessary burden on you or your staff.

A good inventory management and POS system has several important features. Cost is a key feature, so price out installation, equipment costs, and service fees for each. Make sure that broken equipment can be easily replaced, and that the company has a technical team that is accessible, knowledgeable, and friendly. Avoid small companies without track records when choosing your system. Look for an easy-to-use interface, interactive dashboards for generating reports, accurate traceability, and demand forecasting.

HIGH ALERT

Make sure to carefully vet POS systems before choosing one. The marijuana industry is an emerging industry, and the technologies that support it are often fresh out of development. Furthermore, those from the regular retail world are not easily adaptable to the peculiarities of marijuana sales and packaging. Ask for referrals from other dispensaries and see which system stands out.

Recently, my dispensary reviewed several POS systems, looking for an upgrade. We picked our favorite and started asking around about it. After hearing from a trusted associate that it was the "worst thing that ever happened" to them, we decided to keep looking. Take your time and make a choice you can count on.

Selling Medical Marijuana

Marijuana flowers are attractive and fragrant. If you can, place samples of each offering in small dishes and allow customers to see, touch, and smell them before choosing. This can be done at a station on your sales floor, where a helpful staff member is assigned, or by the service clerks at the dispensary counter. Patients use their senses to grade cannabis organoleptically, just as your buyer does, so allowing people to smell, see, and feel the cannabis helps them make the best choice.

Patients also need help choosing the best medicine for them, and dispensary service clerks act as peer counselors to help with this decision. Clerks need to have an understanding of the general effects of each product on your shelf. They must be able to explain how strain, potency, and ingestion method come together to create specific benefits. And they have to understand the potential side effects from consuming too much as well.

HIGH POINTS

Enticing customers to buy additional products at checkout is called *upselling*. Keep impulse items near the register. These may include lighters, rolling papers, books, marijuana grinders, and pipes. Make sure your sales staff mentions these items to each customer, and consider offering an award to the employee who sells the most each week. You can add $5 or more to each sale, simply by adding merchandise to the area near your cash register.

Patient Care

Dispensaries are hybrid companies, serving patients only in retail settings. Some are like clinics with adjunct services such as acupuncture and massage therapy. Others are like pharmacies where staff provides pure medicines in sterile environments. However, most are like high-end food co-ops, with marijuana and a variety of other products sold over the counter to registered members. The staff is generally super friendly and ready to chat about medical marijuana, kale, or the weather with equal vigor.

Regardless of the model you choose, taking great care of patients is what drives your profits. People want to feel like they are part of a community and that they are welcome and respected. Their time matters, and the care your staff provides adds value to it. Each transaction should be a learning experience, where patients are introduced to new products, given helpful tips, and told how amazing and valuable they are to the dispensary.

Helping Patients Choose the Right Medicines

Patients welcome the assistance of your staff. Good sales skills require active listening and attention to details. Customers may not always know what they want or how to ask for it. The job of a sales clerk is to identify a patient's needs and help them choose the correct product.

Potency and method of ingestion play important roles in treating symptoms. Does the patient require high THC or low THC with high CBD? Do they need high CBN for sleep? Are they interested in vaporizing or smoking marijuana? Product cost is a consideration for patients, too, especially for people on a budget. Does the patient have a symptom that can be treated with edibles, inhaled cannabis, or both? If the answer is both, then what will offer the quickest relief at the best price? Listen carefully and the customer will tell you everything you need to know to help choose the right medicine for them.

 HIGH POINTS

When assisting patients in choosing marijuana products, avoid statements like "this will cure your condition" or "this eliminates those symptoms." Such statements can get you in a lot of trouble with the Food and Drug Administration (FDA), as marijuana is not a federally approved medicine. According to their spokesperson, Jeff Ventura, the FDA "has not issued guidance or an opinion on these kinds of products, [but] the agency reserves the right to take action when appropriate to preserve and protect the public health." Instead, educate patients about the products, their potency, and the differences in strains, so they can choose what's right for them.

Patients may not know the range of products available, so you will be introducing them to a variety of choices they didn't even know existed. Marijuana connoisseurs want to see the newest, most innovative items available, and they're willing to pay high prices for the best products. Make sure your clerks point out the items near your cash register, too, adding value to each transaction.

Above all, be polite to every customer at all times. Treat people in a way that makes them want to return, and let them know that you really do appreciate them shopping in your store. Consider building loyalty programs to keep them coming back. Give discount points for each transaction, and consider giving birthday gifts to your patients. Customers return to stores that treat them well.

Managing Medical Marijuana Deliveries

Many medical-marijuana patients get their cannabis delivered. Delivery services are very popular in communities lacking brick-and-mortar dispensaries. They are especially valuable to patients in hospice care or those so ill they are homebound. The downside is that delivery services don't offer the variety dispensaries do and access to adjunct services is nonexistent.

Driver safety is a big concern for delivery companies. Even if drivers have delivered to an address before, it doesn't mean it's safe the next time. You must plan for the worst-case scenario, which is armed robbery. Teach your drivers to always check their rearview mirrors and alternate their driving patterns, never taking the same route two times in a row. Consider also sending them out in pairs to provide greater safety.

Make sure the drivers keep products and cash locked up at all times. Do not allow them to get complacent and keep cannabis or cash in a bag on the front seat. Ensure that delivery vehicles are registered and licensed and that all lights and signals work. Your drivers must always follow the speed limit and obey traffic laws. You don't want them to get pulled over for a traffic violation and arrested for transporting cannabis with intent to distribute.

Keep track of all delivery sales using your POS system. This transaction should be no different than one at your dispensary. Each item must be accounted for when it's delivered, it must go to a registered patient, and the money must match the sales ticket. Use the POS system to help with phone sales, as it provides a handy reference for your staff. A patient may want to know what they purchased in the past so they can duplicate or avoid the same order. Your POS system should be able to run a simple report on customer history and past purchases, and your staff member can offer guidance based on this.

The legality of delivery services is a question on everybody's mind. Few cities and states have written legislation regulating these companies, so they often work in a grey area and remain underground. Many places have historically left them alone, taking no measures to discourage or shut them down. This is mostly because it's hard to locate their headquarters or owners, and as soon as one gets shut down, more open to fill the gap. California is taking a unique approach to delivery services by licensing them under the new medical marijuana laws. In order to receive licensing there, delivery services must operate out of a storefront and not a home or unregulated structure.

Developing a Cannabis Community

Developing your own cannabis community of loyal repeat customers is essential to keeping your doors open. Build your base by offering a warm, welcoming place for patients to gather. Host classes and guest speakers to keep people interested and returning for more. Consider offering adjunct health services as well with sliding scale fees to maximize access.

Celebrate holidays, sponsor festivals, and host offsite parties for your members. Hold annual anniversary events with a free community barbeque to introduce more people to your services. Participate in neighborhood clean-up days, campaign for supportive elected officials, and plug into the local safety committee. Show your customers that you are making the community a better place; keep them informed of your outreach programs and make room for participation. People like to see that their contributions are making a difference.

> **HIGH POINTS**
>
> April 20th, or 4/20, is the biggest holiday in the cannabis calendar. It was started in the 1970s by a small group of Californians who used to hang out at 4:20 to smoke marijuana. By the 1980s, it spread nationwide with countless people gathering in unity to smoke that day. This date in April has become the ultimate day to celebrate marijuana, with New Year's Eve-style countdowns leading up to 4:20 each year. Dispensaries see a huge boost in revenues the week before this day, and visits can easily triple on 4/20. Simply put, it's the Black Friday of marijuana, so be stocked and ready to celebrate.

Understanding Legal Issues

Nothing ruins your chances of success like misunderstanding legal issues and finding yourself outside of regulatory compliance. Keep your finger on the pulse of the legal landscape at all times, ensuring consistent compliance. One of your biggest tasks will be tracking and recording the disposal of cannabis waste, including waste per pound. Some natural shrinkage occurs when breaking down and packaging pounds; you'll lose stem weight and water weight as well. Always track and record that loss.

Using Accurate Weights and Measures

Ensure that your dispensary accurately weighs its products at all times. The scales you use must be of a certain standard and quality, as stated in your state and local regulations. These scales are generally calibrated in accordance with standards set by the National Institute of Standards and Technology (NIST) under the U.S. Department of Commerce. Each state has its own branch of Weights and Measure that takes its lead from NIST. You may be required to have your scales checked and calibrated at least annually.

Marijuana flowers and concentrates are sold in gram units, both at the wholesale and retail levels. High-grade flower grams retail for upwards of $17 each, so even a small mistake in the unit weight can create loss for the dispensary or for the patient. Make sure your scales are calibrated at the start of each day and again at random intervals to assure they stay accurate with use. Some of your clients will have scales at home, and you never want to come up short.

Always use properly calibrated scales to weigh medical marijuana.

Many states, such as Washington and Colorado, have specific regulations explaining how to track and dispose of cannabis waste products. Stalks, stems, and out of date, moldy or otherwise unusable products have to be weighed and destroyed properly. This often includes mixing the marijuana with coffee grounds, dirt, or another contaminant. Depending on the laws, it may be composted onsite or must be properly disposed at an offsite location. Some states require authorization to destroy any marijuana products, while others simply require audit trails to prove it existed and was removed. Make sure you must dispose of all waste according to local, state, and federal regulations.

The Deal Breakers

You must be on the lookout for people who are either accidentally or purposefully violating the laws. By doing so, they wrap your marijuana business up in their crime. If you know about it, you must do something to prevent it. After all, you never know if it's your government regulator or an undercover agent checking to see that you're being compliant with the rules.

There are two big issues—interstate transport and diversion to the illicit marketplace. It is illegal to transport marijuana across state lines, per a U.S. Supreme Court Ruling. Licensed patients aren't even allowed to travel with marijuana medicines between contiguous states (for example, from California to Oregon), even though both states are legal and allow *reciprocity*.

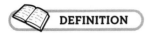 **DEFINITION**

Reciprocity is when one state recognizes the legality of a license issued by another state, such as with drivers' licenses. Some states have reciprocity written into their medical marijuana laws, while others ban access and use by out-of-state patients.

Train your staff to deny access to medical marijuana by any person stating they will be traveling across state lines with the product. The patient needs educated about the laws and asked to return a different day, and only when they are seeking medicines for legal use. Make sure people are treated kindly during these interactions, as it's more likely that the person did not know the rules, rather than that they are intentionally flouting them.

Diversion of cannabis is also a crime except under very special circumstances. In California, medical marijuana patients can supply cannabis to each other and reimbursement is allowed. In most places, though, it's not even legal to share a joint with a nonpatient. While it doesn't seem like a big deal on the surface, it can still be a misdemeanor criminal activity.

Your staff has to be on the lookout for signs of diversion. Any member stating they're buying marijuana for someone else needs to be denied service, explained the rules, and asked to return only under legal circumstances. Be on the lookout for people talking to friends on their phones, asking what to buy for them, and deny service to these people. Make sure your parking lot security is watching for exchange of money between passengers in cars, as this pooling of resources could indicate an illegal group buy. Again, deny service and explain the rules. Your marijuana business must follow the laws, each and every time.

The Least You Need to Know

- Your job as a leader is to empower and inspire your team.
- Good customer service attracts members and keeps them coming back.
- Most marijuana delivery companies are unpermitted and risky to companies because of it.
- It's illegal to transport medical marijuana across state lines, even between legal states.

Heavy Lifting: Accounting, Human Resources, and Marketing

No one said this would be easy, but maybe fun on occasion. There is a lot of heavy lifting when it comes to running a marijuana business, and most of it is not glamorous. The most essential parts of your business are the least fun: accounting, human resources, and marketing. Each takes focus, work, and planning to do well, and trained staff with the skills to run each department.

In this part, walk through each task in detail. Learn how to create your accounting and marketing plans, and see what it takes to supervise their implementation. Find out how to implement a fair hiring process, and how to terminate employees swiftly if needed. Learn how your role as founder is to hire the right team and to provide them with the leadership and tools to excel. You will only reach your goals with a winning team!

Recruiting and Hiring Employees

Hiring and training employees takes up a lot of time when starting a business, but if you hire good employees, you only have to repeat the process when your business expands. It's not easy to find the right people. You need to strategize where to post your hiring notices so people with the skills you need see it. Each position must have a clear job description, which sets your expectations and acts as a guide to the employee.

You need a fair vetting system to find the best candidate from the applicant pool. Cannabis businesses, like any other, must adhere to fair employment practices. There must be no discrimination in hiring. Once the best employees are in place, you need to train them on your standard operating procedures (SOPs), then supervise them as the company grows and changes.

In This Chapter

* Learn to write an effective job description
* Study the use of fair hiring systems
* Consider where to post your job openings
* Find out how to train your staff

Creating a Fair Hiring Process

A fair hiring process includes a lot of steps. You must start with a clear vision of the company's structure and an organizational chart to express it. Create job descriptions for each position, carefully considering the knowledge, skills, and abilities you need for each one. Outline an hour-by-hour staffing plan that illustrates the number of employees you need to run the business. For example, you'll need fewer retail clerks on Tuesdays, than you will on Fridays.

Think carefully about where to post your hiring notices. If you post them on craigslist, you'll get hundreds of applicants, most without qualifications. It bogs down your human resources (HR) staff as they try to wade through them all. Instead, post notices at places like Oaksterdam University or on one of the marijuana industry's online job boards.

Consider using a job application, rather than resumes, as your main method to compare potential workers. This makes it easy to do quick side-by-side comparisons of multiple applicants. Create a script for your phone interviews, so you can whittle down the applicants further by rating each person's knowledge, skills, and abilities as compared to your needs. Bring in the most skilled applicants for in-person interviews, and choose the best person based on their knowledge and preparedness to take the position.

HIGH POINTS

Make sure to do a salary analysis for each position, checking what the same jobs pay in similar industries. Your retail clerks should be paid slightly above the median rate for sales clerks at regular stores, as the job requires a special knowledge base. This isn't a job selling T-shirts; it's peer-counseling people on medicine choices. Your executives should be paid similar to those in nonprofit industries. Marijuana businesses still walk the line between acting as social service organizations and being for-profit entities. Don't get carried away paying high executive salaries, as your community expects you to be modest.

Creating Your Organizational Chart

An organizational chart for your marijuana business should illustrate your entire chain-of-command and the flow of responsibility, authority, and communication. Provide this chart to your staff so they understand how each person relates to one another and to your board, and so they know how you intend to govern operations. List all departmental supervisors and their relationships, not only to each other, but also to nonmanagement employees.

Your goal is to capture the way decisions are made and responsibilities are shared within the company. The organizational chart flows downward from the chief operating officer (CEO) or executive director, who heads the company and is responsible for supervising all other staff.

Below them is the *C-Suite* of executives—the people responsible for supervising the various departments within the company.

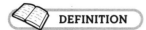

DEFINITION

> A company's **C-suite** of executives refers to the senior team in corporations who generally have titles starting with the letter C. This can include jobs like the chief operating officer, chief financial officer, chief marketing officer, chief technology officer, and chief information officer.

Each C-suite staff member leads a team of people. Below them in the organizational chart, list each person that they supervise. Doing so gives staff members a clear idea of who is responsible for providing them with the tools and training to perform their job well, and who to turn to for various departmental needs. Without a clear organizational chart, your employees will be confused about their own roles and responsibilities and those of their supervisors. The organizational chart will evolve over time as you improve and scale your company. Make updates as needed, and be sure to provide them to every team member.

Writing Job Descriptions for Everyone

Every position in your company has clear and precise duties and responsibilities, which you must list in their job description. Taking time to write these out is important for you as a leader. It provides you the chance to clearly think about the knowledge, skills, and abilities needed for each position, and to imagine the tasks of each job so you can find the right person for each job. By first writing out the job descriptions, you can use them to create job postings and develop questions to ask during the interviews.

In order to write a job description that attracts the best candidates, you must be precise. List the job title, objectives, and a general summary of duties. Include the supervisor to whom they will report, how the job fits into the overall mission of the company, and the required skills or education. Make sure to scrub all bias from your job descriptions, leaving out any mention of gender, race, age, or sexual orientation. None of these have any relevance in hiring the best person, and it is illegal to include them. Last but not least, include the job's salary range. You don't want to waste time interviewing good applicants with expectations or needs beyond your abilities.

Review your job descriptions and update them as your company grows and changes. Provide each new version to your employees so they understand your new expectations. Not only are these descriptions tools for hiring, they're also valuable for evaluating employee performance. Compare the job description requirements to how well each employee has performed them. Use them as guidance if an employee is struggling and offer more training to those who need it.

Using a Fair Hiring System

Your marijuana business must establish a fair and transparent hiring process ensuring complete compliance with state and federal regulations. Your HR manager should oversee the hiring process to ensure it is comprehensive and equal. A fair hiring system helps prevent you from having to explain yourself in court or to a union representative.

Step one is to turn your job description into a job posting. Break the description into two parts. First, list the responsibilities of the job, detailing the key procedures of that position. Highlight the company's mission, vision, and values so potential employees can determine if they are a good fit. Next, list the knowledge, skills, and abilities required for that job. Be concise, but as complete as possible, so applicants can see exactly what you expect from them. Doing so also helps eliminate people who don't fit your needs.

Rather than depending on resumes, create a job application. You can capture all of the data you want for your initial review of candidates on this application. Ask about past employment and volunteer service, and request confirmation of any special skills they possess that you require for the position. Your HR staff should review every application using identical criteria, and only high-scoring candidates should proceed forward in the interview process. For example, you might immediately disqualify all applicants who don't complete the application in full.

 HIGH ALERT

Make sure to keep all applications and any resumes you accept on file for the amount of time required by law, which generally is one or two years. For this reason, don't take applications or accept resumes unless you are actively hiring. If you do, make sure to consider them in the next hiring round. It's best to just return any unsolicited resumes or applications on the spot and avoid the hassle altogether.

Create tough phone interview questions and call only the top people from the application round. You want to vet their skills, knowledge, and ability, so make sure your questions cover a wide range of topics related to your requirements. Ask each person the same exact questions and grade their answers.

Bring the top people to your facility for in-person interviews. Start the interview with a pop quiz. You want to see how they act under pressure, and it is essential to test their knowledge of cannabis, the laws, and your company. If they didn't take time to study these topics before the interview, they are not a good fit for an ambitious, hard-working, and well-prepared team.

After the test, the candidates should be put through an interview process with two or three of your team leaders. Make sure they ask each person the same questions, so their answers can be directly compared. This part of the process is designed to dig deeper into each candidates' skill sets and to check the likelihood of them fitting into your team. Sales clerks should be immediately personable, bookkeepers should be detail-oriented, and your supervisors should have a fun gravitas. First impressions matter, both in your hiring process and to any clients you serve.

Keep the interviews focused: stick to the script, asking the right questions and listening to every answer. Allow the candidates to ask questions as well. Not only will they learn more about you, you'll learn more about them from the questions they ask. At the end of the interview, your team will be able to ascertain who's the best candidate and offer them the job.

 **HIGH POINTS**

> Train your employees to move up. You can avoid unnecessary hiring processes by having staff ready to step into open positions. It's great for overall morale, and you will be able to retain your best people by providing them a path to higher wages and more challenging jobs.

Hiring Quality Employees

The hiring process is long and expensive, but if you take all the right steps you'll end up with a stellar team. The choices you make can have a serious effect on your reputation and image.

Beyond just having a fair hiring process, there's still much to consider. Your company must decide if you are hiring *at will* (where you can terminate the employee without cause) or *on contract* (where each person has a contract stipulating the terms of their employment). You must find places to post your job descriptions that will attract a narrow scope of applicants with the skills you need. Your supervisors and entry-level staff are surely looking different places, so envision where you will find each.

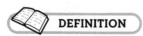 **DEFINITION**

> Hiring **at will** means that as an employer you can fire an employee without cause, and they can end their employment anytime as well. Hiring **on contract** means your employee has signed a contract, which details the terms of their employment and the end of their contracted job.

The better you describe exactly what you're looking for in an employee, the better chance you'll have finding the right employee. Be careful not to sound too demanding or bore the prospect with your requirements; you might turn off qualified people before they apply. Make sure to tell them how the company provides opportunities for career growth. If you want to attract qualified people, show candidates what your company can do to improve their situations.

Keep up to date with social media; people like to work for modern companies that recognize the latest trends. Also you can use social media to screen candidates—this can often tell you more about a candidate than a background check. You can learn about their personalities and sometimes see examples of their work.

HIGH POINTS

The best employees are drawn to the companies that value them the most. Let current and potential staff know that they have room to grow within your company and that you'll reward them with competitive salaries and benefits. Show people that as the company grows and profits, they will, too.

Hiring At-Will or Contracted Employees

The choice between hiring at-will and contract employees depends on your needs. At-will employment means people can be terminated without cause or notice and that they can quit at any time without consequences. Contracted employees have a legal document that outlines the terms of the job and any future exit from it. In either case, employees can still be fired for cause, as long as all employment laws and any contracted terms are followed when doing so.

Companies depend on their leaders and contracting them makes sense. You want to show shareholders, the board of directors, and your staff that the people running the company plan to stay awhile, and that you are committed to them. Consider contracting your C-suite of executives, which shows you are dedicated to them and their growth, and they are dedicated to the business. Get your corporate lawyers involved, as their contracts are binding and the terms should be thought-out and affordable.

Most of your staff will be at-will employees, paid hourly for their work. Your goal is to provide a sweet deal for these people, as you want to keep them around as long as possible. As your company grows, at-will employees should be offered regular raises and bonuses, and you should provide benefits like health care, dental care, and eye care. People have several choices on where to work, and you want to attract and keep the best people for your team. Invest in your at-will employees, train them to move ahead, and they'll be your future executives.

HASHING IT OUT

United Food and Commercial Workers (UFCW) started organizing marijuana industry workers in 2009. They launched a sub-group, Cannabis Workers Rising, dedicated to the industry. Its goal is "to bring more professionalism and stability to this emerging sector of the health-care industry." Since then, UFCW has signed contracts with dispensaries like Magnolia Wellness of Oakland, edibles manufacturers like Bhang Chocolate, and service groups like the Patient I.D. Center of Oakland. UFCW ensures that workers get competitive salaries and good benefits. They also lobby for marijuana regulations and workers' rights at the state and federal levels, bringing experienced leadership and a unified voice to reform efforts.

UFCW organizers launched Cannabis Workers Rising to provide a unified voice to people in the marijuana industry.

Where to Post Your Job Descriptions

Where you post depends on the position being filled. For entry-level retail positions, list the job openings on your social media pages and website and at the dispensary. Your own members make great employees, as they are already familiar with your products and the corporate ethos.

Ask your staff to pass the word around about the job opening, too, and spread the word through your networks in the marijuana industry. You can find excellent employees through your current connections.

For C-suite supervisors, look for people with more specific kinds of educational and training backgrounds. All of these same recruiting techniques work, but you'll need to expand the search. Consider contracting with a staffing agency, especially one specifically for cannabis workers, to fill these positions. Be sure to network constantly, attending marijuana business conferences and pitch events in order to stay connected with the industry's top executives. These people can be a resource for you during the hiring phase, offering referrals and recommendations. And you may be able to capture them for your own staff, when they are ready to move on to a new position.

There are numerous places to post your job openings. Your local community job placement non-profits might be willing to share your openings with job seekers. Check at the local universities and post in their job centers. Hang Help Wanted signs at your local coffee shops, community centers, and anyplace else people with the skills you need gather. You can also post on industry-specific jobsites, such as THC Jobs or 420 Careers, or at industry training centers like Oaksterdam University.

HIGH POINTS

Pioneering marijuana advocate Richard Lee founded Oaksterdam University (OU) in 2007 to train industry workers in anticipation of adult legalization. Lee wrote the nation's first state marijuana legalization initiative, California's Proposition 19, which qualified for the ballot in 2010 but lost the popular vote. This inspired and led to the passage of legalization in Colorado and Washington State in 2012. The federal government raided OU in 2014, but no charges were filed and it reopened shortly after under new leadership.

Choosing the Right People for the Right Job

Not only do the candidates you hire need the right qualifications and skills, they need the right personal characteristics to navigate situations unique to the cannabis industry. From managers to growers to delivery drivers, cannabis industry employees must remain cool and collected; it's the key to success and longevity. When problems arise, your team must be able to adapt in order to keep operations running smoothly.

The marijuana industry blends nonprofit advocacy with retail sales and manufacturing. The industry only survives if its leaders continue to push for workable regulations and legal reforms. Workers have to be as dedicated to the cause as they are to the business. They can't be easily rattled by law enforcement encounters or inquiries by local, city, or state officials. Your sales leader and team must be confident, creative, fearless, outgoing, and calm in the face of adversity. Until marijuana is declared legal at the federal level and each state creates regulations, marijuana workers will wear these two hats.

You want employees who are honest, trustworthy, and willing to do the right thing. Look for people with a history of community volunteerism and whose job references are willing to speak for them. Marijuana workers need thick skins and can't be easily offended. A lot of stigma still surrounds the industry, and the patient base can sometimes be difficult to manage. Ask that potential employees give examples of how they persevered despite adversity, and how they took negative customer interactions and turned them into positive ones. These skills are hard to teach, so make sure your employees arrive with them.

Performing Background Checks

State and local regulations generally require criminal background checks for marijuana businesses. This can be limited to the founders and leaders or extended to all staff. Check your regulations to find out what types of criminal history findings are acceptable. In some states, felony convictions, even felony marijuana convictions, disqualify applicants. Other states believe that prior marijuana convictions should be excluded from the disqualifying criteria. This exclusion prevents good people with no other criminal history from being denied employment at a dispensary or cannabis-manufacturing company.

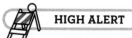

HIGH ALERT

SB 643 establishes new regulations in California creating a statewide requirement for Department of Justice fingerprinting for all applicants. According to California NORML, the "licensing authority MAY deny application if applicant has been convicted of an offense substantially related to qualifications, including ANY felony controlled substance offense, violent or serious felonies, or felonies involving fraud, deceit or embezzlement, or any sanctions by a local licensing authority in the past 3 years (SB 643, 19323-5a)." It's still unclear who will decide which operators are disqualified or what conditions would lead to such a dismissal.

The Department of Justice (DOJ) processes background checks with companies located in every major city and also online to facilitate them. Your state or local regulations may require you to use a certain company. Otherwise, get these checks done wherever you choose and provide the results to the proper authorities. You don't want violent felons, fraudsters, or thieves working at your facility, either, so *never* skip this step.

The Least You Need to Know

- You need an organizational chart to clearly express your company's leadership structure.
- Your marijuana business needs a fair hiring system to find the best employees and to protect itself from liabilities.
- You must post your job offerings in the right locations to find skilled workers.
- Background checks are both a requirement of marijuana laws and a smart business decision.

Managing, Training, and Retaining Employees

Your company's success depends upon hiring the right people for the right positions and giving them clear roles and responsibilities. The management team will execute and oversee your vision, so start by hiring great leaders. You also need a self-starting administrative team, great floor supervisors, and a team of staff members that are happy in their jobs.

It's to your advantage to train the staff well and to make sure they have the tools to perform their duties. Each person needs to understand the company's standard operating procedures (SOPs) and know exactly what to do each day. Making sure you provide ongoing staff training helps with employee retention, and it provides people with the skills to move forward with the company. This is to your advantage, as it will limit the need to search outside the company for your future leaders.

Your marijuana business will have to offer competitive wages to attract and retain great employees. Providing benefits is important, too, and many dispensaries pay full health coverage for their staff. You also have to create a safe and pleasant workplace, where employees enjoy coming each day. Treat your staff well, and they will work hard and with dedication.

In this Chapter

- Understand the role of supervisors
- Learn the importance of staff training
- Discover how to retain employees
- Review management of exit interviews

Staff Roles and Responsibilities

Marijuana businesses need a staffing plan, just like any other company. You need to evaluate your goals, the steps needed to reach them, and what staff positions need filled to get you there.

The company needs a C-suite of executives with talent and decision-making power. This team is responsible for envisioning your standard operating procedures. They will train staff to implement them and update the systems as the company scales and grows. They need the support of a specialized administrative staff, likely a bookkeeper, human resources person, and an office administrator. In early stage startups, people often fill multiple roles. Your chief financial officer (CFO) might also manage the daily bookkeeping; the chief operating officer (COO) could lead hiring; and the chief executive officer (CEO) can act as the office administrator: answering phones, making sure supplies are ordered, and paying the bills.

The team needs talented department managers, who are supplied, mentored, and supervised by the C-suite and administrators. The rest of your staff works under the direction of these people, doing their assigned work using your SOPs as a guide. Among your nonsupervisory staff, you will have senior staff members who have seniority or who came with skills that enabled them to advance quickly. These people are paid more and take a big role in mentoring other staff members. You also have entry-level employees on the team who have been with the company anywhere from a day to a year. It's essential to choose these people carefully, as they hold positions of importance on your sales or production floor, yet are often brand new to the industry.

Finding Your Leaders

Depending on your type of marijuana business, the first employee you must hire will be a chief executive officer (CEO) or executive director, a master grower, a head edible chef, or a production manager. This person will lead the company with the responsibility for systemizing and supervising it. Next you need to flesh out the C-suite, finding the other executives who will help open and manage your business. Especially important is finding a good chief operating officer (COO) or general manager (GM) to share the responsibility for creating and implementing your SOPs.

Most cannabis-industry leaders, especially master growers, are currently employed or leading their own companies, so filling these positions will be challenging. Your networking skills can pay off here, as you'll need to reach out to other industry leaders for recommendations.

Screen all potential leaders carefully and verify their work history. If you're hiring a master grower, for example, you want one with real-world experience in large, commercial cultivation operations. Someone who's only managed a single grow room, or even a black-market grower who filled an entire house, does not have the knowledge to run a 30,000 sq. ft. building full of marijuana.

Finding a COO or GM with cannabis industry experience is difficult, but you may be able to fill these positions from other industries. Much of these professionals' experience is transferable to the cannabis industry, as these roles depend more on leadership and operations backgrounds, rather than on marijuana-specific knowledge. However, they will need to adapt quickly to the specifics of the marijuana industry. Your COO and GM must understand marijuana medicines, inside and out, in order to lead your team.

Exempt versus Nonexempt Employees

The executive director or CEO, COO, CFO, and general manager (GM) are typically salaried, exempt employees. This means they work for a set pay, based on a 40-hour workweek. Occasional overtime is to be expected in these positions, so it's wrapped into the salary. Your executives have to be on call 24 hours a day to deal with any problem or emergency, and they must respond to whatever demands come their way, even if it falls outside of their normal work days. As the leader, you have to watch their overtime. If it starts to regularly exceed more than a few occasional hours, you should give the equivalent in overtime pay to them and consider shifting the extra work to another employee.

Exempt employees make decisions for the company without your direct supervision. They create the SOPs, train the staff to manage them, and supervise the daily operations of the marijuana business. This freedom to make decisions is one of the key bellwethers to measure exempt versus nonexempt employees.

It's likely you will have several layers of supervisors, including nonexempt workers paid an hourly wage. These people work under the leadership of your C-suite, exempt employees, but don't share the same ability to make independent decisions about management of the company. Their job is to assist your leadership team in implementing the SOPs, in training staff, and in managing the daily operations of your facility. Invest time and money into training and improving the skills of these staff members, as they are the future leaders of your company.

 HIGH ALERT

Supervisors are considered to represent the authority of the company, and as such, have extra obligations by law. Manage supervisor liability by making sure each is trained in harassment and retaliation prevention. Their job is to protect the rights of each staff member and to appropriately investigate and respond to problems. Any violations of harassment prevention laws by supervisors pose a serious problem for both the company and for any individual supervisor involved in the problem. Each problem can create high legal fees and come with serious penalties.

Administrative Staff

The administrative staff of your marijuana business might include an office manager, a human resources director, and a bookkeeper. These people manage the essential day-to-day operations of your back office. Small businesses might not have any administrative staff, with the founders or other supervisors sharing these tasks. Large companies might have more positions, adding a payroll manager, administrative assistants, or having multiple bookkeepers.

Your office manager interacts often with the public, answering questions over the phone or in person. Their job responsibilities include packaging, shipping, and receiving of nonmarijuana items. They order supplies, acting as the company quartermaster, keeping a tight budget and making sure each department is stocked with the items needed to function. A good office manager assists the C-suite as needed, providing your executives with a helping hand on a variety of projects.

In a small business, the office manager will fill the human resources (HR) director role, too, screening job applicants and participating in the hiring process. But, any business with more than 20 employees should consider hiring a specialist. HR is a complicated job, with complicated procedures and ever-shifting regulations. Your HR director will manage hiring, training, retention, and termination. They will coordinate scheduling and payroll, organize and track staff trainings, and manage any complaints or problems that arise with the staff.

Your bookkeeper is responsible for keeping track of monetary transactions, including sales and purchases. They facilitate sales-tax payments and act as liaisons between the company and your accountant at tax time. A good bookkeeper will create a daily financial dashboard, so your executives can view the bank balance, sales totals, daily visits, costs, and profits each day. This is a skilled position, so make sure anyone you hire is fluid with accounting software, knows how to track and balance your bank accounts, and is skilled enough to advise the team on spending decisions.

Senior Staff

Nonsupervisory senior staff members fill an essential role at any marijuana business. These people have been with the company a long time and have seen it evolve over time. They know the original processes and what improvements have been implemented. They also know what's not working and have ideas about how to make better systems.

Designate these employees as senior clerks or senior production staff and give them extra pay based on their years of experience and their time with the company. People in these positions are not supervisors and do not come with that added liability. However, they are highly trained employees who often help train new employees and who lead sales and production on the floor.

The goal for these people is to lead by example, showing newer staff how to do the jobs right. They are inspirational team members who help make the job fun and efficient. These are your future supervisors, so train them and treat them well.

Regular Staff

Reception, dispensary, and maintenance staff are just as important as your senior staff. These are the people who make sales, produce products, and keep your facility functional. They have to be trained and well cared for to do their jobs right. Retain them by offering flexible work hours, career-development opportunities, good salaries or wages, and benefits tailored to their specific needs.

Make sure that you and the other executives at your company have an open door for the staff. Develop a relationship with each person, as they count on your leadership for motivation. The company's floor staff has a unique view, dealing hands-on with its products and customers, and you can learn from them. Ask for ideas on improving service and work flow, and reward any employee whose ideas improve the bottom line.

Your job is to lead the entire team, providing coaching and mentoring and improving operations based on everyone's feedback. You watch the bottom line and pay the bills, keeping the operation afloat through good and bad times. Most importantly, you guide the mission, vision, and values of the company, spreading the word and motivating the staff to reach these goals. Each decision and every step your team makes should move the company closer to these, with you leading the effort to get there. Motivate people by reminding them of the social-justice mission to end federal cannabis prohibition and to help people get access to marijuana medicines.

 HIGH POINTS

Motivating your staff can take many forms. Consider throwing them a surprise party to show your appreciation. If you run a dispensary, ask suppliers to donate testing samples for the staff. Collect enough for gift bags, and give them out once a month. Bring in guest speakers for trainings, including marijuana experts, business leaders, or politicians who will provide special knowledge to the team. Host a monthly staff birthday party with cake and snacks, and have occasional lunches where staff can showcase their own home cooking. Building a team that cares about each other and about the company is essential to motivating sales and maximizing production. Simply put, your staff has to care.

Developing a Staff Training and Education Program

Training helps new hires learn their roles and keeps veteran staff focused and on task. A good training program is ongoing and changes as your company expands. It should commence as soon as you hire a new employee and should continue regularly afterwards. Consider sending leadership and top employees to outside trainings, such as to marijuana conferences or to skill building classes.

Develop an in-house training program to prepare new staff for their jobs. Your SOPs provide the guide for this, so write them as step-by-step operational manuals. Plan other types of training for staff, including first aid, emergency response, workplace safety, and harassment prevention. Well-rounded staff members will best implement your mission. Investing in their ongoing education will endear them to the company, and it will keep them interested and involved into the future.

Consider sending staff to a comprehensive training program, such as those offered by Oaksterdam University in Oakland, California. Cannabis universities offer an in-depth education in subjects such as cultivation, strain identification, and dispensary operations. Marijuana businesses favor applicants who have already completed this type of program.

Be sure to keep records of all staff trainings, so you can see that each person is ready to perform their duties. These records help your supervisors hold staff members accountable and form the basis for future job reviews. Your state or municipal regulations may require staff to complete certain trainings or to hold specific certifications. For example, your kitchen manager may have to prove completion of Department of Health food-handling classes. Make sure to keep all records of such training on file and available for audit.

Working Your Management and Operations Plan

Your Management and Operational Plan details each standard operating procedure used to run your marijuana business. The idea here is to create a manual so complete that anyone can read it and follow the steps to run the business. It provides uniformity and authorized instructions, detailing the leadership structure and identifying the staff responsible for implementing the SOPs.

Well-written SOPs aid you in training employees by providing detailed instructions and acting as a reference when needed. Cover all of your operations, including security, staffing, registration, inventory management, sales, manufacturing, and cultivation. Your SOPs should accurately relay required information and enhance regulatory compliance when followed. They should also mitigate health and safety risks.

New staff members should be assigned a trainer to review the SOPs with them. Depending on the complexity of the tasks, this could take several days to accomplish. Supervisors or senior staff members both make excellent trainers. Choose the most productive and outgoing people from each department to educate new staff members, regardless of their rank. Have new employees sign off on each procedure after they learn it, and make sure your HR department keeps a copy of these records. These trainings and the records from them will help your supervisors hold staff members accountable to the requirements of the job.

HIGH POINTS

Create checklists to simplify procedures for your employees. Include all relevant steps and space for staff to initial upon completion of each. Use a checklist for your opening set-up and closing procedures, for cleaning the facility, for processing cannabis, and as a tool to help organize any other task. These will help keep staff on track and establish the productivity of the team.

Staff Training Essentials

A comprehensive training program covers all aspects of staff development in all parts of the organization. Your job as team leader is to determine what this means for your marijuana business. There are three different points of view to consider: your leadership team, the staff, and the people you serve. Each group has different ideas about what training your staff needs and how to prioritize it. Consider doing a survey of each, and use the results as the basis for your training program.

This part of your staff education program goes beyond what is found in the SOPs. These are generally one- or two-hour sessions led by professional trainers and educators. You can plan these before or after opening hours, so the entire staff can attend at once, or hold multiple small-group sessions during work hours. Either way, these are a great way to promote teamwork, while providing your staff with skills that will help them in the workplace and beyond.

HASHING IT OUT

To build skills and increase satisfaction, marijuana businesses should provide ongoing training for their staff. This will pay off by increasing your company's productivity and improving its safety. Consider offering these trainings:

- Leadership development
- Harassment prevention
- Customer service
- Dealing with difficult people
- CPR and first aid
- Fire, earthquake, and disaster management
- Robbery and active shooter response

Make sure your staff understands the laws and regulatory requirements governing your marijuana business, so they can help with company-wide compliance. Consider bringing in marijuana advocates to educate them about the history of cannabis prohibition and the struggle to change the laws. Some of your staff might not remember a time that medical marijuana wasn't legal, so share information about what it was like and how important it is to continue to improve the laws. You might want to host training about the uses of medical marijuana, and which strains, doses, and methods of ingestion help what conditions. And consider hosting "know your rights" and "raid response" training with a lawyer so your staff understands how to interact with the police.

The HR manager should track attendance to make sure that no one misses essential information. Your supervisors should retain the information and skills well enough to share them with people who were absent, but this is not a replacement for first-hand education. Plan follow-up sessions to keep the staff's skills fresh, and so that anyone absent will have a chance to catch up. Consider using online training modules to provide enough information for absent staff members, and for any newly hired employees, between moderated training sessions.

Medical Marijuana Training

Learning about medical marijuana is easy these days. Go online and you can read research studies from around the globe. There are countless websites with information about strains and types of medicine, and anyone can review anecdotal information from patients about how cannabis helped their conditions. People applying to work at your businesses should already be fully informed about medical marijuana. Consider giving applicants a pop quiz, and if they fail, don't hire them.

Everyone from the CEO to the receptionist needs to understand the active ingredients in marijuana, and how the method of ingestion and potency combine with these to create certain effects. The more information you can provide to staff about this, the better. Research primary sources of information and share them in training sessions. Bring in patient spokespeople to give presentations about first-hand experiences. Invite vendors to host trainings where your staff can ask questions based on what your clients need to know. Make sure your staff stays up to date on new studies, and that they understand each new product on your shelf. Nothing turns off clients faster than being served by someone without the knowledge to help.

Keep resources around for your staff and have guides they can refer to for answering tough questions. This should include information on cannabinoids, terpenes, strains, and methods of ingesting medical marijuana. There are several strain encyclopedias that you can keep at the dispensary counter and a lot of cultivation books that would be helpful references. Your staff won't know the answer to every question, but they should always be able to direct patients to where they can find more information. Always have an experienced general manager or floor supervisor on staff with access to resources to help.

Customer Service

Medical marijuana patients want three things. The first is a given—they want the best marijuana at the lowest prices. Second, patients want convenience. They want to be in and out fast, so make sure your systems are efficient. Finally, and maybe most importantly, they want to be served by knowledgeable and kind people. Check any dispensary's Yelp reviews, and you'll quickly learn that if budtenders aren't friendly and well-informed, the entire world soon knows.

Make sure you put the right people in the right positions. Some staff members are well suited for sales, while others do best in packaging or manufacturing. Your front-of-house staff should have customer service and retail sales experience, as well as being fully versed in medical marijuana. They should act like performers, engaging and educating your clients, as well as uplifting them and guiding them to the best products all at once. It's hard to train for these skills other than through coaching, so make sure your supervisors are experienced and able to lead by example.

 HASHING IT OUT

The biggest complaint patients have about dispensaries is poor customer service. The main issue is feeling rushed, rather than listened to, due to the lines of people waiting behind them. You must balance the needs of people in line with those at the counter. It's essential to have experienced dispensary staff to help guide patients' choices, with great customer service skill, so that each client receives individualized care. You develop a loyal clientele by making sure each person knows they matter.

The staff needs leadership, and your founders, CEO, COO, and general manager must provide good ideas. How will transactions work, start to finish, and what special attributes are a part of each one? Will you have a greeter at the door, or have floor staff guiding people to the counter? Will there be a line or will you use a number system, and how will members be cared for while they wait? Imagine each part of the visit from the customer's point of view, and look for sticky points. Your goal is to make each visit smooth. Be innovative!

As in any customer service profession, you'll occasionally encounter difficult customers. Train your staff to take great care with all customers, as successfully dealing with difficult ones sets you apart from other retailers. Treat upset customers with the same patience and dignity as anyone else; be patient and listen to them. Conflicts often arise from misunderstanding, so listening is all that's required to resolve them. Sometimes people are just having a bad time. Offering them a free cookie or small discount can turn their day—and thus their attitude—around. If you just can't win, remain calm and polite and help them as quickly and efficiently as possible.

Retaining Your Staff

Hiring and training employees is both expensive and time-consuming, and turnover costs employers a lot of money. The goal is to hire well, and then to retain your employees. This means you have to offer competitive salaries and benefits, and provide other perks and incentives regularly. Your best employees will be headhunted by other firms as they rise through the ranks and take a noticeable public role. They will also consider forming their own marijuana businesses, using the training they received from you to move ahead as entrepreneurs. To retain them, you will have to start with fair employment packages and continue to improve them over time.

Staff members want to move ahead in the ranks. They hope to gain decision-making autonomy and to see their ideas put into action. Build your team for this, and work to constantly improve the leadership and business management skills of your entire staff. Any person on the team could be the future CEO or COO, so train and mentor them to excel. Foster employee development programs and promote from within whenever possible. Employees like to know that if they work hard they can grow with the company.

Create Great Environments

Design an environment that makes your employees want to come to work, and enlist their help in creating it. Encourage staff to decorate and personalize their work areas; people feel more comfortable when they're allowed to express their personalities. Have a nice staff break room, with cubbies or lockers for belongings, a coffee pot, a microwave, and some light snacks for quick refuels. Have a table and chairs or counters and stools, so people can sit and relax on their breaks. This is a place where staff will have a chance to meet each other and chat off the clock, developing positive feelings that carry back into the workplace.

Let the staff spread their wings. Create opportunities for each person to take leadership roles, even entry-level staff. Give staff flextime to create programs that will drive sales or increase productivity. If someone brings a great idea to your attention, give them the credit, and help grow it to fruition. Your team is talented, so fully deploy them.

 **HIGH ALERT**

Don't let bad apples bring down morale. If you have toxic employees spreading discontent and causing trouble, terminate them as soon as possible. Some people thrive on negativity, and thus can't be made happy. Try to avoid spending time and energy on these futile efforts. Your staff sees exactly what is happening, and they want the person gone, too. Waiting will only cause the team to question your leadership.

Have some fun in the workplace. Consider putting in a sound system to play music at your retail store or manufacturing space. Host events to develop community and to build moral, and get the staff involved in organizing them. Celebrate birthdays, holidays, and births, and show that your company cares. Make staff-only t-shirts and jackets, so people can wear them with pride. There are countless great ideas, so get creative and make each day enjoyable.

Raises, Bonuses, and Perks

Your marijuana business will need to give annual raises to each employee. The cost of living increases each year, and people simply will not stay with you if they cannot afford to do so. This raise should be at least a dollar annually for your retail clerks, and more if you can afford it. Your senior staff and supervisors' salaries should each be evaluated annually and adjusted based on the company's income. Everyone should get an end-of-year bonus. Set this based on the annual net income of the company, and reward your staff for their hard work all year long. Consider giving other occasional bonuses, when they are warranted. This could either be when the company is performing particularly well, or when an individual staff member is excelling.

 HIGH POINTS

Marijuana businesses often give their employees two annual bonuses as a part of their pay. The first is an end-of-year bonus based on the company's net income. The second is on April 20th, which is the nation's marijuana holiday.

Businesses in the marijuana industry generally offer benefits to their employees. Give staff significant discounts on products they purchase from your company. Offer health insurance and pay the full premium for employees when you can afford it. Add dental and vision insurance and a 401(k) program as the company grows and has more net income. Consider offering paid vacation time to the staff and increase it over time.

Institute an employee-recognition program to acknowledge workers' achievements. Consider having an employee-of-the-month program and give the highest producing staff person a gift and award. Offer staff the chance to travel to work-related conferences and conventions. Find ways to involve their spouses and families in your community. Hold an annual picnic offsite or host a special event in your parking lot. You don't have to offer the best benefits or highest salary to retain employees if your company serves a meaningful purpose in an enjoyable workplace.

Firing Staff and Exit Interviews

It's never an employer's intention to hire someone who will need to be terminated later. It's no fun to fire people, especially after you become invested in their success, both financially and as their coach. However, your job as a leader sometimes requires that you set aside emotions and let someone go.

In at-will states, unless your employees are contracted workers, you can terminate them without warning or cause. If you fire someone for cause, make sure there is a clear paper trail and a real reason. It's likely that the employee will fight back, demanding unemployment pay or filing a wrongful-termination suit. Consider offering severance pay to soften any layoff or termination so your employees have time to find a new job.

Some problems require swift action. Employees involved in theft, violence, or crimes of any kind at your facility should be immediately terminated. You cannot afford to risk the loss of product or the safety of your staff. Any employees engaged in criminal behavior should be reported to the police and kept under security's supervision until they arrive. In all other circumstances, do an exit interview with each person, give them their final pay, and ask for return of all company property.

Dealing with Employee Theft

Hopefully you won't have to deal with employee theft, but because it does occur, you must have a process in place to handle it. It's theft regardless of the amount taken. If an employee takes a small amount of money or a seemingly insignificant item, then they cannot be trusted not to take more. Ensure that all employees understand your policy on this.

Prevention is important. Don't give people the opportunity to steal. Keep product out of reach or under lock and key, instead. Have a system of checks and balances to keep loss to a minimum. Do daily cash and inventory counts and reconciliations. Make sure you can track inventory and cash to specific employees, as it moves throughout your systems. Work together with your staff and security to minimize customer and employee theft, and build a caring community willing to protect the assets of the company.

Choose your words carefully when confronting someone you believe has stolen. Talking to someone about a cash-handling violation, as opposed to a theft, will soften and de-escalate a difficult conversation. Regardless, depend on facts. Your marijuana business is likely under full video surveillance, so review the tapes and have proof before you discuss theft with an employee. Never discuss your suspicions with nonessential staff members or with customers, lest you open yourself up to litigation. You do get to choose how to respond to employee theft. This can be anything from a verbal warning for taking office supplies to immediate termination for theft of cash or product. Only you can decide whether to rehabilitate, terminate, or prosecute.

Termination Notification and Exit Interviews

A notice of termination is an official document from the company saying that it has initiated termination proceedings against an employee. These procedures vary depending on the employment relationship. At-will termination is fairly straightforward and does not require an official notice. It's still helpful to create one, though, outlining the status and terms of the termination. Firing contracted employees requires consideration of the details of the employment agreement. This generally means using a termination notification to give notice to the employee.

Whether an employee leaves by choice or termination, it's a good idea to conduct an exit interview. The HR director generally conducts these to help gather data that could be helpful in similar situations in the future. An exit interview also enables you to learn where an employee left off on any current projects and to determine who should take over from there.

Make sure to provide the staff member with their final pay and commissions along with any severance, vacation, and accumulated sick pay during the exit interview. Provide exiting employees with information on the continuation of their health benefits (COBRA) and on how to apply for unemployment benefits. Ask the employee to return any company equipment, including keys, phones, and passwords. Any nondisparagement or nondisclosure agreements should be hashed out and signed in the exit interview; reference letters should be provided; and job placement assistance should be offered, if that is part of the exit plan.

The Least You Need to Know

- Train your staff to be independent decision makers with all of the skills to run the company one day.
- To retain your staff, you must let them grow and prosper as the company's net profit increases.
- Prevent employee theft by having good checks and balances in place and a swift response to any problems.
- Exit interviews fulfill your final obligations to the employee and get the information you need to fill their role.

Managing Your Accounting Plan

Marijuana businesses are under a lot of scrutiny from regulators. The Internal Revenue Service, state taxation departments, and your local marijuana regulators will all likely audit your company at some point. Get prepared by developing a foolproof accounting plan. Make sure every part of your inventory and financial procedures, from seed to sale, are systemized, tracked, and regularly reviewed. You need to have a good system of checks and balances, enabling your team members to be ready to find and solve problems.

The marijuana industry operates on a mostly cash basis—not by choice, but because federal laws limit access to banking services. The dispensaries that have bank accounts and credit-card processing consider themselves lucky. They also know that their accounts can be terminated at any time if the bank gets squeamish. Ensure you stay fully compliant by running tight systems with provable results.

In This Chapter

- Discuss your team's roles
- Find out how to create an accounting plan
- Learn about cash substantiation
- Discover the importance of budgeting

Deploying Your Accounting Team

Your marijuana business needs an accounting plan that clearly outlines the roles and responsibilities of every person on its inventory and finance teams. Ideally, you will have a chief financial officer (CFO) or a finance director on staff, who will work with you to craft, implement, and supervise the plan. This person will help you find the best employees and make sure that they are trained to do their jobs.

Your accounting plan should detail how you manage the resources of your marijuana business. This includes how you will track inventory, cash, your bank accounts, and all other resources on the company's *balance sheet*. Make sure you hire a leader with an understanding of the peculiarities of marijuana business laws and taxation. Find someone flexible, as new regulations are constantly being implemented and better systems are coming on the market for compliance tracking and data management.

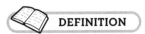 **DEFINITION**

> Your **balance sheet** is the spreadsheet that lists your assets, liabilities, and retained earnings, and provides a snapshot of a specific day.

Team Members

Find a great CFO or finance director, as that position holds the most important role in your company besides the CEO. The CFO is responsible for creating your finance department and must be experienced and ready to lead. They supervise a vast number of tasks, including the creation of job descriptions and standard operating procedures (SOPs). They do the tax planning, compliance reports, and watch the daily books to make sure inventory and finances are in balance. They are responsible for budgeting and analyzing data and have decision-making power, along with the CEO and COO, on financial decisions.

In small companies and start-ups, CFOs might also train and supervise the staff, manage inventory counts, input data, pay bills, and solve daily problems. In larger companies, they are paired with a controller or in-house bookkeeper to assist with these processes. These people work closely with the CFO, helping develop and implement the financial SOPs. They input and analyze the daily sales and spending data, balance the company's checkbook, and identify mistakes. You might also consider hiring an outside bookkeeper to check the work of your in-house staff and to reconcile the books monthly.

On the other side of the team, you need an inventory staff. This includes two key positions: your inventory manager and the buyer. The inventory manager is responsible for tracking all of your marijuana and your manufacturing materials. If you are running a cultivation or manufacturing facility, they are responsible for tracking plants and manufactured units using your inventory software. In a dispensary, they track active and back stock marijuana and nonmarijuana products.

Depending on the type of business you run, your buyer works with the inventory manager to secure marijuana products for your dispensary menu or with your production head to purchase raw materials for manufacturing or cultivation. Make sure your buyer has a good understanding of budgets and is experienced with inventory management and bookkeeping software. It's not a glamorous position, with a buyer chilling out buying marijuana all day. It's a stressful job, which includes budgeting, negotiating prices, and paying bills.

Your accounting team also needs outside staff to provide checks and balances. A key player is your treasurer, who holds the ultimate responsibility for assuring that the company's accounting is accurate. They oversee tax reporting and payments, with the assistance of a certified public accountant (CPA) . Your CPA will prepare state and federal taxes and provide you with information on what, when, and where to pay them. Make sure you find a CPA who understands 280e tax accounting for marijuana businesses. Marijuana businesses have special taxation rules, which you need to clearly understand and follow.

Working the Plan

Founders have to keep a close watch on their business, top to bottom, but nowhere more so than in their inventory and financial departments. It's essential that you and the company's CFO work closely together making key decisions and solving any problems early. Your bottom line can quickly shift, depending on the whims of the retail market; by watching trends closely, you can pivot to meet demands.

Set up a comprehensive accounting plan, and detail each inventory and money-management procedure. Establish the chain of command to supervise and implement each, and make sure that each staff member is trained and has the tools to do their job. The marijuana industry is rapidly changing, so make sure your CFO is forward-looking. You want to have the best possible systems to manage your company, and a CFO's job is to ensure your company stays innovative.

Your inventory and finance teams must do accurate work. There's no place on the team for people who are not experienced with data entry or who can't learn it fast. Mistakes are hard to find and correct, and errors can be costly. Make no mistake, your data will absolutely be audited. The IRS, your state, and your local regulators all want to be sure that you are paying them accurately. Each piece of data contained in your system needs to be substantiated, with back-up paperwork, cash register receipts, and multiple levels of staff checks and balances.

HASHING IT OUT

The following are key elements of a good accounting plan:

- A department organizational chart
- Job descriptions for each person
- Product purchasing procedures
- A system to manage and track cash payments
- Data entry processes
- Management of bank deposits and payments
- An inventory-management plan
- Point-of-sale procedures
- Account-reconciliation procedures
- Management of variances
- Tax preparation and payments

Working with Limited Access to Banking

Marijuana businesses work on a largely cash basis. They make cash sales, buy products, and pay their bills with it. If they are lucky, a nearby business will have an ATM machine that the dispensary members can use so members can have cash ready for these transactions. Otherwise, dispensary sales suffer, as they generally do not accept credit or debit cards.

Securing a Bank Account

Marijuana businesses are seriously limited in their ability to secure bank accounts. The FinCEN guidelines make it clear that any bank working with cannabusinesses is violating federal law. This means that the bank's assets could be forfeited and its staff arrested for opening these accounts. Despite this, it's possible to open an account. FinCEN also details the necessary steps, which outline the burdensome oversight and reporting processes required to do so. If the banks follow these steps, it won't stop a forfeiture or arrest, but it will de-prioritize the enforcement of federal laws.

The very first requirement is to tell the bank that you are a marijuana business. Don't break this rule and pretend to be another type of company. The bank will find out and close your account immediately. It could also prevent you from getting any bank account in the future, as your Social Security number can be red-flagged. All of your bank accounts could be closed, even those unrelated to your cannabusiness, and you could be denied future banking access.

Try talking to local banks and see if any of them will grant you an account. You might find one willing to comply with the FinCEN rules and unconcerned about the risks of forfeiture and arrest. In theory, the Rohrabacher-Farr amendment should provide the banks with protection from enforcement, and hosting accounts for state legal businesses should be fine. There are a few companies offering banking services who have sourced banks and will arrange introductions to selected marijuana businesses. But these arrangements come with high account fees and charges of up to 10 percent per transaction. Be wary of these deals.

HIGH POINTS

Illinois National Bank (INB) is contracted by the State of Illinois to transact tax payments for all of its marijuana businesses. No banks applied when the state first posted this contract solicitation. But, INB eventually submitted an application after receiving additional guidance and assurances from state and federal banking regulators.

Cash Accounting

Without access to banking, most marijuana businesses have to depend on cash accounting. They sell retail or wholesale to clients using only cash—not checks, credit cards, or debit cards. This, unfortunately, means there is less of an audit trail, with no banking records to prove the provenance of the income or the recipient of payments. Without proof, auditors can easily question whether the funds came from legitimate sales or if payees existed at all, bringing concerns about money laundering into the scenario.

To solve this problem, each transaction must be substantiated. Proof must exist that the money came in legitimately and that it was given to a rightful payee. Your goodwill and promises are not good enough; the proof has to be in the paperwork. This means your CFO and controller or bookkeeper have to be firmly in control of the process of buying and selling marijuana, and that all transactions must have multiple, provable systems of checks and balances. With careful management of sales income and oversight of procedures, it's possible for dispensaries to pay for all of their marijuana products, bills, employees, and taxes with cash.

HIGH ALERT

Paying your employees in cash does not mean going underground. You must report and pay all of the tax withholdings and payroll deductions required by law. Consider hiring a payroll service to help calculate your wages and to help direct these payments.

Check out these scenarios to understand more about cash substantiation:

Scenario A: Purchasing Wholesale Marijuana Products

1. The offices where your bookkeeping, payments, and marijuana purchasing are located must always be under video surveillance.

2. Your buyer, controller, bookkeeper, and/or inventory manager should meet each week to create a purchasing and payment plan.

3. Based on the inventory needs for the dispensary, your buyer should set a daily appointment calendar to meet with suppliers.

4. Each morning, the buyer should confirm with your controller or bookkeeper that funds exist for each planned cash payment, and the buyer should present the bookkeeper with copies of invoices for all funds requested. The buyer should retain all original invoices on file until the vendor comes for payment.

5. The bookkeeper should prepare a cash payment receipt for each transaction that day. Each should have the invoice copy attached, and should be signed by the bookkeeper. This data should be entered into the accounting program each day.

6. The bookkeeper should count out cash payments for each vendor, sealing them in an envelope, ready for pick up that day.

7. When the vendor comes to drop off inventory and pick up payment, the buyer should carefully weigh and count the product, matching it to the invoice. Any adjustments should be noted on the invoice and should be initialed by both the buyer and the sales agent.

8. The buyer should open the pre-prepared cash envelope and count the funds to verify they match the invoice total. If not, the bookkeeper should be consulted and the mistake solved.

9. If it matches, the funds should be given to the supplier, who must count the funds as well. If everyone agrees on the cash total, the buyer and seller should both sign the invoice to acknowledge the transfer of product and funds.

10. The signed invoice should be provided to the bookkeeper to keep on file for internal and external audit purposes.

In this scenario, the entire transaction is on video. The cash is counted and signed for by three separate individuals. The inventory is carefully verified and matched to the payment. Each appointment is listed on a calendar, to provide back-up verification that it occurred, and the signed invoices and receipts are all filed and available to any auditor.

Scenario B: Purchasing Supplies

1. All requests for supplies should be directed to the bookkeeper, controller, or their designee. This person should create a daily budget for petty cash purchases and a weekly and monthly purchasing budget for general supplies. Petty cash expenses should be limited to less than $300 a day.

2. When an employee requests to purchase an item from petty cash, the bookkeeper should evaluate the purchase, and approve it, deny it, or schedule it for the future. If it's approved for immediate payment, the employee should provide a purchase order request for it, detailing the price with estimated tax included.

3. The bookkeeper should record the expense on a cash receipt with the purchase order attached. They should count the cash out from petty cash and provide it to the employee, who should also verify the count, and sign the cash receipt.

4. The employee should get a sales receipt for the purchase and count all change at the register. They should initial the receipt and make sure it clearly states the name of the store, its address, the date, and the items purchased. These can be handwritten on the receipt, if necessary.

5. They should return the receipt and any change to the bookkeeper. The bookkeeper should verify with the employee that the change, the cash out, and the receipt all match. The cash receipt should be adjusted for any discrepancies, and the bookkeeper and employee should both sign it.

6. The sales receipt should be attached to the cash-out receipt and purchase order, and this data should be entered into the accounting program each day. This paperwork should be filed and kept for audit purposes.

Again, three people count the cash and the change: the bookkeeper, the employee, and the sales clerk. The cash register receipt provides proof of the purchase, and the in-house cameras record the cash going out and the change and receipts coming in.

In each scenario, the bookkeeper or controller oversees all daily spending and budgeting. All of the data is regularly entered into an accounting program so that the controller, bookkeeper, or CFO can investigate any anomaly. The treasurer and accountant review the data at least quarterly, and both agree to its validity before reporting it to various regulators and tax agencies. Any employee unable or unwilling to learn or follow these procedures has to be cut from the team. There are no exceptions to this, as mistakes as small as flipping a couple of numbers during data entry can take hours to unravel.

HIGH POINTS

The Internal Revenue Service requires that all receipts contain the following information to be considered as deductible business expenses:

- Date
- Place's name and address
- Item(s) purchased
- Purchaser's name or initials
- For meals and entertainment, list the people being treated and why

Write this information directly onto any related receipts or create a cash-tracking form that has blanks to complete for each field, and attach that form to each receipt.

Using Seed-to-Sale Tracking Programs

Substantiating your inventory is just as important as tracking your cash. Be prepared to prove how much marijuana you purchased or produced and how much you sold and to whom. You have to record each dollar—both where it came from and where it went—and keep all of the records to prove it. This is an enormous amount of data to manage, and you'll need a functioning seed-to-sale tracking system to manage it all.

This system will provide you with data to track purchasing trends and to guide the decisions of your buyer. It will show you how each staff member performs at the register, helping you decide who needs more training and who might be ready to be a trainer. These are, or soon will be, required by most of the laws in medical marijuana and adult use states. You are required to have one in order to keep your permit, so expect to be audited.

Finding the Right System

The requirement to track marijuana from seed to sale is generally found in state law. Any business granted the right to cultivate, manufacture, or sell marijuana has to be able to prove that none of their products were transferred to the illicit marketplace or sold to unqualified people. These laws are designed to prevent transportation of marijuana to nonlegal states and to ensure that the funds from selling it are not used for organized crimes.

You will face regular compliance checks and tax audits, so prepare in advance by having an inventory and point-of-sale management system, and trained staff to operate it. Your CFO should lead the effort in selecting and getting a system installed. They are also responsible for making sure the supervisors and staff are all trained and for keeping the system updated and compliant.

HASHING IT OUT

Before reviewing seed-to-sale tracking systems, create a checklist of the features. You should look for:

- An easy-to-use interface
- Reasonably priced equipment
- Competent and available support staff
- Local installation and training assistance
- Able to manage your member and contact database
- Able to differentiate between active and stored inventory
- Point-of-sale tracking
- A customer reward program
- Able to manage multiple taxation levels
- Able to produce meaningful reports

There are a growing number of these systems in the marijuana marketplace. Most are brand new, designed by entrepreneurs with tech backgrounds eager to serve the industry. You might not want to risk being the beta-mode experiment for a new company. But if they're well run and the company takes off, you'll likely secure a lifetime of free or discounted service for helping them in their start-up mode. It's safer to find a system that has some provable experience complying with marijuana industry regulations.

Search online for information on these systems or attend one of the growing number of marijuana industry conventions. Develop a list of five to ten companies whose seed-to-sale programs are a complete fit for you. Have your CFO or their designee phone each and ask detailed questions about their systems. The goal is to compare them to your needs and to vet their staff. If you have a problem getting a return call for a sales appointment, assume the tech team will be just as hard to reach. You may want to look at several non-cannabis systems for comparison and to see if any may fare better.

Choose the best three systems and delve in deeper. Ask your inventory manager, CFO, and book-keeper to spend an hour or more meeting with each company. Request a presentation on their systems and spend time asking questions. Check the references for each, and ask around in the cannabis community for recommendations. This is a serious decision, so make it from a fully informed perspective.

Once you zero in on the best system, develop an installation and training timeline. It could take 60 to 90 days to receive the equipment and get it up and running. Staff training takes time, too. Start with your supervisors, who are likely to have more general experience with POS systems.

With an intuitive system, their training should go quickly, and then they can train the rest of the staff. If you're replacing your existing system, expect to have one crazy day while the entire staff learns the new system. If you are starting from scratch, you should take a day or two to train staff using mock transactions before you open your doors. Your inventory manager, bookkeeper, and controller all have more specialized roles in the system, which also will require special training. Make sure to back up your CFO as they manage all of this; it's a lot of work, and your leadership and assistance is essential.

Daily, Monthly, and Annual Inventory Counts

The data in your seed-to-sale tracking must be regularly reconciled to the actual products and plants on hand. This is an essential part of the system of checks and balances involved in proving to your regulators that you are running a compliant marijuana business. Your physical inventory should match what the computerized records show on hand, with only explainable shrinkage.

The average retail shrinkage is about 1.5 percent of the total inventory. Investigate any variance higher than that to look for theft and/or mistakes and to identify products that are breaking or losing water weight. You should also be concerned if your shrinkage is too low or zero. This could mean that someone is stealing or committing fraud and balancing the books exactly in an attempt to cover it up.

At retail dispensaries, count the active stock daily, as your inventory manager removes it from storage and assigns it to staff sales stations. The staff member accepting it should also count it, and both should sign off, agreeing on the totals. Your bookkeeper or controller should record these daily counts, and they should match the closing to opening stock. Any unexplained variances should be investigated and solved. Count your back stock at least monthly, comparing the *book inventory* to the physical stock.

 **DEFINITION**

The **book inventory** is the amount of inventory your seed-to-sale tracking system says should be in physical stock.

In manufacturing businesses, you must count and track all of the products produced each day, and do a monthly count of back stock to match it to the book value of your inventory. Your controller will compare your production numbers and sales to the stock on hand, looking for shrinkage. For cultivation facilities, each plant has to be tracked in the system, and any losses need to be clearly explained. Both cultivators and manufacturers have to establish acceptable variances, and must be able to account for any shrinkage.

All marijuana businesses have to do an end-of-year inventory for accounting purposes. The IRS and state want their tax money, which is partly based on the value of your inventory. This is one of the main reasons to track shrinkage and to investigate variances; if you are audited, tax agents will insist that you explain any abnormal shrinkage looking for criminal activity and attempts to evade payment. Using a simple, well-functioning seed-to-sale tracking system and performing regular physical inventory counts will prevent problems and keep you prepared for compliance audits.

The Importance of Budgeting

Your annual budget is the tool that helps you figure out how to use the company's resources to maximize its ability to create more resources. Your CFO should help create this document, using their experience to interpret the company's financial records and to predict future growth or losses based on its history and on market trends. Regularly compare your budget to the actual financials and adjust future monthly and annual expectations regularly. This way, you can spot concerning trends in sales, see potential profits, and plan for growth.

Using Your Starting Projections

To secure funding, your marijuana business predicted its income and expenses with as much accuracy as possible. Now, it's time to use these predictions to guide spending in your first months in business. Once you open and start making money, the budget can be more accurately predicted. Within a few months, your CFO should be able to understand its income growth trends, know the real costs of your startup, and more closely predict future spending needs. Then you can adjust your three-year budget and create a first-year budget that acts like a road map for income and spending, and if anything gets off track, you can find out why.

It's helpful to evaluate the budget monthly so you can look at real income and expenses versus predicted. Your controller needs to understand how much money is available to pay the bills, and your CFO needs to be able to accurately predict future income and plan for what's ahead. You'll want to understand it all, in order to be prepared to answer to the board or shareholders. Expect to be called on to explain any problematic differences between the predictions and reality, and to have a plan to cover any shortcomings or to wisely invest any surplus funds. Use your budget to regularly evaluate your wholesale margins and hard costs, and make sure they balance. Base decisions on widening this gap, and aim to create a cushion of profit to safeguard the company.

Your CFO, controller, or bookkeeper must have the skills to manage budget. You'll work closely with this team to track the company's income and expenses, and to understand the assumptions behind any predictions about future income and expenses. Research your competitors to understand the future market in your area, and get as much comparative data as possible for your projections. You'll likely borrow money or take on shareholders to launch your startup, which is a huge responsibility. Create reliable, realistic goals, and make sure you can meet these commitments.

Your projections should be well researched and accurate so you can depend on them to keep the company on track. The company's funders will expect their monies to be used as promised, and any variances will have to make sense. Your ability to go back to them for more money later requires earning their trust through good financial stewardship and by meeting the promised goals.

> **HASHING IT OUT**
>
> Marijuana businesses are at the forefront of changing national consciousness and building responsible, sustainable businesses. Make sure to build annual nonprofit giving into your budget. Support organizations in your community and at the national level who support ending the marijuana prohibition and mass incarceration, and who are working to create jobs and more gentle and tolerant communities.

Doing Annual and Monthly Budgets

At the end of each fiscal year, your cannabusiness must take inventory of all products and reconcile it to the book value. Once any variances are investigated and cleared, you'll have a clear and reconciled annual profit and loss statement. You and the CFO should then spend time comparing this report to your starting projections. Evaluate each category to see where you met, exceeded, or fell short of the original expectation. Review the strengths and weaknesses of your original plan, and use this data to project a budget for the next three years.

Keep a monthly budget to guide spending, starting with the projections found in the three-year budget. Your company has mandatory fixed costs, such as rent and employee healthcare, and variable costs, such as packaging materials and nonprofit giving, which change based on need and ability. As the company's leader, you need a firm understanding of its income and expenses. If the income exceeds expenses, you are in the lucky position of being able to wisely grow the company. If it doesn't, you need to swiftly respond to the shift and lower your costs and production, while increasing sales.

Work with your monthly budget every day. Make sure your bookkeeper keeps the sales and expenses data up to date. You need the ability to regularly compare the projections to reality. If sales are slower than predicted, you may need to change the monthly spending plan or plan a marketing event to drive up income. Watch out for unexplainable variances and investigate shrinkage right away. Something as simple as bad data entry can wreak havoc, leaving you overconfident or scaring you for no reason. Your sales and manufacturing output will fall into a predictable rhythm. Anything falling outside of this is likely a mistake or problem. You have to watch the financials daily in order to assure that the company can pay its bills and to see that it develops a financial cushion.

The Least You Need to Know

- Marijuana businesses need experienced people on their financial teams.
- Cannabusinesses need a system for cash accounting, which substantiates every transaction with clear checks and balances.
- Seed-to-sale tracking systems are a requirement of state marijuana laws and an important tool for inventory management and decision-making purposes.
- You should create an annual budget to set goals and to measure successes.

Create a Winning Marketing Plan

A good marketing plan is as important as a good business plan. Both sell your company, one to investors and the other to its clients. You want people to purchase your products, and your marketing plan is the guide to make that happen.

Your cannabusiness has to set itself apart, which takes planning and resources. Use the company's mission, vision, and values to form the foundation of the plan. The goal is to introduce the company to potential clients and to show them why they should support it. Your marketing plan acts as a road map, establishing measurable goals for growth and guiding your team to reach them.

In This Chapter

- Learn to create your marketing plan
- Discover the importance of branding
- Plan your preopening strategies
- Discuss different types of marketing campaigns

Developing Your Marketing Plan

The goal of your marketing plan is to drive wholesale or retail customers to purchase your company's products. You need to build a noticeable buzz, based on the strength of your values and the quality of your offerings. To do this, it's essential to understand the marketplace, inside and out, and to showcase your strengths within it. You must know who and where your clients are and how to interest them in your product.

Be innovative and forward thinking. The legal marijuana industry is bursting with creative and driven competitors, and your company has to be bold in order to stand out. Be prepared to spend money to catch your client's attention, using thought-out campaigns with measurable results. Be smart when spending advertising dollars and make adjustments based on real-world results. Don't set your plans in stone; make frequent adjustments to reflect changing trends and to target new markets.

Take time to determine what your company wants to achieve with its marketing plan. You have to know what success looks like in order to plan how to get there. Is your goal to sell a set number of products or to reach a particular dollar amount for the year? Are you looking for a market share or to promote brand awareness? Are you trying to increase the number of clients you serve or is the goal to increase the amount each spends with your company? Can you keep your budget consistent throughout the year or should it change seasonally? Make sure to consider all of your important *key performance indicators (KPI)* and create a plan to reach them.

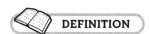 **DEFINITION**

> **Key performance indicators (KPI)** are the metrics you set to prove your success. Dispensaries might aim to increase daily visits and the total amount value of each sale, while manufacturers may want to expand their product line and increase the number of wholesale accounts. Set at least five major goals each year, and measure the company's ability to reach them.

Doing a SWOT analysis

Start by doing an analysis of your company's strengths, weaknesses, opportunities, and threats (SWOT). Your team needs to understand the current industry environment and what the future might hold. Host a focus group with core team members to discuss the following questions:

Strengths: What exceptional skills, knowledge, and abilities does our team possess? Does the company produce a product that surpasses others in the market or that is altogether unique? Is our location superior to others? Are we well funded, and can we spend heavily on client acquisition? What other strengths does our company have that give it an advantage in the marijuana marketplace?

Weaknesses: What skills, knowledge, and abilities does our team lack? Is the company distinct enough from competitors? Is the location too remote to attract retail clients? Are the company's manufacturing practices standardized, and is the customer experience consistent? Are we short on funds? What other weaknesses does the company have that need to be shored up?

Opportunities: Can we position ourselves to lead our segment of marketplace? Is the company able to attract top talent? Are there new trends we can take advantage of? What new technology exists that can help the company? What other opportunities exist now or over the next year that the company can take advantage of?

Threats: What competitors threaten our market share? Is anyone making the same products better? Are the local, state, or federal marijuana laws shifting unfavorably? Have neighbors complained about our business? Are new marijuana businesses flooding the marketplace? What other threats exist that could hamper the business?

Compile these results into a comprehensive report, creating a priority list of the best ideas and the biggest worries. Work with your COO and chief marketing officer (CMO), if you have one, to create a marketing plan based on these answers. Use your team's time and dollars to highlight the company's strengths and to take advantage of its opportunities. Pay close attention to shoring any weaknesses uncovered during the analysis, and work to lower the risk of the threats. Do a new SWOT analysis each year, and compare the annual differences to understand what activations were successful and which failed to reach targets.

Creating a Marketing Team

Your marijuana business needs an ambitious marketing team with clear roles and established goals. Start by finding an experienced team leader. Your CMO or marketing director has to come into the business with the skills, knowledge, and ability to reach the goals. Your plan will surely encompass social media, advertising, earned media, internal marketing, and street teams, so look for a leader with a broad range of experience running campaigns and motivating teams.

Each part of your marketing plan requires work, and your CMO will supervise these assignments. Small marijuana businesses don't have big marketing budgets, so tasks are likely to be spread among the existing team. Your floor manager might manage the social media accounts, the receptionist might help with graphic design, your CEO might manage press campaigns, and the COO might manage internal marketing projects. Each person in the company should be focused on client acquisition and sales, and your CMO can help envision creative ways to maximize your ability to recruit and keep clients.

As the company grows, it can afford to expand the team. Hire an outreach director to manage tradeshow booths and to run a street team. Getting your flyers and promotional materials directly into the hands of potential clients is a great recruitment technique. Bring on a graphic designer to create materials to distribute, to build advertising campaigns, and to help create branded products. Find a part-time social media coordinator to maximize your reach across all platforms, making sure each site is regularly updated and interactive. Communicating directly and regularly with your clients is a great way to build brand loyalty.

HASHING IT OUT

Set specific goals. You want measurable returns from your marketing plan, showing which campaigns should be scrapped and where your dollars were well spent. For example, newspaper ads should equal more dispensary visits, and magazine ads should mean more interest in your wholesale products. If not, don't repeat the effort without changing it to succeed. Social media posts should increase website visits and lead to sales. Otherwise, change up the strategy, and find campaigns that work. Set specific goals, measuring the number of website visits, new clients, and sales that result from each. Use the findings to determine where to invest your money and time.

Developing a Marketing Budget

A budget is an instruction manual for handling money. Be as accurate as possible when projecting your marketing budget and disciplined enough to follow it. Start by evaluating the overall company budget and determine how much can be spent on this. You have to build your clientele, and doing so will take a large part of your discretionary spending budget to start. Likewise, launching new products is costly, so make sure you have the funds to get the word out before you invest in expansion plans.

Make sure you don't overspend on marketing projects. There are plenty of innovative ways to develop sales and reach without breaking the bank. Get what you need done, but don't go into debt doing it. Listing each line item expense on the budget is helpful. You can cut any non-essential costs and focus on spending money where it will provably bring in income. Make sure your CMO and CFO are monitoring the budget closely, regularly comparing projections to the actual amounts spent, and all wasted expenditures are trimmed.

The following steps will help you to develop a sound marketing budget:

1. List the segments of your marketing strategy, such as research, testing, communications, and results tracking.

2. Find out how much market research will cost.

3. Estimate the cost of all the marketing strategies you plan to employ.

4. Plan the cost of tracking and supervising your marketing campaigns.

5. Add up the costs to determine whether or not you can afford each campaign.

Pick your marketing campaigns carefully. Each dollar spent should lead directly to website clicks and sales. This means spending on building your brand's reputation and reach, and on creating campaigns that make it magnetic. Your campaigns should be so exciting that clients are ready to search out its products. Budget carefully and build on measurable successes, and your company can take a top position in the marketplace.

Creating Your Brand

Your marijuana business needs a strong brand that represents your mission, vision, and values. Branding is your business's identity; it's how you define yourself and your team. It should speak to your customer base with a specific tone and message that inspires a long-term relationship. Think of your brand as a person and define its characteristics. Bring life to the company and your clients will respond.

Your goal is to create brand equity so that the brand itself has a measurable value in the marketplace. Work with your core marketing team to create this look. Never copy others; the goal is to develop your own unique style and message. Consistency, authenticity, relevance, and differentiation make a brand successful. Let yours be bold and daring.

Use branding to create a unified vision across various parts of your company. Branding creates the look and feel of your business, and a good brand is instantly recognizable to its clients and staff. Create a style guide, detailing the various components of your brand. This will help your marketing team clearly understand and adhere to the vision.

The goal of a successful brand is to match the look of the company to its vision and values and to be instantly recognizable in the marketplace. Create a style guide to establish guidelines for the following aspects of your marijuana business:

- Logos
- Signs and symbols
- Color schemes
- Social media handles
- Hashtags
- Taglines
- Labels

- Facility design

- Staff uniforms

Your brand is also the image you present to the public. Stay consistent and make sure all team members represent the vision and values in their actions and core messaging. Any iconography used in your advertising should match these same goals. Create a uniform brand and spread its message widely.

Design Your Logo and Look

Your logo is the visual representation of your company. It's one of the first things potential customers see, so it needs to grab their attention. You want a logo that is instantly identifiable and incorporates your vision. Hire a graphic designer to help with this—it may be expensive, but a good logo will continue to pay off for as long as you're in business.

You have a lot of choices. It can be like the logo for Google or Facebook, where the logo is a stylized version of the corporate name. Or, you might choose to use a symbol like the Nike swoosh to represent your company. Either way, your logo should be clean and functional, and its color scheme should fit the style and message you intend to convey.

 **HIGH ALERT**

Make sure your logo is simple enough to print. Too many colors and lines and it won't read right on flyers. It will also be impossible to put on t-shirts, lighters, or other items used to promote your company. Keep your logo simple and attractive.

You're going to live with your logo for many years, so take the time to choose the right one. That said, it's always a good idea to update your look occasionally, making small tweaks to your logo to update its look. Don't feel stuck with it; your marijuana company should be flexible and able to change course when needed.

Brand Everything

Set out a brand strategy in your marketing plan. Decide what, where, how, and to whom you will promote the company. Don't go headfirst into marketing campaigns without completely thinking them through. Instead, build your brand equity with consistent strategies. Always keep your brand in mind when communicating with others, but remember that stamping it on everything is not necessary. Find the balance between branding and wasting effort and resources.

Use your logo and color scheme on signage, stationery, and on business cards. Use components from your style guide to design advertising, to create your website design, and to help with the look of your packaging. Note, you may not want to brand your company vehicles or the drivers could be targeted on the road. In addition, don't post big signs on your facility if the local laws or the tenor of the neighborhood make it problematic.

Join with like-minded companies to manage co-branded marketing campaigns. Combine your resources to host special events; to buy advertising; and to create unique, limited-release products. Make sure to review all plans carefully though, and be sure each fits your corporate vision and values. You need to be sure that someone else's bad idea does not become your marketing mistake.

Preopening Marketing

Planning your grand opening is one of the most exciting things you'll do when starting your business. Create a buzz that will drive customers to your door and start you off with great sales numbers. This requires more than just advertising; it requires a preopening marketing strategy.

The first step is to know who your clients are and how you'll reach them. Decide which products you'll carry and their price points, and target your preopening marketing plans to reach the most likely buyers. If you're looking for high-end retail clients, consider adverting in local alternative newspapers and in marijuana magazines. If your dispensary will serve local clients, create a campaign to get flyers out to local cafes and community gathering spots. If you want to mass market, do a press campaign and manage community and government relations' efforts. Think about your audience, and create a plan to reach them directly.

Create a detailed budget for your preopening marketing strategy. Advertising is expensive, as are other traditional marketing tools such as mailers, billboards, and radio ads. Social media outreach takes time, which means money, as does any media campaign or community outreach efforts. Analyze your ideas and their costs before launching. Make sure you are reaching as many potential clients and community influencers as possible with each dollar spent.

Hosting an Open House

Host a prelaunch open house to generate excitement about the business and its products. Your goal is to bring in clients and important community members to showcase the offerings and give a presentation about the company. Consider giving attendees a behind-the-scenes look at the company, showing off the backrooms before the inventory is installed and the spaces become tightly controlled.

Build a preopening online presence to create excitement. Spread word about the event on various social media sites, and feature it on your corporate website. You can also generate interest by putting up signs and passing out flyers ahead of time advertising the event. Gear up your marketing team to build a comprehensive outreach plan with a clear budget and targeted return on your investment. If you want 200 people to attend, set the goal and make a plan to reach it.

On the day of the open house, greet everyone who stops by. Don't sit in the corner; mingle with your potential new clients and community members. Let them know that you are there for them and that you want to be their one-stop solution. Make sure to check with your municipality if you want to invite nonpatients to a dispensary. You may be limited to hosting an event in the parking lot if you plan to invite the community at large. Consider hosting two events, one for the community (maybe a barbeque with speakers and information), and one for patients and suppliers to showcase inside the facility.

HIGH POINTS

An open house is your chance to showcase your goods and services. If possible, offer demonstrations, tastings, and samples. Consider giving a behind-the-scenes tour before you stock the facility with its full inventory. People love this, and it gets them very excited. If not, take photos of the offerings, and have staff be ready to talk about them in detail.

Put together a nice program for attendees. Invite local celebrities and your elected officials to attend and ask them to give a short presentation. Have a ribbon cutting, and invite the press to document the moment. Nothing stirs up excitement faster than an event surrounded by news vans with a crowd of eager people listening to inspiring speeches. Have yours ready, as this is the chance to get your community excited about your mission, vision, and values. Pass out free t-shirts to the crowd and provide food and drinks to keep them around for the speeches.

Listen to feedback from visitors. The ideas you get at this event might be vital to improving the business before you open. Look for flaws in your operational plans during the event. Did your security plans hold up to expectations? Do the entry and exit plans work? Poke holes in the entire operation during the event, and fill them back up with better working systems.

Attending and Hosting Community Events

Attending community events is a great way to network and bring in business. It's also a great opportunity to check out other marketing campaigns to see what inspires you and what fails. The marijuana industry, as a whole, produces an enormous amount of events. You'll need to choose carefully where to spend your time so that you reach your most likely clients. The large conventions might not always work best. Staying local and attending a local marijuana festival might be a better way to meet your potential clients.

HASHING IT OUT

Before you open, get out in your local community and spread the work about your mission. Consider attending events like Lions or Rotary Club meetings to reach people and to start building professional brand recognition. Let people know what you have to offer, and answer any questions to help destigmatize the uses of marijuana.

It can be beneficial to host events yourself. Consider gathering smaller groups of people at places such as coffee shops, senior centers, and other community hangouts to educate them about marijuana. You can host open-mic nights, trivia contests, and musical events, infusing them with your vision and letting people know about your business along the way. This can be expensive and time consuming, but the benefit is that you build a dedicated community with a passion for your goals.

Types of Ongoing Marketing Campaigns

Marketing campaigns communicate the value of your company to your potential customer base. Good campaigns carry a central theme that gets people excited and motivated to pick up your products. The marijuana industry employs the same types of marketing strategies used in any other industry and achieves similar results.

Not all marketing campaigns cost money. Get your entire team involved in outreach and client retention and recruitment. Ask them to brainstorm and help implement zero-dollar marketing ideas. The staff at any marijuana business is full of creativity, so deploy their skill to build your base. It motivates your team to see their own ideas used in the company's marketing campaigns.

Of course, most of the time, marketing does cost money. New cannabis businesses should expect to spend 10-20 percent of gross revenues building their clientele. Established companies can lower it to 5-10 percent, as long as they retain their dedicated base. Advertising, social media management, printing, and staffing all cost your marijuana business money. Use the metrics established in your marketing plan to evaluate each campaign, and make sure they worked to bring in money. Quickly dump poor-performing campaigns and build on those that succeed.

Marketing to Your Members

Advertising to your customers when they're visiting your business is known as *four-walls marketing*. They're a captive audience for as long as they're in your establishment. Your goal is to keep them coming back. You want your clients to leave happy and to keep them intrigued about the future. It's much less expensive to keep these people coming back than it is to recruit new clients. Make retention a main focus of your marketing plan.

DEFINITION

Four-walls marketing is when a company's sales staff spends time promoting new in-stock or soon-to-arrive products or services to clients who are shopping on the premises.

The most important task is for your staff to be helpful and friendly. Each person working there represents the company's values, and their actions should match. Great customer service will keep people coming back. They may have lots of choices of where to shop, but customers want to go where they feel treated well and valued. Establish this as a requirement of the job and make sure each customer is greeted with kindness, helped with alacrity, and exits satisfied.

Use signs and flyers to get information to your clients. Hand out coupons to people as they exit and encourage them to come again for the discount. Hang banners inside detailing your specials and make sure the staff points them out to clients. Get people excited about the days of their favorite discounts, and let them know to return then. Host demos where clients can sample products and offer discounts that day. Encourage people to return regularly for other tastings and to pick up a stable supply of their favorites.

HIGH POINTS

Create beautiful product displays in your dispensary. Your clients want to be wowed, and nothing is more exciting to them than being able to see all the various marijuana products on display. Make it fancy—display the marijuana flowers in jewelry cases and put the other products in locking cases of various shapes and sizes. Let people browse the offerings, and have staff nearby to guide, answer questions, and help people make choices. The experience matters, so dedicate time to making it interesting and of value to each person.

Zero-Dollar Marketing

Zero-dollar marketing ideas cost little or no money to produce. They deploy the talents of your team, without requiring a big outlay of funds for materials or advertising. Of course, great customer service is the easiest way to do this. Provide kindness for free, and people will keep coming back for more.

But, there are lots of other great ideas that will spread the word about your company. Social media is a no- or low-cost means to promote your company. Consider joining Facebook, Twitter, Linkedin, and Pinterest, and designate a staff member to build your following. This can be done during slow times throughout the retail day, or staff can set aside time daily to manage online communications. As the leader, you should be willing to put the word out through your own social networks, too. Share stories from the company's pages to your own, and build unique content on your sites to link people to the company. Your staff is likely willing to do the same, if you create time in their workday for outreach. The team's personal networks are a great source of potential clients, so utilize them well.

If you have writers on staff, get them blogging. Create unique and interesting content for your website and social media sites, and share the articles around widely. Post them on online forums such as Reddit and cannabis-specific sites to stimulate conversation and to let people know about your products and services. You may have to pay staff their hourly wages for this work, but it's still an inexpensive way to start conversations and to direct people to your products.

Bartered trade deals are another good method of getting the word out about your company. If you operate a dispensary, make a deal to provide premium shelf space to manufacturers whose marketing campaigns drive clients to your facility. Offer ad trades to your allies, where you list them in your ads for reciprocal listings in theirs. Doing so doubles your reach for no more money. Offer to send volunteers to an event in exchange for a co-sponsor listing or trade listings. The ideas are limitless, so find fun ways to build your brand alongside likeminded allies.

There are plenty of other zero-dollar marketing ideas to explore. Consider doing an online newsletter, and blast it to your mailing list once a month. Add in an exclusive online coupon and measure how many clients use it. Become a local thought leader and a media source. Publish press releases when major marijuana news hits and for any special events you host. Make sure that your group becomes known as the local expert, and that it's you the local news calls for any story.

Paid Advertising

Paying for ads in mainstream media outlets is common for cannabis businesses in legal states. Local entertainment weeklies are often full of cover-to-cover industry ads. Marijuana users are well aware of this fact, and use these papers to look for deals and special events. Strategic advertising in these outlets will drive clients to your dispensary.

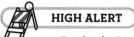 **HIGH ALERT**

Facebook, Google, and Twitter all forbid marijuana companies from advertising. Even trying can get your company's account canceled.

Paid advertising on online cannabis communities such as Leafly and Weedmaps can also bring in customers. Build brand recognition by making sure your dispensary comes up first in their search results. The cost of listing on these sites can be overly high, though, and in a competitive market it may not be the best option. It's worth considering advertising in marijuana magazines, too. You can often get a good deal on an ad that comes with a content marketing deal. In other words, if you advertise, the magazine will write an article about your company, too.

If you want to go big, consider taking out billboard space. Some state and municipal laws limit or forbid this type of advertising, so check your governing rules first. Billboards draw attention, often generating news stories when they first go up. However they are costly, and it's hard to tie views to visits. Without the availability of metrics showing increased visitors, a billboard could end up being a costly folly.

Organizing a Street Team

Consider creating a *street team* to get the word out about your grand opening. They can be very effective, especially when the people on the team have a sense of inclusion in the mission. Make sure the team feels passionate about the company and its products; they'll pass that enthusiasm on. Hire an experienced team leader who keeps everyone motivated and on track with the goals.

 **DEFINITION**

> **Street team** is a marketing term for a group of people who hit the streets to promote a product, brand, or event. They pass out flyers, hang posters, and generally spread the word about the campaign.

Recruit outgoing team members with a background in sales, and give them the training and materials to succeed. Make sure to have measureable goals for the group. This might be something like increasing the client base from a specific neighborhood or building overall daily visits. Evaluate how each effort contributes to the goals, and eliminate ideas that don't meet expectations. You might send your team to a local concert, asking them to pass out discount cards. The expectation is that new and returning clients will come in with these over the next few days. But, if this doesn't happen, consider trying a different audience next time or skipping the idea altogether. Use your metrics to save time and money, and to send the street team where they will create the most value for the company.

Planning Your Grand Opening

You made it this far, which is a reason to celebrate! It's a serious accomplishment to incorporate a marijuana business and to get it permitted. You set up a budget and got the company funded. You established your SOPs and hired a staff and trained them to run the place. You developed a marketing plan and set it in motion. Now is the crucial moment: It's time to open your doors for business.

Determine what kind of launch your team envisions. Will it be a big party or is the focus on getting people in and out fast? Either way, decide how much you can afford to spend, and use it to make the day memorable. Decide which customers, product suppliers, contractors, and media outlets to invite, and give plenty of lead-time to design and distribute invitations and promotional materials. Plan each detail, from entry to exit, and assign staff to manage the tasks. You want the day to go like clockwork, as it will set the tone for all operations to come.

Hosting an Event

Whether you plan the grand opening yourself or hire an event planner, this is a chance to show the world what you stand for. You will meet your customers and begin establishing long-term relationships. Remember that first impressions count. Getting off on the right foot requires accurate market research and meticulous planning. You have to have the products people want, served by knowledgeable staff in a pleasant environment. If you are missing any of these aspects of service, you are already off to a poor start.

Plan a fun party, surprising people with various event happenings. Have live music and offer delicious food. Consider inviting performance artists to add to the atmosphere. This could be something fun, such as having a local artist paint at the event and giving the painting away as a free raffle prize. Or, invite stilt walkers, fire dancers, or slam poets to participate to add a memorable spin to the day.

Invite clients, suppliers, and the community in general, as well as reporters, bloggers, and other thought leaders. Create a good press release, and hope it gets picked up for a feature story. The more buzz you can create on day one, the faster you can grow your marijuana business.

Congratulations! You Are Open for Business

Congratulations! You have joined the ranks of business owners in America's new billion-dollar industry. The marijuana community is vibrant and caring, and you will likely enjoy every day of this work. Even the hard times are worthwhile, as participants in this socially responsible, values-based industry make a difference in other people's lives each day.

Now that your company is open, your job as founder shifts to thinking ahead. Get ready to take advantage of each viable opportunity, and use your knowledge to sidestep bad ideas. Marijuana's future is being built right now, and the innovations ahead are limitless. Your frontrunner position will afford you benefits and opportunities that others won't have, so maximize your position. Gain market share fast and early, and ensure your profits for the long run.

And don't forget to enjoy the experience! Marijuana is used to improve health, and it helps people feel better. Make sure to take time to experience the flowers!

The Least You Need to Know

- Your marijuana business needs a marketing plan and budget to guide its outreach and advertising goals.
- Set key performance indicators (KPIs) to establish a means to evaluate the success of your marketing plans.
- Some of the best marketing ideas are free to implement, such as making sure your staff is kind and efficient.
- Your job as leader is to be forward thinking and to anticipate and prepare for opportunities and threats.

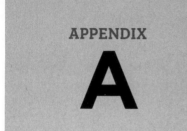

Glossary

angel investor   Someone who loans their own personal money to a company.

below combustion   A process that enables a user to benefit from the cannabinoids found in marijuana without having to inhale the burning plant material.

beneficial insects   Insects that pollinate plants or help control invasive insects of other species. In the marijuana industry, ladybugs are used in grow rooms to fight spider mite infestations.

book inventory   The amount of inventory your seed-to-sale tracking system says should be in physical stock.

cannabinoids   The main active ingredients found in marijuana. They are neuro-regulators, facilitating communication between cells.

cannabis broker   The person who arranges sales between the supplier and the buyer, working directly with cultivators and manufacturers to source supply.

cannabusiness   Term used in the industry denoting a cannabis business that touches the plant: dispensaries, extraction labs, and edibles manufacturers.

capillary action   The process that causes liquids like water to move through another substance, even defying gravity to travel upwards.

clean-room or clean-zone environment   A contamination free space, where outside particulates are eliminated through use of protocols for entry and exit, airflow, clothing, and product handling.

convertible loans   Also known as *convertible notes*, the loans allow the holder to convert monies owed into company stock at a future date. The terms are established from the start, including the timeframe of the potential conversion and value of the shares to be exchanged.

C-suite The senior team in corporations, who generally have titles starting with the letter *C*, such as the chief operating officer, the chief financial officer, the chief marketing officer, the chief technology officer, and the chief information officer.

dabbing A cannabis delivery system where cannabis is delivered into the body via a dab rig, providing a faster and more efficient delivery of cannabis than smoking. Users heat a metal piece called a nail with a handheld torch, apply a small amount of cannabis concentrate to the hot nail with a metal dab tool, and inhale. The concentrate instantly vaporizes and provides a strong hit.

decarboxylation A chemical reaction that occurs in cannabis when heated, which removes a carbon molecule from the plants THCA, changing it to its psychoactive form, THC.

first-mover advantage The competitive lead gained by companies founded early in brand-new industries. It can take forms like securing exclusive vendor contracts and developing market share and consumer loyalty.

forced flowering When outdoor growers cover plants with dark material beginning in the summer, thus leaving them in darkness for 12 hours a day, tricking the plants into believing it's fall and time to flower.

forfeiture laws Laws that enable prosecutors to file claims against property owned by the person or people accused of a crime.

green zone The area in a city or county designated by law for marijuana businesses.

heating, ventilation, and air conditioning systems (HVAC systems) Systems essential for all indoor and greenhouse grows that provide a stable temperature and fresh, pure air for plants to thrive.

HEPA filter A High-Efficiency Particulate Air filter used in grow rooms to purify the smell of marijuana from the air and to eliminate incoming airborne matter that could contaminate the plants.

hydroponics A method of growing marijuana where water, rather than soil, delivers nutrients to the plants.

intra-state commerce Economic activity that takes place entirely within a state's borders.

Investigational New Drug Program Part of the drug approval system supervised by the U.S. Food and Drug Administration (FDA) that allows the FDA to license experimental substances for researchers to use during drug trials. It's also used to distribute drugs on an emergency basis, when lengthy approval processes would harm lives.

key performance indicators (KPI)   The metrics set to prove success. Dispensaries might aim to increase daily visits and the total value of each sale, while manufacturers may want to expand their product line and increase the number of wholesale accounts.

keystone pricing   When the retail price of an item is increased by 100 percent from its wholesale cost, so that 50 percent of the sale price is profit.

laboratories of democracy   A phrase coined by Justice Brandeis in the 1932 Supreme Court case, *New State Ice Company* v. *Liebmann,* which determined that the Tenth Amendment gives states the right to exercise autonomy and to act as social laboratories for change.

loss leader   A product you advertise and sell at a loss in order to attract customers in to buy profitable items.

marijuana tinctures   Cannabinoids extracted from the plant using ethyl alcohol, glycerol, vinegar, coconut or olive oil where THC and CBD bond to these carriers, leaving an infused liquid behind after the plant matter is strained. They are packaged in dropper bottles, so patients can take measured doses straight or infused into beverages.

master growers   Cultivators who are experienced in management of industrial-sized cannabis facilities. They have proven experience producing consistent, high-test plants and are often marijuana breeders who have created award-winning strains.

neuromodulators   A messenger in the central nervous system that facilitates communication between neurons, ensuring that each fulfills its proper function.

perlite   A form of obsidian (volcanic glass) that enables proper drainage when used as a plant-growth medium.

pitch deck   A succinct slide show presentation about your funding opportunity. It includes a problem statement, your solutions, team biographies, and a brief description of the investment and its expected payoff.

pocket listing   A property that a broker is under contract to sell or rent, but is not publically advertised.

positive-pressure rooms   Sealed areas with airflow systems that exchange the air at least 12 times per hour, using HEPA filters for purification. These rooms generally have an antechamber, beyond which street clothing is not allowed.

reciprocity   When one state recognizes the legality of a license issued by another state, like with driver's licenses. Some states have reciprocity written into their medical marijuana laws, while others ban access and use by out-of-state patients.

Reefer Madness   A 1936 propaganda film that bolstered public opinion in advance of the 1937 vote to prohibit marijuana. The term is now used to describe the mind-set that swept the nation and led to cannabis prohibition.

runway   The amount of time your company can operate in start-up mode without going out of business.

scaled business   A fine-tuned and ready-to-expand business that has sustainable procedures and the ability to ramp up or slow down operations as needed. It's stable to the point that it could be franchised, sold, or replicated with ease.

Sea of Green   A method of cannabis cultivation that maximizes the use of indoor space and resources to get high quality cannabis in the smallest possible area.

Section 280E   A section of the Federal Income Tax Code that restricts tax deductions for any business involved in trafficking a controlled substance. Marijuana businesses generally pay at least 25 percent more than other companies in federal taxes.

seed-to-sale **tracking**   Each marijuana plant is documented and traced from the moment the cultivator acquires and plants the seeds, through its harvest and any manufacturing processes, and until the final product is sold at a licensed retail facility.

shrinkage   An accounting term describing the difference between what your inventory-management reports and what is actually on hand, stemming from problems such as lost items, theft, and human error. Businesses expect and can predict average shrinkage and investigate when losses exceed these amounts.

standard operating procedures (SOPs)   Step-by-step instructions for employees that guide each role or activity and ensure all tasks are completed in a uniform manner during regular work shifts. SOPs are critical to compliant cannabis operations, and in many states must be submitted prior to receiving a cannabis license.

street team   A marketing term for a group of people who hit the streets to promote a product, brand, or event. They pass out flyers, hang posters, and generally spread the word about the campaign.

throughput   The maximum number of customers you can serve in a given amount of time.

transdermal administration   Using patches, creams, or implants to deliver medicine.

trichomes   Resin glands on the leaves and flowers of the cannabis plant. They consist of a stalk and a head, similar in shape to a mushroom and contain the plant's cannabinoids and terpenes.

toxic funding   Funding with such a high interest rate that payoff will be impossible and default to the funder is imminent.

vaporizing   A process that transforms liquid to aerosol at a low temperature. Cannabis patients use vaping pens to injest medication.

vermiculite   A lightweight, highly absorbent magnesium- and aluminum-based material used in soil mixtures.

vertical integration   When your dispensary plays some role in the manufacture of certain goods it retails, which helps lower the cost of these items, increases quality control, and improves their profitability.

Resource List for Advocates

Check these sites for reliable marijuana information:

High Times
www.hightimes.com

Smell the Truth
www.smellthetruth.com

Leafly
www.leafly.com

Marijuana Politics
www.marijuanapolitics.com

International Association for Cannabis as Medicine
www.cannabis-med.org/english/bulletin/iacm.php

These companies are mentioned in, and helped with, the creation of this book. Check them out:

Magnolia Oakland
www.magnoliawellness.org

Green Rush Consulting
www.greenrushconsulting.com

Drug War Facts
http://www.drugwarfacts.org/cms

Investing in Cannabis
http://investingincannabis.tv

Liana Limited
http://lianaltd.com

Steep Hill Lab
www.steephill.com

BAS Research
http://basresearch.com

These organizations work hard for marijuana law reform:

Drug Policy Alliance
www.drugpolicy.org

California NORML
www.canorml.org

Americans for Safe Access
www.safeaccessnow.org

Project CBD
www.projectcbd.org

Marijuana Lifers
www.marijuanaliferproject.org

Marijuana Policy Project
www.mpp.org

National Cannabis Industry Association
http://thecannabisindustry.org

National Organization for the Reform of Marijuana Laws
www.norml.org

These groups help marijuana businesses get funded:

Gateway Incubator
www.gtwy.co

Arcview Group
https://arcviewgroup.com

Canopy
www.canopyboulder.com

WeedClub
www.weedclub.com

This is a list of the agencies responsible for the medical and adult use programs in each state, with the exception of new programs created by the November 2016 elections.

Alaska
Marijuana Registry, Bureau of Vital Statistics, Division of Public Health, Alaska Department of Health and Social Services
http://dhss.alaska.gov/dph/vitalstats/pages/marijuana.aspx

Alcohol & Marijuana Control Office, Alaska Department of Commerce, Community, and Economic Development
https://www.commerce.alaska.gov/web/amco

Arizona
Medical Marijuana Program, Arizona Department of Health and Human Services
https://medicalmarijuana.azdhs.gov/

California
Medical Marijuana Program, California Department of Public Health
https://www.cdph.ca.gov/programs/MMP/Pages/default.aspx

Bureau of Medical Cannabis Regulation, California Department of Consumer Affairs
https://www.cdph.ca.gov/programs/MMP/Pages/default.aspx

Colorado
Marijuana, Colorado Department of Public Health & Environment
https://www.colorado.gov/pacific/cdphe/categories/services-and-information/marijuana

Connecticut
Medical Marijuana Program, Connecticut Department of Consumer Protection
http://www.ct.gov/dcp/cwp/view.asp?a=4287&q=503670&dcpNav=|&dcpNav_GID=2109

Delaware
Medical Marijuana Program, Division of Public Health, Delaware Department of Health and Social Services
http://dhss.delaware.gov/dph/hsp/medmarhome.html

District of Columbia
Medical Marijuana Program, District of Columbia Department of Health
http://doh.dc.gov/service/medical-marijuana-program

Hawaii
Medical Marijuana Program, State of Hawaii Department of Health
http://health.hawaii.gov/medicalmarijuana/

Illinois

Medical Cannabis Pilot Program, Illinois Department of Health
https://medicalcannabispatients.illinois.gov/

Maine

Maine Medical Use of Marijuana, Division of Public Health, Maine Center for Disease Control
& Prevention, Maine Department of Health & Human Services
http://www.maine.gov/dhhs/mecdc/public-health-systems/mmm/index.shtml

Maryland

Natalie M. LaPrade Maryland Medical Cannabis Commission, Maryland Department of Health
& Mental Hygiene
http://mmcc.maryland.gov/default.aspx

Massachusetts

Medical Use of Marijuana Program, Massachusetts Department of Health & Human Services
http://www.mass.gov/eohhs/gov/departments/dph/programs/hcq/medical-marijuana/

Michigan

Michigan Medical Marihuana Program, Department of Licensing and Regulatory Affairs
http://www.michigan.gov/lara/0,4601,7-154-72600_72603_51869---,00.html

Minnesota

Medical Cannabis, Minnesota Department of Health
www.health.state.mn.us/topics/cannabis

Montana

Montana Marijuana Program, Montana State Department of Public Health & Human Services
https://dphhs.mt.gov/marijuana.aspx

Nevada

Medical Marijuana, Nevada Division of Public & Behavioral Health
http://dpbh.nv.gov/Reg/Medical_Marijuana/

New Hampshire

Therapeutic Cannabis Program, New Hampshire Department of Health & Human Services
http://www.dhhs.nh.gov/oos/tcp/

New Jersey

Medicinal Marijuana Program, State of New Jersey Department of Health
http://www.state.nj.us/health/medicalmarijuana/

New Mexico

Medical Cannabis Program, New Mexico Department of Health
https://nmhealth.org/about/mcp/svcs/

New York
New York State Medical Marijuana Program, New York Department of Health
https://www.health.ny.gov/regulations/medical_marijuana/

Ohio
Ohio Medical Marijuana Control Program, State of Ohio Board of Pharmacy/State Medical
Board of Ohio/Ohio Department of Commerce
http://www.medicalmarijuana.ohio.gov/

Oregon
Oregon Medical Marijuana Program, Oregon Health Authority
https://public.health.oregon.gov/DiseasesConditions/ChronicDisease/
MedicalMarijuanaProgram/Pages/index.aspx

Recreational Marijuana, Oregon Liquor Control Commission
http://www.oregon.gov/olcc/marijuana/pages/default.aspx

Pennsylvania
Pennsylvania Medical Marijuana Program, Pennsylvania Department of Health
http://www.health.pa.gov/My%20Health/Diseases%20and%20Conditions/M-P/
MedicalMarijuana/Pages/default.aspx#.WBe3cfkrK00

Rhode Island
Medical Marijuana, State of Rhode Island Department of Health
http://www.health.ri.gov/healthcare/medicalmarijuana/

Vermont
Vermont Marijuana Registry, Vermont Crime Information Center, Department of Public Safety
http://vcic.vermont.gov/marijuana-registry

Marijuana, Agency of Human Services, Vermont Department of Health
http://healthvermont.gov/adap/drugs/marijuana.aspx

Washington
Medical Marijuana, Washington State Department of Public Health
http://www.doh.wa.gov/ForPublicHealthandHealthcareProviders/
HealthcareProfessionsandFacilities/MedicalMarijuanaCannabis

Washington State Liquor and Cannabis Board
http://www.liq.wa.gov/mjlicense/marijuana-licensing

Legalities Checklists

Starting and running a marijuana business requires owners to follow all the legal regulations for their locality. Use this checklist to help ensure your company complies with all legal marijuana business laws and regulations. Again note that state-by-state regulations vary, so be sure to research your state and municipal laws as you complete this checklist.

Organizational Documents

❑ Write your business's articles of incorporation or incorporation documents.

❑ Create and file your business's annual report with your state's secretary of state.

❑ Get a registered agent for service of process.

❑ Obtain your business license and tax permit.

❑ Obtain your local permits.

    ❑ Alarm permit

    ❑ Building Department permit

    ❑ Health Department permit

    ❑ Occupational Department permit

    ❑ Signage permit

    ❑ Zoning Department permit

❑ File for your Federal Employee Identification Number.

❑ Register your businesses with your state's Internal Revenue Service.

❑ Obtain your cannabis business license.

Corporate Governance

❑ Create your initial list of officers and directors.

❑ Mail out your business's officer and director acceptance and notification letters.

❑ Mail out your notice of meetings.

❑ Note shareholders' and directors' meetings' minutes including all motions, at every meeting.

❑ Create your business's by-laws or operating agreements.

❑ Create your business's mission, vision, and values statements.

❑ Create your business's buy/sell agreement.

❑ Create your business's subscription agreement.

❑ Create your business's shareholder agreement.

❑ Write the corporate monthly and annual goals lists.

Financial Management

❑ Create your statement of the location of your business's stock ledger.

❑ Obtain stock certificates.

❑ Create a stock transfer ledger.

❑ Create a capitalization table showing allocation of all shares.

❑ Create annual budgets.

❑ Create and keep on file copies of all cash tracking receipts.

❑ Obtain and keep on file copies of all loan documents.

❑ Obtain and keep on file copies of all leases.

❑ Obtain and keep on file copies of all contracts.

❑ Obtain and keep on file copies of tax returns for 7 years.

Insurance Policies

❑ Obtain workers' compensation insurance.

❑ Obtain general liability insurance.

❑ Obtain product liability insurance.

❑ Obtain directors' and officers' liability insurance.

❑ Obtain insurance for errors and omissions.

❑ Obtain theft, fire, and earthquake insurance.

❑ Obtain health, dental, and vision insurance for you and all employees.

Human Resources

❏ Write job descriptions.

❏ Create job applications.

❏ Create a grading system for applications, phone interviews, and résumés.

❏ Write on-site interview questions.

❏ Create a termination process.

❏ Write and distribute your staff handbook.

❏ Write and distribute to managers your employee training manual.

❏ Create an employee review process. Negotiate your union contract, if unionized.

❏ Create and distribute staff schedules.

❏ Create and keep on file all payroll records.

❏ Obtain and keep on file copies of I-9 forms and identification.

❏ Write new hire reporting forms.

Operational Documents

❏ Create your Standard Operating Procedures.

❏ Create your Marketing plan.

❏ Create your Accounting Management plan.

❏ Create a Chart of Accounts.

General Documents

❏ Write and enforce your good-neighbor policy.

❏ Write and enforce building rules.

❏ Write and enforce your member rules.

Cannabis Legal Information

❏ Perform a monthly review of your state laws related to cannabis.

❏ Follow important judicial rulings related to cannabis.

❏ Review and conform to state marijuana business guidelines. Review and conform to the federal Attorney General memos related to marijuana law enforcement.

❏ Review and conform to local cannabis laws.

Sample Standard Operating Procedures (SOPs)

The marijuana industry is highly regulated and businesses have to run with tight standard operating procedures (SOPs). Take time to establish these procedures using fair systems for the best results. The following procedures are adapted from those used at Magnolia Wellness, a licensed dispensary in Oakland, California.

Registration Form

Your registration form is a contract between your company and its clients stating all of the rules. Collect your members' information in a database and save a backup of the form itself, either digitally or in print.

MEMBERSHIP AGREEMENT

All patients or caregivers are required to agree to and comply with the following Membership Agreement. The dispensary reserves the right to terminate membership for any violation of this agreement.

- Only legally qualified patients and caregivers may register as members. Only members are allowed to access services at the dispensary.

- You must be at least 18 years old and have state-issued identification to access the dispensary.

- All members are required to show state-issued identification and must have their membership validated by the dispensary prior to accessing services.

- No alcohol, illegal drugs, or weapons are allowed in or around the premises.

- No consumption of cannabis is allowed around the property or in the surrounding neighborhood.

- Members must never sell or otherwise distribute the medicine they obtain at the dispensary.

- There is no loitering allowed on or around the property. Please be friendly and support our neighbors with your patronage.

- For your safety, place all medicine and plants out of sight before leaving the building.

- In the event of an emergency, please follow the instructions of our staff.

I hereby affirm that I have read and understand this Membership Agreement and agree to follow it. I understand that my membership may be terminated for violating these policies.

Printed Name:

Signature:

Date:

Address:

Telephone Number:

Email address:

Emergency contact name:

Emergency contact number:

I authorize my recommending physician to verify the validity of this medical marijuana recommendation to this dispensary.

Signature:

Date:

For staff use only:

Intake staff signature:

Recommendation verified by:

Date:

Expiration date of Recommendation:

Member identification number:

Standard Operating Procedures

Each process in your marijuana business should be documented, step by step, in a Standard Operating Procedures (SOPs) manual. Look online for examples and templates to get started writing your own SOPs, or hire a consultant to review your systems and document them for you. Update the manual as processes change, and provide it to each employee so they know exactly what their responsibilities are and how to manage them. Use this outline as a starting point and add your specific processes to it.

Outline for Your Standard Operating Procedures Manual

- ❑ General
  - Hours of Operations
  - Opening and Closing Procedures
  - External and Internal Signs
  - Nuisance Prevention
  - Control of Litter, Debris, and Trash
  - Maintaining Proper Indoor and Outdoor Lighting
  - Management of Air Treatment Systems
  - Coordination of Marketing Plans
  - Adherence to the Americans with Disabilities Act (ADA)
- ❑ Registration
  - Check-in Procedures
  - Membership Limited to Patients and Caregivers
  - Age Limits on Membership
  - Maintenance of Records
  - Confidentiality of Information

❑ Inventory Management
- Determination of Necessary Inventory Additions and Reductions
- Safe Receipt of Cannabis Deliveries
- Appropriate Payment for Cannabis Medicines
- Maintenance of an Electronic Inventory-Management System
- Safe Storage of Cannabis
- Product Handling Procedures
- Managing Recalls

❑ Point of Sale
- Supervision of Dispensary Operations
- Limits on Dispensing
- Labeling of Marijuana Products
- Maintaining Sales Records
- Posting prices and Products
- Sales of Nonmarijuana Items
- Discounts

❑ Staff
- Hiring and Termination Plan
- Mandatory Criminal Background Check
- Age Requirement for Staff
- Staff Training
- Payroll Management
- Scheduling

❑ Security

  • Supervision of a Detailed Security Plan

  • Staff Training

  • Use of Alarms and Panic Buttons

  • Use of Security Cameras

  • Security During Product Deliveries

  • Preventing Loitering and Nuisance

  • Window, Door, and Perimeter Checks

  • Managing Security Emergencies

Employee Handbook

Marijuana businesses need to provide each employee with an Employee Handbook, which outlines the rules of the facility, your expectations from staff members, and their rights as employees. Use this outline as a guide to create your own staff manual. There are a lot of employment laws you must follow, so you may want to ask a human resources (HR) specialist or a lawyer to review your staff manual to ensure that it's comprehensive and legal. Making mistakes in the HR department are costly, and the corporate shield doesn't protect you in these matters.

Starting Outline for Your Staff Manual

❑ General Employment Policies: harassment and retaliation prevention; right to revise the manual

❑ Hiring: new hire information; job duties

❑ Leaves of Absence: medical, bereavement, military, victims of crime, vacation, sick time, and more

❑ Benefits: paid holidays; medical, dental, and vision insurance; workers' compensation

❑ Management: performance reviews, personnel records; open-door policy

❑ Company Property: bulletin boards, parking, electronic and social media, and guests and visitors

❑ Employee Conduct: conflicts of interest, news media contact, off-duty conduct, customer relations, and business conduct and ethics

❏ Wages: scheduling, deductions, advances, overtime, meals and breaks, and payment of wages

❏ Safety and Health: ergonomics, security, and driving

❏ Termination: progressive discipline, reductions in force, and resignation

Writing Job Descriptions

Before hiring anyone for your marijuana business, take the time to write clear job descriptions. This will help you clarify the company's needs, and it will narrow down the qualifications you are looking for in a candidate. It's standard process to base your jobs descriptions on three key principles: knowledge, skills, and ability.

Potential Qualifications for a Retail Dispensary Clerk:

❏ Knowledge: general effects of sativa, indica, and hybrids; major terpenes and their effects; and recommended doses for types of medicines

❏ Skills: data entry, cash counting, retail sales, and customer service

❏ Ability: required to stand, stoop, or kneel; able to lift up to 30 pounds; able to type and talk or capable of typing and talking

❏ Qualifications: 21 years or older, high school diploma or equivalent, two years' experience in retail sales or customer service, and history of nonprofit volunteerism

Organoleptic Grading of Cannabis

Your dispensary's buyer can determine the quality and potency of marijuana flowers with a simple organoleptic test using their senses. Patients choose their medicine this way, too, with a quick look, squeeze, and smell to guide them. Use this simple formula to rate the potency and quality of cannabis, and set your prices accordingly.

Sample Organoleptic Grading Form:

Name: Jack Herer Sativa

Rate each category on a scale of 0 to 6.

Smell: 5.5

This flower has a strong terpene smell with no detectible molds or mildews. To a trained nose, it smells like Jack Herer, which is a distinctive sativa.

Feel: 5

The flowers are dense and do not have any give that indicates dampness.

Appearance: 5

The flowers are green, with red hairs, and are covered in visible trichomes.

Trichome Quality: 5.5

Under a 30x microscope, the trichomes have all the stems and heads intact, and they are widespread throughout the flowers.

Total: 21

Average the score by dividing by 4: 5.25

With a 5.25 rating, your buyer can price it at $50 or $55 an eighth at the dispensary counter. This will help them negotiate a wholesale price that can be fairly marked up. If the marijuana has a lower rating, negotiate the price accordingly. If the quality is high with lots of trichomes, but the appearance is low with leafy flowers, your buyer can get a lower price. You will be able to provide potent cannabis at lower prices by carefully choosing how to stock your shelves.

Any marijuana flower that received a 0 rating in any category should not be purchased or sold. If it fails on just one count, your members will not want it.

Here is a sample form with a failed result:

Name: OG Flower

Rate each category on a scale of 0 to 6

Smell: 0

This flower smells moldy.

Feel: 2

The flowers are moist and squishy when pinched.

Appearance: 1

The flowers are dark green and have untrimmed leaves.

Trichome Quality: 3

Under at 30x microscope, the trichomes are spaced out, although all the stems and heads are intact.

Total: 6

Average the score by dividing by 4: 1.5

This batch should be rejected for the zero rating in the smell category. There may be times when your buyer accepts a 1.5-grade cannabis flower. For example, they may find a baker's grade of cannabis with small flowers and not much to feel, but with a high trichome count and a pleasant smell. Priced low, members will use this to bake at home and to mix with their high grade for use in joints. Your buyer should carefully judge your selection of products and set both purchase and sales prices based on organoleptic and lab testing results.

Index

D

E

F

G

S

T